The Dark Horse Speaks

Little White Bird

PasserPress

This edition first published by Passer Press in 2013, Plantsville, CT.

Printed in the United States of America.

Cover Art Copyright © 2013 by Shelley Ott

Computer graphics input: Special thanks to Katherine Chordas

ISBN-13: 978-0-9890679-2-8

Library of Congress Control Number: 2013908707

FIRST EDITION
10 9 8 7 6 5 4 3 2 1

For My Mother

who stood by me through all of this

and still loved me when it was done.

Contents

November

December

January through mid-February

Tatanka Ska

Epilogue

Hello my dear friends,

I know it's been a while since I've written to some of you. Know you are each in my heart always.

I need to let you know about a change in my life. First, please reach me via this new e-mail account:

xxx2@hotmail.com

I don't know when I will be able to check it, but I will get to it first chance I see a computer with internet hook-up. I will include a snail mail address for you all as well. Christmas cards, etc.

Second, I am moving to Wounded Knee, South Dakota. I am leaving Maine on Halloween and driving the two thousand miles out to the Lakota reservation where I will be living for the winter, at least, if not much longer. I had hoped to move home to CT, but kept encountering roadblocks, the doors opened one after another to move to the reservation and I must follow where they lead.

I need a change. My spirit is so dead here in Maine and I can't take another winter. I need to go somewhere where I feel impassioned about something and I felt that in Wounded Knee this summer when I went out there for Sturgis bike week.

I made a friend out that way. We've been writing and he asked me to come stay there and take care of his grandkids.

I felt alive for the first time in so long on the reservation. It's like a third world country and it is a shame the U.S. government has taken so much from these people. Maybe I can make a difference out there. If I can't, I'm sure they will make a difference in me.

You can write to me the old-fashioned way at:

xxx xxx c/o
Chief Two Bear Paws
P.O. Box xxx
Wounded Knee, S.D. 57794

I love you all.

XOX.

Introduction

To most people, they are known as "Sioux." Many are not aware that "Sioux" is an offensive name for the Lakota. To a Lakota Indian, "Sioux" is as hurtful as the "n" word to African-Americans.

I am here to speak honestly about events in my life on the Oglala Lakota Pine Ridge Reservation.

I feel love and hurt, admiration and fear, hope and sadness, all at the same time. The human heart is a vessel large enough to hold every emotion at once. This is what you will find here. My heart.

I am not here to make friends. I am not here to make enemies. This book will offend both sides equally. And honor both sides. I am here to speak. My words are not black and white. My story illustrates how black and white blend together to create a grey ground. A place where one can stand wrong and stand right, both in the same moment of time.

This is not your usual romantic Indian story, nor is it your usual "white is right" fairytale told in history books.

This is a story of Truth.

Those who follow on this journey should not pass judgment with haste. There is much to say from many sides.

It is best to read the entire book before committing to how you feel.

I must also say, "Indian" is the term I was asked to use by the Lakota. It is the word they have chosen and the term I shall use with respect.

I ask you, please, both Indians and White Man and all who gather here in this circle, leave your prejudices at the door.

Enter with a clean heart and mind. Open. Listen.

Hear this, my story.

Zintkala Ska Chikala Win
"Little White Bird"
July 2012

AUGUST

CHAPTER ONE:

The Reasons for Everything

Wounded Knee is a two-sentence, minor event in U.S. history books. If it is mentioned at all. In the heart of the Lakota people, where their true history is written, it is a massacre that cannot be forgiven. One for which they have never even been offered an apology.

Wounded Knee is on the map in southern South Dakota. It is part of the Pine Ridge Indian Reservation located in Shannon County. Shannon County is the poorest county in the entire United States. Think about that. The *entire* United States.

Picture the worst city anyone can think of. Think about the shootings, the violence, the sickness, hunger, and poverty. Picture these, the "bad areas" people avoid to stay "safe."

Shannon County is worse than any place you can imagine. Worse than any place you know or have heard of. It is a third world country right here within the United States. And it is where I wanted to go with all my heart.

I first heard of Pine Ridge when I was attending the University of Maine in Orono, Maine. I received my books for next semester, among them was *Lakota Woman* by Mary Crow Dog. It was part of my summer reading list and the thinnest book in the pile, so I thumbed through it. The black and white photos caught my eye and captured my heart. If a picture speaks a thousand words, I heard those and then some.

The images of poverty juxtaposed with a sense of unbroken spirit spoke to my soul and moved me in a way I had never felt before. I had an unexplainable desire to experience the heartbreak and history for myself.

I skimmed thirty or so pages around the photos. Somehow, the few words I gleaned were "Pine Ridge" and "Wounded Knee." I looked at a map and discovered this place was 120 miles from where I was headed in a few days, to the Sturgis Motorcycle Rally in South Dakota.

If I had actually read the book, it would have made more sense to plan a visit to Mary on the Rosebud Reservation where she currently lived, instead of setting my sites on the Pine Ridge Reservation, about an hour and a half away from Mary in Rosebud. Actually, if I had read the book, it would have made the most sense to avoid the whole situation.

As it was, I immediately idolized Mary and convinced myself she was an untouchable celebrity removed from the reservation, adrift on the winds of her great fame. I told myself it would be impossible to meet her. I decided instead to journey to Wounded Knee, the heart of all the action in her story.

I had no idea Mary was a budding feminist from a reservation near my destination. I also had no idea she is half white. Her Christianized mother is Brulé, one of the many bands of "Sioux." Perhaps it is best I was so far off the mark, as I ended up feeling the pulse of the beauty and tragedy I was seeking in Wounded Knee's history by joining up with the Lakota Oglala "Sioux" band who are Crazy Horse's people.

I quickly found myself in over my head with a full-blooded Lakota chief twenty years my senior, a Wounded Knee local steadfast in the old ways and traditions. Within a month of opening Mary's book, I was immersed to the point of drowning in a culture which was much more than I could comprehend.

When I picked up *Lakota Woman*, I wasn't your typical college student and I wasn't running away on a whim. I was thirty years old. And I didn't plan to run away, I simply wanted to visit the area in order to enrich the college class discussion of the book next semester. I enjoy living what I learn; life is a journey and I have always done things a little differently.

I did not have the money or the scholarships to attend

college in a four year block of time. I took classes piece meal, "a la carte" as my sister Amandah always joked. It had taken me twelve years to finish my freshman year of college. The mailman would catch me studying at work and tease, "At the rate you're going, by the time you graduate, you'll throw out your hip when you toss up your cap!"

It might take me a while, but I was determined to get there. I didn't follow a strict curriculum, which also delayed my official progress from freshman status. Before I moved to Maine, I took art classes in Connecticut at the University of Hartford. When my life moved me to New Hampshire, I studied diverse topics of interest at Keene State College, such as a senior year level Literary Analysis and Theory class, which I loved.

Wherever my life brought me, I continued to take a few classes that interested me. I built a base so strong in subjects I cared about that, in time, I found myself in a level 500 graduate study Sociology class at the University of Maine. Admittance to this hand-selected group of fifteen required an interview and the professor's signed approval. They let me in, I worked hard and was one of only three students who earned a final grade of 'A.' I enjoyed giving all I had to the classes I chose. As an older student, I carried in my life's experience viewpoints and remained open to creating new ones. I lived life voraciously, because I was alive every moment.

Good grades were simply a bonus that came from a passion for learning. I never focused on the outcome, I cared only about the joy I felt. I graduated high school with a 3.875 GPA with a 4.0 being a solid 'A.' But, it was not enough for college scholarships; I did not fall within the top 10. I never even knew "top ten" was a goal until my senior year of high school. The guidance counselor told me how close I was to being in this elite group of ten who are honored and adorned with monetary awards. It was the first I'd heard of it.

I was shocked I had done so well. I expected our meeting

would address my poor performance. Armed with my "I'll do better" speech, I was instead praised and pushed harder. I shrugged to myself and thought, "All these years, I've just been doing it for fun. What a shame I never knew it was all for something."

Our first class reunion was our ten year, which meant a commute to Connecticut from my apartment near Bangor, Maine. I attended, amused by how these twenty-seven and twenty-eight year old women proudly and arrogantly flashed their diamond engagement rings. At this point in my life, I had been married and divorced twice, with no children. I laughed and said, "You'll learn. The first one's just practice. Talk to me at the 25th year reunion," which was the next one we had planned. Yes, you could say I was jaded. Or, you could say I was the biggest romantic always searching for the grandest dream. I fell in love hard, open, honest, every time. My mother would say I give too much of myself too quickly, but I would say if you are not real, it's not worth it. As long as the good outweighed the bad, I was in with all I had.

My parents were not role models for my failed marriages. They're Southern Baptists who recently celebrated their 35th wedding anniversary. My dad is from Kentucky and my mother Indiana; they met while working at a JCPenney in Ohio. They married; my father got a promotion that came with a job transfer to a new store opening on the East Coast.

That's how I was born in Connecticut instead of the Midwest. It also explains why there is a calling in my blood which does not allow me to feel at home in the East. Or perhaps anywhere, as this calling contributes to my overall sense of wanderlust.

My parents were over-protective and worried about everything. Naturally, it made sense to me when I ran away from Connecticut on my eighteenth birthday to the woods of New Hampshire with only a hundred dollars and a milk crate full of clothes.

I lived alone in an old, broken down chicken coop with no electricity, phone, bathroom, chickens, or heat. I bathed in a babbling brook, I roofed houses by day, and worked as a waitress by night. I walked everywhere I went, as I did not get a driver's license until a few years later. When the moon wasn't full, I lit my way through the night woods with my Zippo lighter. Coyotes and black bears would sniff at my door; however, my shotgun could not protect me from the coming cold weather.

That sounds tough, but I never shot anything. I would just hug the gun like a teddy bear while sniffs and snarls seeped through the cracks in my battered door during the lingering dark hours. What scared me most was the cold. I had no source of heat. Any smoke would give away my squatter's location to the town officials. I got married too fast the first time mostly because winter was coming and my coop was drafty.

Marriage seemed my only option, as I was not welcome back home with my parents and two younger sisters. I was "too worldly now." My sisters were still in middle and high school, they needed to be sheltered and protected from my rebellious ways. I was seen as promiscuous, even though I had only been with two people at this point in my life, yet both out of wedlock. I was not allowed to come home when I asked. Not even when I begged. I had no other relatives to turn to, so I created my own.

Being respectably married did not bring my birth family any closer; they did not even attend my wedding. When my first husband died suddenly, I mourned but moved on. I was alive and I planned to make the most of it. I always searched for something more out of this life; it had to be bigger, better. I would not get stuck in a rut and hang my head, trudging through the motions, beaten down like others I see.

I got married again, he was also a small-town New Hampshire local. My family really liked this one and the relationship with them got a little better with time. This marriage lasted for six years. He was a kind, gentle biker almost two decades older. After less than a year of dating, we got married at Laconia Bike Week, a New Hampshire motorcycle rally. Some said we eloped because nobody was invited and we kept our plans a secret. We had both already been through the drama of a big wedding, we wanted something more private and personal this second time around. We told our families the news when we got back home.

He truly loved me and was always good to me. There is not a bad word I could ever say about him, the fault was all my own. I gave the American dream a chance inside his house. His first wife was gone and I picked up where she left, living the white picket fence life, being a good wife until I could do it no longer. A healthy relationship and a normal situation were too commonplace for me; safety and security became suffocating boredom. My feathers were too bright for the caged life. There had to be something more than this daily routine.

As I was divorcing him, I moved to Maine with my two parrots. My goal was to finish my college degree at the University of Maine even if it took the rest of my life.

In between my new, unmarried life and work, I took classes. Three years into it, I finally finished the core classes I needed to officially complete my freshman year. This is when I discovered *Lakota Woman* in my stack of books. It was required reading for my sophomore year Women's Studies class. The photos in Mary's book opened my heart like nothing had ever done before. This was real. This is what I had been searching for.

The first Wounded Knee took place on December 29, 1890, not that long ago, really. This is the Wounded Knee students might be familiar with from history class. In the 1890 Wounded Knee, the remaining members of Custer's 7th Calvary took revenge on the Lakota *(Luh-koh-tdah)* people by slaughtering them in a bloody massacre. Hundreds of Indian bodies, including women, children, and infants, were gunned down in a frenzied racist rage and then abandoned. Days later, the frozen, twisted bodies were unceremoniously dumped together in a mass grave. Mary's book spoke at length about the second Wounded Knee. The occupation from 1973 when Indians took over the village of Wounded Knee for 71 days from February 27th 1973–May 8th, 1973. They made a stand for their rights against the powers that oppress them, including the FBI sent in to stop them.

I admired the Indians' strength and their passion for life, which I shared. A few photos in Mary's book showed images of destitute poverty. I could not believe people with such spirit lived in this manner, here in the United States, in modern times. This was not an old story. The mistreatment was still happening. I had to see it for myself. I had to offer my heart. Perhaps, if I could find the right person, give some words of understanding . . .

It was in this moment of longing that I looked at a map and discovered the Pine Ridge Reservation was not that far from Sturgis, South Dakota. Coincidentally, I had already made plans to travel to the Sturgis Motorcycle Rally. I was headed west in just a few days. *Lakota Woman* had come into my life at the most perfect moment.

I would soon learn, however, that if a book is going to change your life, perhaps it's best if you actually read it first.

CHAPTER TWO:

Sturgis

I have been riding motorcycles since I was twelve. Motorcycles are roaring passion, something real to make me feel alive. I enjoy the sport, either on the back or on my own.

In this, the summer of 2005, a few months after my 30th birthday, I had a teal and silver Sportster and big, bald biker boyfriend who had a big, bad Harley. His shaved head was as shiny as his bike's mirror-polished tanks and fenders. My long, golden brown hair was past my waist. We made quite the pair.

Big Biker and I had love for and pasts filled with motorcycles, but we had never been to Sturgis. Heading out there in August for the Sturgis Rally is a milestone in a biker's riding history. We would be part of the 65th anniversary celebration.

Each year, about 500,000 people attend the week-long event. To a biker, Sturgis is a feather in your cap, like Indian boys who earn their eagle feather and become a warrior. Riding your own motorcycle out there is a badge of honor much admired by other riders. Plus, it's a heck of a lot of fun! Sturgis means you've made it. It's a right of passage. If you've been to Sturgis, you're a real biker.

Riding your own out there is even more impressive when home is somewhere on the East Coast. Big Biker and I were planning to make the 2,150 mile ride—each way—from Bangor, Maine to Sturgis, South Dakota. We decided to ride together on his purple and silver Heritage Softail.

We weren't towing it on a trailer behind a more cushy vehicle like many do. We weren't flying out and then renting a

Harley once we got there like others do. We were going to prove we were hardcore bikers by riding over 4,000 miles out and back. We'd tack on another thousand or two touring everything we could possibly see out there. By the time we returned to Maine, his Harley would have close to 6,000 new miles on the odometer, logged in about fifteen days. That's enough miles to travel across the entire width of the United States coast to coast—twice.

I asked him if we could make a detour 120 miles south and see Wounded Knee. Big Biker looked at the map and said it was possible on the way home. We could travel through the Badlands, then head down to Wounded Knee. It would put us on some different road choices for the way back to Maine.

Big Biker was born and bred in Boston, he was a truck driver who put decades of his life into transporting goods across the U.S. He upgraded to owner-operator and now ran a local Boston/Maine route for the company he was leased on with. He liked saying, "Everything you have, except your baby, was delivered by truck." He still lived in Boston and would come up to see me in Maine on weekends. When he didn't have his blue Kenworth truck, he'd bring the Harley. We were always out riding, sometimes we'd put on 300 miles in the few hours I had after work on a Saturday.

Since driving was his life, he decided we'd try something different and take a very northern route out to South Dakota. He promised it would be more relaxing to head up through Canada instead of fighting our way through Chicago city traffic. He was a mastermind outsmarting time because the Canada route was shorter than traveling through the U.S. the entire way. We examined and re-examined the maps, we chose to leave GPS and cell phones behind. Our excitement kept building, each passing day bringing us closer to beginning our journey, and bringing me closer to Wounded Knee.

We'd be cowboys riding with only a paper map and our sense of adventure to guide us. I traced our route with my fingertips. It would take us over the tops of a few Great Lakes, we'd cross between two of them at Sault Ste. Marie, Ontario, then drop down into Wisconsin. The plan sounded great until it was enacted. The roadmap had been misleading. It promised fun blue and red lines on a green background. Not all routes are as equal as they seem when traced by an excited finger that's never been there before. Going up through Canada turned out to be a very lonely, long, and grey way to go. I don't think I've ever been so bored on the back of a motorcycle as I was on that endless, desolate, Canada highway.

To make matters worse, all the road signs were in French. This really messed up Big Biker's sense of direction. Especially since neither of us knew the French word for "east" or "west." And the Canadians weren't about to tell us. Well, that is, if there was anyone around to ask, which there wasn't.

I was of no help, as I had not yet been trained by the Indians to look up at the position of the sun to tell east from west. When they trained me, it never did me any good, anyway. I'd turn around and everything would get reversed, then I'd be lost again. The Indians could tell the time of day and their coordinates on the globe just by checking the position of the sun. They could tell one clump of prairie grass from another to find their way through locations that all looked the same to me. I need landmarks. Like, "Turn left at McDonald's."

Growing up, my dad always said it was our Kentucky heritage that made us this way. He said people from Kentucky use landmarks, not street names.

With hillbilly pride, Kentuckians give directions: "Whatcher gonna do's turn left at Betty Joe's old barn. It blew down last year, so ya won't be seein' that, but yuh'll know the spot cuz its where that big ol' oak tree stood. You know, the big un Li'l Johnny chopped down last fall. So, ya won't be seein' that oak tree, neither. But yuh know where it useter be."

No wonder I'm always lost. I have no sense of direction. I get lost finding my house on the way home from work every day. As a kid, I couldn't even color in the lines and now I'm supposed to drive and park between them.

Big biker didn't look up at the sun either, for he was also a White Man. Besides, the sun doesn't shine on Americans when they are in Canada anyway, everyone knows that.

I think Big Biker was rattled because this alternate route was his idea; he was trying to impress me and knew it wasn't working. His stress made things worse as he got wound up. We pulled over. I walked away so he could figure it out on his own without me breathing down his neck, which was easy to do since I was on the back of his bike.

I strolled down the road, trying to find anything interesting. It was a hopeless quest. Bored, I gave up and just stood on the side of the Canada highway staring at the grass and dirt, waiting for him to check the road atlas. I couldn't believe how the soil beneath my feet was the same shade of grey as the bleak sky. It was like standing in a muddy watercolor painting with nothing to break up the horizon. Just flat grey earth, flat grey sky, even the roadside weeds had grey flowers. To me "gray" with an 'a' is a harmless American neutral color, but on this afternoon, I understood "grey" with an 'e' to be the colour of despair, oftentimes influenced by some British affiliation. Needless to say, this was the worst part of the trip.

Since I was removed from the situation, he got a handle on things rather quickly. The bike roared into life, we did seven hundred miles in one day just trying to get out of Canada. If I fell asleep on the back of the bike, I'm sure I had bad dreams of running in place.

I was never so glad to kiss Wisconsin soil. Finally, there was color in the world again and we could read the road signs. Now back in the U.S., we were well past Chicago and the scenery had changed dramatically. Lots of farmland, big round hay bales, windmills, and irrigation systems later, we were finally in South Dakota. We had been traveling hard for three days, about 1,700 miles. South Dakota is six hours wide and we were aiming for the west side of the state.

Not too long into the ride, we started seeing billboards and little "Burma-Shave" style signs promoting Wall Drug Store in Wall, South Dakota. "Free Ice Water since 1936" doesn't sound like much, but I was looking forward to it. I started asking, "Are we there yet?" when we were still three hours away. I don't think I would have made it if it wasn't for the hope of Wall Drug and its persistent advertising signs. I kept thinking, "Well, somebody lived through this, they put these signs up."

The ride across South Dakota is desolate. There is just one long highway across the state, it can be a hundred miles or more between gas stations. The fun, little signs for Wall Drug made the ride more interesting. The signs became familiar little buddies popping up along the way like friendly little prairie dogs saying hello, keeping a traveler company on the long, lonely road. The signs start advertising about three hundred miles away from Wall in either direction of the place. Upon arrival, Wall Drug is a welcomed break from the endless isolation.

From the outside, Wall Drug looks like a building on a western movie set, the street complete with horse hitching posts. Once inside, I was glad to see its name is honest; it really is a drug store with aspirin and Pepto-Bismol. The rows of pharmacy products were lost among the crazy postcards, T-shirts, and unique souvenirs. The place is huge, about a city block long. There are places to eat and little stores filled with tourist knick-knacks and kitschy Western wear. There was a giant brontosaurus and a jackalope. My favorite was a roaring T-Rex complete with fierce red lights and smoke. I took photos of everything.

The free ice water ended up being a long copper horse trough about waist high. Water streamed out the faucets into the trough. Looking back, I might have been drinking from the restroom hand washing station, but I thought it was the free ice water. At any rate, it was refreshing and noteworthy, since even motels out this way proudly shout from billboards: "Rooms with running water!" as an enticing perk. They are serious. Water is a big deal out here where it is so dry and thinly populated.

We got a no-frills motel room down the road in the town of Wall. It had running water. I was happy. One of my nicest memories was taking a late afternoon shower at the motel, putting on a light cotton dress with sandals, and riding a few blocks down to the main street for dinner. After about ten hours in the iron horse saddle with the hot sun, road dirt, and all that heavy leather gear, it was refreshing weightlessness to leave everything in the motel room and hop on the bike for a three minute easy ride down the street.

It was so different being on the Harley in a dress with no leather jacket, no helmet, no boots, no socks, no jeans, just a simple dress with no underwear. Fresh out of the shower, the wind lifted my loose and lightly damp hair back just enough at a slow, breezy speed. I felt so pretty and clean. I closed my eyes and smiled. I imagined an eagle effortlessly soaring, letting the warm and cool air currents carry him without flapping. If I were to define perfect, that moment in my life would be it. There was nothing wrong or out of place, I had not a care or worry. I simply felt so light, floating in the evening air which was slowly slipping into twilight.

The next day, we finally made it to Sturgis. The town of Sturgis was crowded with motorcycles; pedestrians were hazards in the street. We took a slow ride down the most popular streets in the heart of the celebration. It was an experience complete with hooting, hollering, revving engines, standstill traffic, and a general party atmosphere.

We parked, got T-shirts, and I had my first taste of Americanized Indian life, an Indian taco. It begins with Indian fry bread, a staple in the Lakota diet. It's like fried dough but sweet and dense and not as greasy. Take that little slice of Indian heaven and top it with normal taco fillings and you have yourself and Indian taco. They are fabulous. Even the Indians like them, and they didn't seem offended by the name.

I'm a vegetarian. It's not a family tradition or a religious thing. It has been my own free will choice for over 30 years. I don't get self righteous or loud about it, I just speak softly and order a big salad. South Dakota is the heart of buffalo and cattle country. It's not the place to be a vegetarian. A vegetarian in South Dakota makes people gasp; they look at you as if you just swore in the microphone at church. Double beans, hold the meat. Yes, I'm a freak. Way to ruin the Indian taco. Despite the extra glares and blasphemous loss of beef, I found it delightfully scrumptious.

We checked out a famous campground near Sturgis and saw a rock concert that evening. The daytime general party atmosphere turned to insanity here. It was an outdoor Harley hell nightclub. Campers offered whiskey shots in return for promiscuous displays by women. I gave only smiles and accepted nothing. Harleys roared, cruising on monorail platforms over the crowd while eruptions of fire burst below. Since every biker is family, I didn't even think to have any fear. These were all my relatives, good people just having a good time. I also had a big, bald biker boyfriend to protect me, a crazy Irishman who used to get in way too many barroom brawls back in his drinking days last year. Yep, I had no worries.

The big food attraction here was "pitchfork fondue." A huge slab of buffalo meat skewered onto a farmer's full-sized pitchfork, then devilishly dipped into a fifty-five gallon drum of boiling oil. Big Biker loved it; I thought it was amazing to watch them cook it. After the concert, we rode back to our motel in Hot Springs with a distant thunderstorm rocking the midnight sky.

It began with a serious light show of multi-colored lightening bolts: blue, white, purple, yellow. A Midwest storm is something of wonder, power, and beauty. It is possible to see a storm happening miles away because it's so flat out there. In the daytime, there could be blue sky without wind or rain, but look in the distance and there will be dark clouds and a wall of water five miles away.

At night, there are no streetlights, no lights of the city. Just a flat blackness, the road lit only by the motorcycle's headlights. Huge animals can easily step into the road; it is quite dangerous. The storm made it worse, changing shadows into moving things, twisting the road with flashes of white light overhead. The black sky in the distance danced with the most amazing display of color. It was about an hour back to Hot Springs and we were on the edge of our seat the whole way. The rain never came down, but the light show was always chasing us.

The next day, we explored some old Wild West towns outside Sturgis which have more charm than the city atmosphere. Hundreds of bikes were parked in the street in one remote tumbleweed town, while a hundred others cruised on by together in a group. I'm sure bikers outnumbered the local population count something like a few thousand bikers to two locals.

I sat on a bench while Big Biker took a bathroom break. Alone and looking pretty, I was soon accompanied by an old biker who looked like Willie Nelson. He sat beside me and said the real Sturgis party happens on this very street at three in the morning, "Cuz that's a when the wimmens ride naked."

Big Biker had given up drinking and I had quit, too, in support. I've never seen anybody up on the wagon hootin' and hollerin' naked. Sober, participation in public nudity wasn't about to happen.

It's true the most thrilling parts of Sturgis Bike Week are not in the town of Sturgis. And I don't mean the parties, drinking, and crazy scenes. That's just some of the people and those people tend to stay put in their campgrounds or hotel parking lots. The people who give bikers a bad reputation are a minority and far outnumbered by those who came to ride.

The best part of Sturgis Bike Week is the scenery. There are so many natural things to see that are truly breathtaking. Out in western South Dakota, once a year, a few hundred thousand motorcyclists agree. We were never alone on the road; thousands of our family members were always around us. Hundreds ride together on the same mile of road, seeing the same sights, breathing the same air, becoming one together with flesh, earth, sky, wind, mountains, and machine.

Despite their tough exterior, bikers are soulful people who love to feel the spirit of the ride. There is so much magic in South Dakota, we were constantly in awe of the beautiful, scenic views and intensely diverse landscapes.

Some of the places we saw were Mount Rushmore, Devil's Tower, Wind Cave, The Black Hills, and The Badlands. Ironically, these famous tourist attractions are all sacred places to the Lakota Indians. In their heart, this land is still theirs. The U.S. Presidents' faces carved into Mount Rushmore are a giant scar slashed into their sacred Black Hills. A deep wound inflicted by White Man. A constant reminder the wound still bleeds.

The most beautiful gem of land we saw was named after General Custer, who was defeated by the Lakota at The Battle of the Little Big Horn in 1876. Custer's resentful, remaining men of the 7th Calvary would later commit the massacre at Wounded Knee in 1890. This beautiful land was stolen from the Lakota and named by White Man to honor the Lakota enemy.

The Lakota should have their sacred land back. Give them back their Black Hills, let them live, hunt, dance, and pray there. Keep the White Man out. Or let the Lakota charge a fee to non-Indians, let them specify the areas non-Indians can take part in. That seems fair to me. Custer State Park is gorgeous, luscious, teaming with life. It is what the Lakota should have instead of a barren reservation grassland.

The park holds the highest natural point east of the Rocky Mountains, Harney Peak, a sacred Indian mountain White Man named for the General who fought the Brulé band of Lakota in 1855, killing women and children to claim its golden title. It is surrounded by the Black Elk Wilderness, named after a spiritual leader of the Lakota. Yet, White Man builds campgrounds around it and charges admission.

Custer State Park is a rich and glorious 71,000 acres, easily seen are bison, pronghorn antelope, mountain goats, bighorn sheep, mule deer, and elk, which are huge. Some of the animals get so used to people such as the adorable wild burros who are known to poke their heads into open car windows, gently nudging shoulders and hands, looking for snacks.

The park is home to a herd of thirteen hundred bison, always "buffalo" to the Lakota. In the old days, the Lakota hunted buffalo and they used every part of it. It is their revered spiritual animal. White Buffalo Calf Woman gave the *chanupa (chuh-noo-puh)*, the sacred ceremonial pipe, to the Lakota people. In modern times, I never saw any buffalo roaming on the Indian reservation.

The buffalo herd is usually found spilling into the road in Custer. Silly tourists use about fifteen seconds of judgment to decide grazing buffalo move slowly, so they must be harmless. Buffalo can suddenly charge. They are powerful and can move quite fast. I have seen males butt heads with each other, pawing the earth into clouds of dust around them, suddenly breaking into a run, creating thunder on the ground with their hoofbeats. Buffalo might look shaggy and docile, but they are not giant stuffed animals.

Buffalo mothers can be the most aggressive. Protecting her calf is her top priority. She will charge anything that gets too close including people, cars, and motorcycles. A motorcyclist doesn't have a car's metal bubble of protection, which leaves a biker very vulnerable if attacked. It also leaves one very open to hear the stupid ideas of tourists.

"Oh look, Johnny! Buffalo!" A car has decided to wedge its way in between the motorcycles, it parks next to us. "Let's get out and take some pictures with Johnny and the buffalo, ok, dear?" The wife gets out of the car and picks her toddler up in her arms. The husband follows with the camera. To my absolute horror, the mother walks right up to a grazing buffalo and sets her three year old son on its back. She laughs as they have their picture taken. I realize my mouth has been hanging open in shock the entire time, my face so white it lost its suntan.

The kid spends a few minutes bouncing on the buffalo's back, as if quarters were just put into the plastic horsey outside K-mart. Mom and dad pose for more pictures with junior, they get back into their car and drive away as if nothing reckless has happened. Never realizing how careless they have been with their child's life, and their own.

We ride onward. The most amazing road lies ahead. Needles highway is full of thrilling switchback turns and breathtaking mountains. The Harley curves around sharply, then tilts the other way, looking back down on the road just traveled. As the bike climbs higher, I maintain my balance looking backwards and downwards, capturing some of the most fabulous photos of the journey.

A hundred other riders cruise along with us, enjoying endless blue sky, passing through forests with adventurous, twisting roads, overlooking pristine lakes and sharp mountains.

Suddenly, a narrow tunnel appears. A square hole blasted through the magnificent mountains, it looks barely big enough to fit a camper. The rock walls are cold and wet inside. These tunnels were cut by man; through the mountain was the only way to the other side.

As if that wasn't cool enough, after passing through several holes in the mountains, the light at the end of the tunnel becomes the faces of Mt. Rushmore. It is possible to snap a photo of the faces framed by the square tunnel cut into the mountain. I know because I did just that; my postcard worthy photo was a prize in the scrapbook I would soon make, detailing our journey.

Many white mountain goats climb about the steps and scenery around Mt. Rushmore. American flags fly proudly on this sacred Indian land. If one stops amid the tourist traps, allows the mind to unfold and thinks with compassion, it might be possible to see why Mt. Rushmore carved into the stolen Black Hills is blasphemous to the Lakota.

Once thinking along these lines, it is understandable how mindful, well-intentioned people can come to the erroneous conclusion that visiting the nearby monument to Crazy Horse is a better, more politically correct thing to do. Those people may visit Crazy Horse Memorial out of guilt for also visiting Mt. Rushmore. To atone, they drop an extra twenty in the donation bucket in addition to their admission fee, believing they are helping "Native Americans." They never know the Lakota do not benefit from Crazy Horse Memorial. One of their great leaders is used as a marketing ploy.

Soon, I would get to know a headsman of an Oglala Lakota family bloodline, a man chosen to guide his people; he, after brave deeds, had earned respect and been honored with the title of Chief.

He was born with Crazy Horse's blood in his veins; he told me the Lakota hate the Crazy Horse monument, too. He said the project is run by a white man and his son. Decades have passed but no work gets done. Yet, the tourists pour in with increasing numbers every year. They pay admission and make donations. The money collected never goes into finishing the project; it just goes into a rich white man's pocket. He does not give to the Lakota people he is supposedly honoring with the project.

What offends the Lakota most is the bar built next to the warrior and steed immortalized in stone.

Now, people can sit and drink the poison which White Man brought to the Indians while they look over their shoulder at the money making monument of a legendary Lakota leader, Crazy Horse.

It wasn't enough for White Man to steal Indian land; he had to steal his spirit and strength by introducing alcohol to their people.

White Man murdered their people, stole their land, lied, and made them drunk. This is what the Lakota see in the Crazy Horse Memorial.

CHAPTER THREE:

Wounded Knee

On our last day, Big Biker and I get up with the early morning fog. Surrounded by a damp, gray mist which holds no sense of despair, we pack our things into the saddlebags. We check out of the motel and head up to Sturgis for our final goodbye to this town and the week-long event. Once there, we make sure we haven't forgotten anybody on our souvenir list. From Sturgis, we travel south through the Badlands; we will stop at Wounded Knee as I requested, then head back to Maine.

Nothing we have ever seen could prepare us for the Badlands. Photos do not do it justice, but I took plenty anyway. It is stunning, majestic, and almost eerie. White mountains with brown, red, and yellow streaks rise in the distance. They come close enough to touch, then pull away, falling for what seems like miles. Towering, sharp peaks turn into plateaus, then drop away, only to be caught by more colorful and taller spires.

I just had to touch it. We pulled over. The bits of rock I picked up broke apart into granular balls with hardly any pressure from my fingers. I tasted the dust, thinking it might be salty or smell like a mineral. It was clean, fresh, and light, with no smell or taste.

The occasional flat patch of grass was the only plant life I saw and the only animals were vultures swirling overhead. Many tourists with an over-eager sense of spirituality might mistake them for hawks or eagles, but to a bird watcher, these had the wings of vultures. It was appropriate, since I cannot see how anything could live out here for long. It is beyond desert.

It is the moon.

Celestial mountains and valleys turn into a flatter, less flashy part of the Badlands known as the South Unit. Ninety-nine percent of the annual visits to the Badlands occur in the breathtaking, gorgeous part we just passed through. Here in the South Unit, Big Biker and I are the 1%ers. There's nobody else here but us. The land is barren like a desert, but it has more grass and scrubby vegetation.

This part of the Badlands was given back to the Indians, then taken away again shortly after the U.S. entered WWII. The government wanted to use the Indians' sacred land as a U.S. Army Air Force bombing and gunnery test site. Hundreds of Indians were given a week to vacate their land. Ten years of testing left the ground scarred with craters, some unexploded bombs still lay buried in the land. Old cars were used as military targets; their blasted carcasses can still be seen on the grassy badlands back roads.

Big Biker and I passed through the South Unit and entered the "Sioux" Reservation. The land suddenly changed. I recalled all the places Big Biker and I had seen in the past few days. The majestic, lush Black Hills were gone, the breathtaking mountains and sudden deep canyons of the colorful "moon rock" desert of the Badlands was gone. The wildlife we saw teeming in Custer State Park was gone. Crystal clear lakes were gone. White Man seemed to have taken most of the trees, too. We had ridden out of everything grand and beautiful into a scrubby, dry, useless, flat prairie.

"*This* is the land the White Man chose to give the Indians?" I was ashamed, mournful, disgusted. "This is where they segregated them? This, the land nobody wanted? Wow." I had tears in my eyes.

What had started off as the fizzled-out end of the Badlands turned prairie. We stumbled upon a classic ghost town; I never saw a person or vehicle. There were abandoned, broken buildings with animal skulls tacked to the weathered wood.

Then miles and miles of just plain nothing, only this long, lonely dirt road through the prairie. It was so rough in places, Big Biker wasn't sure the motorcycle could make it through. Later, I learned there are other ways into the reservation easier to navigate, but all paths are desolate for a long ride.

For an hour's time there were no buildings, no gas station, no food, no hospital, no police, no ambulance, no firehouse, no school, no mall, no shelter of any kind, no Starbucks, no McDonald's, no general store, no houses, no parking lots, no busses, no taxi, no cars or any other signs of human life, not even another human. I mean, there is literally NOTHING.

There is a vast geographical as well as emotional separation between the White Man's United States and the reservation. The Tribal Police are not White Man's police. White Man's police do not enter the reservation. The Tribal Police do things their own way on their own land. Stepping onto the reservation is stepping under Red Man's Law. Everything you, the outsider, think you know and everything you think protects you is gone. Even the law is not on your side. You are the minority and your presence is resented. If you lose your transportation, there is no tow truck or repair shop— and there's no taxi or bus or airplane out of there. If it takes a desolate ghost town hour to ride in, imagine how long the walk would be to get out. Based on my experience, I would say you'd be lucky to see the other end of that journey.

The Lakota have their own, sometimes seemingly broken, form of government with representatives at the tribal, state, and U.S. levels. To enter the reservation is to truly leave "American" soil. Setting foot on reservation land, one abandons American law and becomes subject to Indian Law, Ancient Law, and that of the tribal police. One enters a third world country.

The reservation is so completely removed from "the real world" as we know it that, in fact, about a year after I lived out there, respected elders went to Washington, D.C. and declared their withdrawal from the United States. There is talk about the Lakota Nation developing their own passports, currency, driver licenses, and charging non-residents to cross the reservation border—if they are allowed in at all.

Letters have been written to other countries declaring Lakota independence, seeking political support. Elders speak on talk radio, they visit states in the U.S. and make a stand for their independence to politicians and locals who will listen.

They speak at lectures and hold meetings, they ask the common man as well as Hollywood producers and actors for donations in support of their cause. They declare openly and publicly the Lakota nation has withdrawn from all treaties and agreements imposed by the United States. They will reclaim the land stolen from them; they will set right grievous thefts which left them with only lies and broken treaties. They want their land back. They want their pride back. They want their heritage, hunting, dancing, spiritual, and living rights back.

Their struggle is a current event happening every day. Even though white society acts as if Indians are something extinct mentioned only in history books, these people are real. Lakota, Dakota, and Nakota Indians are still very real, yet they are lumped under the same terminology by white man as "Sioux," but there is so much more to learn. For just the Lakota, there are seven different bands, each similar yet different. Visiting the Pine Ridge Reservation may seem like taking a step back in time, but their voices cry daily in our modern world. White Man's majority closes its ears and looks the other way.

The Lakota are fighting for a noble cause when they declare they have withdrawn from treaties of the United States and are now their own independent sovereign nation within the U.S.

However, from my experience living out there, I can say probably only four people actively support and believe in this movement and it is their voices being heard to represent many who may not agree with the concept. And between those four active supporters, two are split against the other two and those two are split against each other, developing their own ideas on how it should be. There is so much arguing amongst themselves that not much can come of it.

In fact, the BIA, The Bureau of Indian Affairs, an agency of the Federal Government representing 566 federally recognized Indian tribes, dismissed this withdrawal as 'not really real.' The BIA is a long-time enemy in some Indian's eyes. The Lakota elder I would soon meet hates the BIA and would snarl at the mention of its name. He claims the BIA is corrupt, which is why he favors AIM, the American Indian Movement, instead. AIM was an influential part of the 1973 Wounded Knee occupation and is still strong today.

The few outspoken people supporting the new Lakota Nation talk big about it, like it's really happening, while their people live off unhealthy government rations, drink White Man's whiskey, and get into gang related fights. The Lakota youth are more interested in wearing bandanas on their foreheads and slouching their pants low with gangster style than they are in listening to the elders tell the stories of their ancestors. Only 14% of Lakota Indians can speak their native language. The average speaker is 65 years old, which is seventeen years past the average life expectancy for men. Their own youth is not listening as the old ways cry out.

I wanted to listen. I wanted to hear it all, soak it in, understand and become Lakota. But, bottom line, I am white; my heart cannot change the color of my skin. My father's grandparents were both directly off the boat from Germany, they settled in Kentucky. My father was proud of his heritage; but, to his dismay and doubt, for my entire childhood mom kept telling us we were Cherokee.

When it came time for college, I went against the grain of my father's upbringing and investigated my Cherokee heritage. I realized I needed tribal enrollment for scholarships. I wasn't enough Indian for college . . . and my Cherokee blood wasn't thick enough for the Lakota, either.

Lakota women would speak with me about my heritage and laugh, shake their heads, and say, "Every time a white person claims they 'have some Indian in me' it's always Cherokee. Those white Cherokees never know to which family name their blood belongs. Cherokee blood was too watered down by Whites." Lineage is important to the Lakota. Besides, Cherokee is not Lakota; they like to stick with their own.

My mother would mourn the Trail of Tears and tell us Cherokee stories when my father wasn't around. She said he would not "let her be Cherokee." He never acknowledged her desire to walk the Red Road; to him his children are German because that is his heritage.

I recall a family vacation to my dad's homeland in Kentucky which included a visit to Mammoth Cave and a drive up into the Smoky Mountains; the Cherokee Indians have a long history with these sacred mountains. My mother cried all the way up into the foggy sky. At the blue misty summit she was so overcome with emotion that she spoke of her people. My dad encouraged her to be still and she hushed. I wish I had listened more to her stories.

When my mother was very young, she knew her Cherokee grandmother only as "Squaw," which was the only name her white husband would use to address her. "Squaw" was a full-blood Cherokee who spoke little English, wore traditional dress, and had black hair in two long braids. My young mother watched as her beloved elder was ordered around harshly. "Squaw" had been plucked from the reservation and married to the white way of life.

Growing up in White Man's rural Indiana, my mother often felt misplaced and alone. She said she would run away to sit on a mountaintop and dream. She would feel the wind in her face and hair and stare off into the clouds. She'd wish to fly away into the distance, knowing she did not belong in this world.

Her father, a man with a heavy hand towards women,

would find her, call her "Little Chief" in a demeaning way and send her home to do the dishes.

Maybe that's the kind of Indian I am. A dreamy, mountaintop Indian sent home to do the dishes.

CHAPTER FOUR:

Chief Two Bear Paws

Big Biker and I came out of the wilderness and suddenly stumbled upon the heart of the reservation. We rode his twenty thousand dollar shiny Harley past the real dwellings of the Lakota. These structures were not traditional tipis of the ancestors, but creations of garbage and scraps. These were not houses, but piles of rusted corrugated sheet metal, tattered tarps, and cardboard stacked together to create shelters.

This horror was home to most. Those lucky enough to live in dilapidated trailers had lethal black mold, leaking roofs, and wind blowing through eroded holes in thin walls. Trash is stuffed into the cracks, scraps of carpet and plastic food wrappers plug holes in uninsulated walls and deteriorated ceilings. Hope keeps out the rain in the summer, the snow and cold in winter.

Many Indians die each winter from hypothermia; it's easy to see why. A sheet of cardboard leaning against a metal drum worn with holes is no protection against eight foot snow drifts and thirty below zero temperatures. Dozens of people pile into one trailer just to survive. A rare few fortunate enough to have gas ovens will heat their small space by leaving the oven door open on the very cold nights.

An Indian froze to death one night when I was living on the reservation. The community's solemn, mournful sadness was touched by an underlying fear and tension. This chill ran through each one of us when we heard. Winter is a merciless beast which cannot be hunted and killed.

Later, when I lived on White Man's land an hour from the

"rez" (Indian slang for "reservation"), I heard the news another Indian died when a wind gust blew his trailer over on top of him. I felt heavy with sadness and I could hardly move. My feelings were in the minority.

White people in white towns around the reservation such as Rapid City and Hot Springs talked of this tragic incident like it was a cheerful good morning greeting. I overheard two local white men in a townie restaurant hollering hello to each other.

"Hey, Larry! You hear about that trailer blew over on the rez?"

"Yeah, that was hilarious!"

"I know! So typical! Stupid old prairie nigger got crushed by his own trailer and died. Ha! When will they ever learn?"

Blatant racism like this is a normal day in the white border towns surrounding the reservations in South Dakota. White Man laughs at Red Man's misfortune while the Lakota mourn, worried they or a loved one might be next.

Upon my first introduction to the Lakota and their modern way of life, tears streamed down my face as Big Biker and I rode past the unimaginable horrors these noble people call home.

One after another, piles of stacked garbage dotted the prairie. Some trash shelters were big enough to stand up inside, others were long enough so a family could huddle together. Scraps of plastic sheeting served as door coverings, a corner might be tacked up on a nice day. Adults sat on cinder blocks, slumped over and dejected while children played outside. Everyone looked up to watch the Harley go by. Nobody waved.

My heart was breaking and I couldn't stop crying. We came upon a dark brown, one story, round building. It was painted with big faded white spots midway up around the side.

Chief Two Bear Paws, whom I would soon meet, had appealed to a global charity organization to build this round building for the Lakota community in October of 1999. It became a museum in the year 2000 and recently in the year 2013 it was named "Holocaust Museum at Wounded Knee."

Although the local Lakota community wants to use the structure as a soup kitchen, Chief Two Bear Paws holds strong to the belief the building is needed as an educational facility open to the public, a special place to "Remember Wounded Knee."

The main round room is the museum. It is also the place donations were piled when an 18 wheeler truck arrived from an Ohio charity early one winter day.

The truck brought gifts of clothes, toothpaste, tooth brushes, coloring books, warm winter coats, socks, shoes, boots, etc. for the entire Pine Ridge Reservation.

When the delivery truck arrived at the round building in Wounded Knee one cold, winter morning, Chief Two Bear Paws's family and I unloaded it, we sorted the contents into piles. He only let his close family know the truck had arrived. Secretly, he let them into the locked building for the next few days, giving them first choice of all the good things laid out on the tables. His family took the best for themselves. There wasn't much left for the hundreds of other families who were also cold with young children when they were notified three days later that the truck had arrived.

Members of Chief's close family live in the storage areas off the main museum room, their private shelter covered by curtains and hidden from summer tourists. Due to lack of indoor plumbing, the building has an overwhelming smell of urine year-round. On the summer day of my visit, the smell was strong despite the open door. Big Biker and I parked in the dirt driveway. Many Lakota people were gathered around the road selling handmade crafts like dreamcatchers and necklaces for a small price, usually seven to fifteen dollars.

The building had a heavy, ominous feel. It called out to be noticed, but then threatened intruders to leave at the same time. It pushed and pulled my energy, making me want to go crazy with fear and love. It was also the first solid building I had seen on the reservation that seemed as if it could withstand a hail storm, wind, and winter.

The Oglala Lakota flag and the American flag flew above the building. The Oglala flag was higher. I touched the handlebars of the bike and discreetly removed the florescent yellow band which announced in bold, black letters: "Custer State Park." The band had been our admission ticket to explore the park; I got a feeling Custer's name was more than not welcome here.

I said to Big Biker, "Come on, let's go inside."

"Nope." He crossed his arms over his chest and leaned back against the motorcycle seat, the engine was ticking as it cooled. "I'm stayin' right here with the bike."

"What are you talking about? We do everything together! We've come this far, don't you want to see what's inside?"

"Don't you see what's *out*side? How about those crappy houses they live in, did you see those? These people are shady. If I go in there with you, I'll come back here to my bike in pieces. You go on ahead. I'll be right here."

I could feel our relationship breaking as I walked away from him. I thought he was heartless and lacking compassion. In hindsight, I can say he was probably smarter than I gave him credit for.

We were both right, and we were both wrong. All at the same time.

I entered the round building alone. The walls inside were covered in handwriting. Black paint was stark against white. Neatly written, bold words stood out and formed huge, blocked paragraphs. Words and drawings covered the curved walls; it was eerie, like cave paintings done in blood. This place told the stories of the Lakota people, murdered by White Man. Old photographs were taped to the walls and ceiling showing slaughtered Indian bodies frozen in snow during the 1890 Wounded Knee Massacre. The images were startling, frightening, horrific. This was reality, harsh with honesty. I felt as if I had walked into the pages of someone's private journal, as if I was not supposed to be here. The pain and accusations were so strong on the walls, they screamed. I forced myself to look around the room. There was not much else inside this small, round enclosure except a folding table near the door.

There were some crafting supplies spread across the table next to a large metal lock box labeled "Donations." Behind the table sat the only other person in the room. He was the first pure blood Indian I had ever seen in my life. He was a living, breathing legend with dark golden skin, long black hair tied with leather and a real eagle feather, a turquoise earring in his ear, and a crisp, formal black dress shirt with beads and ribbons. His black cowboy hat had a red feather; it sat on the table next to his crafts.

He kept working, looking down, while I gazed upon him. His face was a map of weathered lines filled with decades of first hand experiences. The legends of those read about were the stories of his personal life. He was the Truth I was seeking. He was this building in the flesh; the words were alive in him and he was alive in the words. The cold images were frozen burns in his heart. I wanted to be so close I was consumed by it.

I yearned to hear his stories, to earn his trust and hear his Truth. I wanted to open myself completely and feel his emotion inside my veins. I wanted to turn my blood into something that belonged to him, something that flowed for him. I had been married twice before, but all others faded in his presence. I was mesmerized.

I did not know how to begin, what to say. Choking on my first words, I realized I had not been breathing. I exhaled and relaxed. My vision panned out from exclusively focusing on him and his aura to now include the wall which wore his shadow. The tale of woe continued to spread out around him.

White Man was clearly the hated enemy, called out directly, harshly named and accused for sins against the Red Man.

There were more garish, enlarged photos of twisted, frozen elders. Their dead, outstretched hands clawed the 1890 Massacre's horrid truth into the eyes of the observer.

It was overpowering. Dizzying. Everything shouted at once and screamed with outrage. I shifted my gaze from the horror of immortalized corpses; yet, my eyes and mind found no relief. Instead, my gaze fell upon a large, upside down American flag tacked to the wall beside the door. This disturbed me. It affected me in a different way than the words and images. It drove me to action.

I had to know why the flag I respected, the one *my* forefathers had died for, was displayed in such a disrespectful, shocking manner. My anger gave me courage to speak. I asked, "What's with the flag?"

He calmly turned his head towards the flag and said, "U.S. flag stars-down means distress. Our Indian Nation is in distress. Look, see how we live. The U.S. government turns its back on the Lakota. They do not want to see what they have done. But we are still here, even if they do not look. This flag shows our pain. It is the right way for us to hang it."

He presented his side so well. What had once shocked and offended me, I now embraced. I wanted to run home and turn the flag outside my apartment door upside down in support of the Lakota, to spread the word of their distress when others questioned my flag's positioning.

But I did not do that; I turned my life upside down in support of the Lakota instead. I don't regret it. They let me in deeper than most. I got closer to the truths that only the Lakota know.

Everything the Lakota show outsiders is done in layers, they peel back the lies based on how they feel about you. But nobody knows the unmasked core except Lakota blood. It protects their culture from non-blood who would exploit, commercialize, and misuse traditions, customs, rituals, and stories. Secrecy keeps the old ways sacred, but it also enables the forgetting of Truth. They have protected their true culture so fiercely that they are killing it in the process.

The few remaining elders who are left will open up and share Truth with only Lakota blood. They try to teach and hand down the old ways to the next generations, but the Lakota youth are not listening; they are distracted by the influences of White Man's ways. The youth play rap music instead of traditional Lakota songs, they learn gangster words instead of the language of their ancestors.

Lakota is an oral language, the spelling of words can fluctuate from person to person when attempting to put it on paper in modern society. Lakota language must be passed down from the mouths and life experiences of elders. It must be listened to with the heart, then handed to one's own children. That is the right way.

The stories of the past help build the honor within an individual. With pride in oneself and culture, hope for the future is created. Sharing secrets of hunting, cooking, and craft making unite young and old. These ways need to be given to the future seven generations through first hand day to day life. The Truth is fading.

Such is the struggle of one of the last remaining elders, Chief Two Bear Paws, the pure blood Lakota I met here in this special place. Each day he fights to keep Lakota traditions alive. He does his best to teach his family how to follow the old ways and soon he would do his best to teach even me.

I looked at the craftwork he held in his hands. He was painting on leather, making buffalo shields. His brush strokes created an Indian face in strong shadow with eagle feathers in his hair. Later, I would learn this is the symbol for AIM chapters, the American Indian Movement. Chief Two Bear Paws is a strong supporter of Indian rights and a devout early member of AIM. He had been actively present at the second

Wounded Knee in 1973, the takeover, occupation, and aftermath.

He is 'a very dangerous wanted man who should not be approached by anyone except law enforcement' according to police reports, which I had not read, but would later encounter. I only looked upon Chief Two Bear Paws with love, respect, and desire.

"You do very nice work," I said, admiring his skill. "Will you make me something?"

"It costs forty dollars."

"Okay, that's great." I tried to hide my shock at the price; it was all the cash I had left, except for a few singles and a five.

"It will take time to make. Go outside and visit the mass grave site."

I was confused as to what he was talking about. I was never much of a history student; I never had a passion for it in my school days. And I don't remember being taught about this incident—or any Indian besides Sacagawea, anyway.

I had been moved by the photos and words on the museum's walls; it was really the first I'd heard of it. I guess I thought maybe the grave wasn't that close. Or perhaps I just hoped the horror was stuck back in 1890 and not really here in modern times.

He lifted his chin towards the direction of the site. "Up on the hill. I will send for you when it is done."

I nodded and said okay. I had an unexplainable desire to listen and obey everything this man said.

CHAPTER FIVE:

Voices of the Ancestors

I went outside, up the hill to a chain link fenced in area marked by stone pillars and a metal archway. The enclosure embraced a small area of respect for the dead. I carried the walls of the museum with me, they were heavy in my heart. I saw the faces of the frozen ancestors, I remembered the photo of white men digging the large hole, the mass grave, where hundreds of Indian corpses from the 1890 massacre were tossed carelessly like cord wood into a collective grave after they were murdered by U.S. soldiers.

Here I now stood, near headstones and a large monument engraved with the names of the dead. Cloth and ribbons tied to the fence in honor of the dead beckoned like arms waving me onward.

I walked through the archway into the fenced in graveyard to pay my respects. I cried at the monument and the headstones. I stood there, tears softly falling, surrounded by Lakota colors, the prayer ties hanging on the fence in remembrance. The ribbons blew around me as if to say, "Welcome, we've been expecting you." I felt like I wanted to leave something personal to show I cared. I took the colored elastics from my hair, they had been with me for the entire journey from Maine. I tied them together in a looped knot and put them on the ground at the base of the stone monument etched with Indian names. My knee on the ground, my head bowed and my long hair loose around me, I pressed my open palm to the earth and wept. I cried harder and apologized for the wrongdoings of my people. I offered myself and my heart openly; I asked the wind what I could do to help.

I heard the Ancestors from the 1890 Massacre calling to me. Their dead voices became alive, rising from the ground, screaming from the sky and earth, their whirling whispers swirled around me, creating the wind.

"We Are Here. Only You Can Help. Hear Us. Help Us. Help Our People."

Dry wind surrounded me from the outside, chilling my old self, making it cold and dead inside me. I was rocked apart by their voices. I fell to both knees inside myself, both hands on the ground, I howled with the pain of their sorrows. I was transformed. The Ancestors were inside me and I was the wind. Everything inside my body and mind, heart and spirit, was swept away. Like the sirens singing to the Greek mythological warriors, luring them to their deaths as their sweet, hypnotic voices made their boats crash upon the rocks, the Ancestors called to me. They possessed my mind and every fiber of my being; I was drawn.

I was arrogant like my white ancestors. Like them, I thought I knew what was best for the Lakota. I was self-righteous, thinking I mattered so much that I could decide what was best for a nation not my own. The wind lifted me to my feet, arms outstretched, face and palms up to the sky. Reborn, I stood there on sacred ground, never making the connection that it was not holy to the blood born into my veins. What first attracted me to the reservation is what almost killed me: my huge, empathetic heart. It heard the whispers of the Ancestors, their voices became a hum resonating ceaselessly inside me.

I stood there, hearing the voices of great Lakota Ancestors who were not mine and my life suddenly had meaning. I felt awake, alive, and sure of my decision. I needed to help these People. They needed me. This moment at the mass grave site was the turning point in my life.

My intentions were to find purpose for my existence by making up for, the best I could, the wrongdoings of White

Man. But now, in the end, I am humble. I apologize for my misled judgment. I thought I could matter. I thought I could make things better. Even just a little.

An Indian mother walked along the outside of the fence beside me, she had her five year old daughter in tow. They both carried willow branches formed into large teardrop shapes. The center was woven with an easy dreamcatcher design using blue yarn. The weaving job was so loose that the yarn sagged and ballooned out into a dome shape with the breeze. They were following me. They looked so sad. The mother spoke in a mournful tone, "Please. There is a funeral now at the church right there behind us. If we cannot raise money, we will not be able to bury our dead. We need money for the burial and for the feast after. If you buy a dreamcatcher from us, it will help us and you can come have some food when we are ready to eat in a few hours."

"Oh, I am sorry to hear of your loss. I am buying something from the museum, it will cost all I have left, forty dollars. Will that help with your funeral costs?"

She snapped out of her sadness and pulled her daughter in close, wrapping them both in the protection of her tightly closed shawl. She shifted her focus to rage for the round building. "You are not buying something from *him* inside there, are you?" She spat the word "him" and accused me with her eyes. "He is a bad man. He takes all the money for himself and does not give back to his people. He takes the money and uses it for electricity and heat for himself and his building. It is not a museum. He only lets people in that he wants to go in there. The building is not for the community as it was meant to be. He keeps it all for himself. He is greedy. He is a very bad, bad man. Stay away from him."

I must have thought she meant some other man, although Chief Two Bear Paws was the only person I saw in the building. I refused to believe her. I let her words drift away as jealousy. I gave her two dollars so she would leave and stop following me around the cemetery. I did not buy anything from her. I did not like her attitude, plus her dreamcatchers were made from slack cotton string and did not look very nice. Her daughter looked so sad. I did not want memories of that energy hanging above my bed.

At a later date, when I discussed this woman's words with Chief, he said, "There was no funeral in the church. That church has not been used in many years. The woman was after donations for herself. She was angry because she wants all the money. She is jealous of the museum. Dogs are always barking at my tipi."

A little bit of money going around and news travels fast. A teenage boy and girl came from behind the building, they were selling necklaces. They played up the meaning of the materials chosen and colors used. They told a good story and their jewelry was expensive, twenty dollars. I gave them a five dollar donation; they smiled.

A group of young men on the side of the road hollered for me to come over to their booth with a straw thatched roof. I didn't make it over that way; I was out of cash, plus, something about their approach didn't feel right to me. Later, when I spoke with Chief again, I mentioned the other crafters out there. He said, "Do not go to the one with the straw roof. It is a bad place." I was glad my intuition had been right and I had avoided it.

The Truth Chief Two Bear Paws taught was the only Truth I wanted to know. And I wanted no other craft but his. It wasn't the money, even though I was short on cash with no ATM in sight. It was the fact I wanted something only from Chief himself, something he touched and made and nothing from anyone else. I only gave donations to others; I did not take their energy in the form of buying their art. I saw there were so many different viewpoints here on everything; I decided Chief's beliefs were the only ones I wanted to adopt as my own. I shared this philosophy with him once we were together; his smile seemed proud as he said, "*Hetchetu*. That is right. It is the only way."

As I left the mass grave sight on the day of my awakening and rebirth, a beautiful young girl about eleven years old came up to me and said, "It is ready." I asked if the man in the building was her relative. "Yes, he is my grandfather." She disappeared, but her memory stayed with me for she was someone I loved the moment I saw her.

Two Bear Paws had put the buffalo shield inside a large, clear, zip lock bag along with a handwritten business card. A mailing address, email, and phone number were on the card, which came in handy for me once I got back to Maine. He did nice work. I gave him the forty dollars. He asked if I was on a motorcycle, he gestured towards my jacket; it was black leather with silver conchos and fringe all around.

"Yes, that's it right outside. The purple and silver one." I said this as if I needed to distinguish it from the crowd of others outside the door. I could see Big Biker standing guard, arms still crossed, his back to us.

Chief glanced at me for the first time. "We get a lot of motorcycle riders here. They visit us in the summer. I want to get a motorcycle ride started here. Get more people come to Wounded Knee. If you want to work on this, that is good. Get it going for next year."

My heart swelled with joy. I could not believe my good fortune; everything I wanted was coming true! I would see this man again, talk with him again; he had invited me to work on a project with him, for his people. My head was dizzy with honor. "Yes! That sounds wonderful! I will contact you when I get home and we can make plans."

He nodded and went back to his crafts. Chief Two Bear Paws was a man who spoke softly and seldom met my gaze. The brief moment of eye contact we shared marked me as his for all my days.

I got back on the Harley, but my spirit stayed at Wounded

Knee. I changed. Forever. What had started out as a heartfelt interest in the topic of a future college class discussion had ended up transforming my soul. Part of me was back there, or, part of it was inside me. I cried and cried. Tears were the rain in my hair and the storm blew all around me. Big Biker said, "What's your problem?"

"It's just so sad. They are living in this country, right here on our doorstep, yet we close the door to our hearts and turn a blind eye. I want to help them. I want to save them all. I have an idea. I talked about it with the man in there. He said he always wanted to get a motorcycle ride started out here. It's a great idea and I can help. Many bikers come to Sturgis, it should be easy to get them to visit the reservation. It will bring some money to their economy, help out, you know? And it will give them a chance to tell their story. I think it could really make a difference. I want to try."

Big Biker yelled back over his shoulder, competing with the roar of the engine. He was speeding away as fast as he could, recovering lost time and making a mad dash to safety by putting this place far behind him. "All I saw were con artists there. That guy, he saw dollar signs when he saw your leather jacket and this bike. So, he played into that, suckering you in. If you would've said you played soccer, he would've suggested you get a soccer tournament going for them instead of a motorcycle ride. You're being foolish. You're being conned. Let it go."

SEPTEMBER

CHAPTER SIX:

Letters

Big Biker saw con artists; I see a beautiful apple: red, luscious, shiny. This is the Lakota untouched by White Man. White Man "discovers" the apple and plucks it from its life source. He does not understand what he holds in his hand, so he must destroy all that is different from himself. He injects poison; it kills the apple's spirit and makes it dull.

Descendants of White Man feel bad about the damage. This new white man does what he thinks is right and cuts out the wounded spot. But the decay goes all the way to the core and it cannot be healed. All that is left is tragedy.

A once perfect apple plucked and poisoned has had so much cut out that it can never be whole again. There is nothing that can fix this; no amount of money can bring back what has been damaged and lost, there is no salve to heal this wound.

Any type of contact from the well-meaning white man does not make it better; he cannot heal the apple and make it what it once was before his forefathers interfered. It does not matter if the biggest, good intentions come at the apple with a silver spoon, all the while crying and praying over the apple, showering it with understanding and love. The damage remains.

Sadly, the descendents of the givers of poison decide it's a lost cause. All that can be done is to preserve what remains and hang the apple in a museum. They turn the rotted side towards the wall and admire what is left. They idealize the perfect beauty it held so long ago. They forget the bad and pretend they have done no harm. Nothing but the memory of what used to be can be saved.

Yet, the memory of those looking through the glass is not accurate. Only the apple who was once a proud part of the Sacred Tree can truly understand the suffering and pain it has been through and feel the wrong that has been done to it. The apple knows the Truth. Silenced behind glass, it sings and remembers.

All the way back to Maine, I evaluated and re-evaluated my life, my choices, my past and future. I searched for meaning, spirituality, belonging, family. I believed I found all those things there on the reservation. I wanted to give my life to this cause since it already owned my heart.

I knew I could make a difference in this world if I made the motorcycle ride a success. At the end of my days, I could look back and see my life had mattered, especially to the Lakota, the great People who held my heart. And I could do it all without a college degree; college was taking too long and getting me nowhere.

I had always been looking for a loophole out of life. I needed to feel alive every day and the reservation would surely do that. I wanted a better, diverse life rich in meaning before money. I desired to learn things my heart truly cared about. I craved to follow the path less traveled and when I died, I wanted to see I had truly lived. There was no choice but to give my life to this cause I believed in.

I had always been different from the norm, although I had tried for so long to fit in with what society expected of me: marriage, college, jobs that turn into careers, careers that in turn suck the life from your soul and leave you empty on your death bed, wondering what it all was for. I wanted to have as few regrets as possible when I died; I wanted to live with passion and make a difference by helping the poorest place in the United States, helping good people who deserved the best because it was their right by birth to have what settlers had stolen. A way to do all this without college was perfect; it could happen right now and it was something original, something that mattered. I had found my calling.

Back in Maine, back in my apartment with my parrots, back at my job, I still thought of Chief Two Bear Paws and the Pine Ridge Reservation; even life's dull day to day routine was not enough to diminish my desire and make me forget. I felt I belonged there but I could not figure out how that could work as there were no apartments on the reservation, no "for rent" ads. A part of me still remained back there at the mass grave sight. I had to do something.

I sent an email to the address on Chief's card. A week went by with no reply. I mailed a letter. I described the person I'd met, stated I wished to speak with him, please give him my address. I wanted to help in any way I could.

A few days later, I got a reply. Chief had cursive handwriting which was precise and elegant. He said he remembered me from my visit, he thanked me for my interest in his people. He said he does not get near a computer often, so he did not receive my email. He asked if I owned a computer or if I had emailed from the library. He stated mailing letters was the best way to communicate. He asked many questions and encouraged me to send another letter.

He told the story of the sacred Black Hills and spoke of the strength of his People. He used many Lakota words and translated them to teach me. He wrote a list of numbers and showed me how to count to ten in Lakota with a pronunciation and hand gesture guide.

He said he is Headsman of his family name; out of respect and honor for his bravery they call him Chief, even though he is humbled by this name, feeling the great leaders of the past deserve this title more than he. He is a direct lineal descendant of Crazy Horse himself, he mentioned other great leaders to whom he is blood related. He said he holds a high title in the local AIM chapter and he is a warrior of many battles and brave deeds.

He told me about his house; he was sure to let me know he did not have a wife. He asked if I had a car and house, a husband or kids.

I wrote another letter, this time I included a hundred dollar check. I told him to buy something nice for his sweet granddaughter. I told him I had my own computer, a pickup truck, and an apartment, where I lived alone with my two pet birds. I liked my job at the book store, I was not married but had a boyfriend and I did not have any children. I also asked him politely and humbly which name he and his people prefer to be called. I suggested the ever popular and seemingly politically correct term, "Native American."

Chief thanked me for the check and told me to lose the boyfriend. He explained the term "Native American" is offensive to his people. They are not fond of the word "American," since their land was never "America" before the white man stole it; their spirit is not native to a land with that name. AIM uses "American Indian" Movement because it denotes to the world the geographical land mass its supporters are from, as there are native people on every continent. Plus, "AIM" is a great acronym. He later told me that part in person with a laugh.

He wrote he prefers to be respectfully called "Indian."

I saw a few baseball hats on the rez which stated "Native Pride." Other than that, "Indian" was the only terminology I ever heard them say besides "Lakota."

"Indian" is the only word I was ever asked to use. It is the choice I continue with today, although it sometimes shocks non-Indian people who think it's racist and I have to explain myself.

Chief's boldness at telling me to "lose the boyfriend" excited me. I liked how he took control and said what he wanted straight out with no games. I laughed his words away, but the seed was set in my mind.

I found myself thinking about him every moment of the

day, romanticizing a life with him. I found myself desiring to stand by his side in all that he did. Every day my private, unspoken dreams grew stronger.

With this letter, Chief Two Bear Paws sent me an AIM patch. I hung it above my bed next to the AIM shield he had painted for me when I visited his museum. We exchanged three letters each way, every one of mine included a hundred dollars. After the first personal check I'd sent, he told me a money order was better, so I started sending those. I also sent him phone cards to call me. I was honored a Lakota chief would speak with me and I was excited to hear his voice. He told me stories, we discussed plans for the motorcycle ride we envisioned together; I really thought this event could work to help his people.

Every morning and each night, I would touch the buffalo shield Chief had painted and lay my fingers on the AIM patch he'd sent. I would cry and pray, still feeling the wind in my veins. My prayers became wordless open energy released in a swirl of hot breath like a wolf howling at the frozen moon.

I felt pain for my white ancestors' actions mixed sharply with love for the Lakota. These were oil and water emotions with razorblade edges that can never mix; instead, they abrade each other, drawing blood. Blood is pain, yet blood is life; it was beauty and tragedy at the same time, pain and love. It was passion. And it burned. All I could do was silently howl as searing tears streamed down my cheeks.

Just a year before, I had seen the grandest fire in Bangor. An old brick building downtown caught fire from the inside out, but the brick exterior never burned or collapsed. The fire burned for four and a half days in subzero temperatures with high winds. The fire department dumped thousands of gallons of water per minute on the blaze, but the water froze on contact. The exterior of the building became encased in white marble several inches thick—a castle of ice—while the fire raged inside.

Fists of fire curled around the outside of the building through broken windows, grasping oxygen but never becoming extinguished themselves, they lapped the edges of the ice without melting it as the white, frozen water only grew thicker. Fire and ice existed in breathtaking harmony for days until there was nothing left inside to burn. It was tragic and it was glorious, scary yet the most beautiful thing to behold. Seemingly unreal, it breathed before my eyes.

I felt like this about the Lakota. The fire of the Ancestors burned inside me as I found my old self becoming only a shell of ice. I let my old self go, I let the building fall, ice and fire, everything melted away and was gone. Alone, I touched the darkness and found the energy of the Lakota ancestors inside me, their spirits dry leaves rustling within me. I carried them and their haunting sound ever since the day they entered me on the hill of the mass gravesite, outside the museum. Meditating in my bed in Maine, I listened. I promised them I would return and do all I could.

One morning, I woke half in and half out of my body. I was in a dream state that felt real with my body wrapped around Chief Two Bear Paws. I touched the charms above my head and I surprised myself by becoming aroused. Later, when I was in his bed on the rez, I admitted this had happened. I blushed and told him he was so good in bed he could have relations with me from two thousand miles away.

He laughed and said he already knew, which was a bit frightening to hear. He said his magic is real. It had been named in an Indian ceremony when he was a boy. His elders had a vision of his gift and told him he had the rare "power over women." When he spoke the Indian name for his power, my eyes went black and dead. It was like the devil had commanded me to hell.

My mother, always my angel, saw right through Chief's agenda. I refused to believe her, even though her track record for being right was stellar in my life. She read the letters he'd sent me. She looked horrified. "He asks if you have a computer and says he needs one. He asks if you have a good job, a car, a house, and credit cards. He told you to leave your boyfriend and he said how he needs a wife. Can't you see he's just after what you have and what you can do for him?

"He will take you for everything and leave you with nothing. You will cook and clean for him and have his babies. He will leave you at home with the kids while he goes out to hunt and hang out with the men.

"Then, one day, he will bring home a younger, prettier wife who is not used up yet and sleep with her while you cry in the next room, listening to them together in your bed. There will be nothing you can do or say to stop it. He may even let the other men rape you, but you will never be Lakota and you will never belong to him or his culture, even if you bear his children."

I remember yelling at her, telling her how wrong she was, how white she was, how her heart was not as understanding as mine. I regret that very much. I orphaned and estranged myself from my real birth family in order to cling to a blood who would never claim me as their own. And, hauntingly, my mother was a hundred percent right, as she always had been. Maybe she was really Indian after all.

Big Biker found the letters from Two Bear Paws and freaked out. He said I was cheating on him. I told him he was crazy and I was tired of being accused of cheating. Our time of great motorcycle rides and laughs together ended with a fabulous photo scrapbook of our Sturgis vacation and a huge fight.

Memories were all that remained; I kicked Big Biker out the same day he found the letters. I told him Chief was right, I needed to "lose the boyfriend." I changed the locks on my door, threw away my cell phone, and bought a tracfone.

My life was spiraling in a new direction very fast.

OCTOBER

CHAPTER SEVEN:

Arrival

Chief read the news Big Biker was out of my life. He called me at work using one of the phone cards I'd sent. He said, "You belong to me now." He was taking the three hundred dollars I had included with my letters and buying a train ticket. He was coming to claim me.

None of his relatives had ever traveled to Maine, he said he would be the first in his family and they were awed at his journey. He expected I pick him up at the Amtrak station in Boston; he would be there in three days. Only a few weeks had passed since Big Biker and I had returned from our Sturgis vacation.

While Chief was still en route, he phoned once. He did not have a cell phone, so he borrowed one from another passenger on the train. He called to let me know he was on schedule and would be there tomorrow. I thought that was sweet.

I took my pickup truck to Boston and waited at the station. His train caught on fire. The diesel engine leaked fuel and exploded into flames. The passenger cars were separated from the burning engine in Iowa.

Chief, uninjured, was severely delayed. I would wait with my heart in my throat for as long as it took. I was so deluded that I never thought his train burning was a bad omen.

Hours passed by, but time did not affect me. Dazed, I stood by the glass door which had a view of the tracks and passenger platform. I peered into the darkness, almost holding my breath for the first light of his arrival, imagining his first step onto the platform, knowing it would change my life.

I held a bouquet of daisies dyed blue and purple. Red and yellow carnations popped among the velvet, exotic daisies. People in Boston actually stopped me to ask where I had gotten such lovely flowers. I had searched up in Maine for the most beautiful and unique flowers I could find to welcome Chief upon his arrival. I tied their stems together with Lakota colors, yellow, red, black, and white. The colored ribbons hung long from my hands.

I saw his train coming towards me down the track. All was darkness until the halo of my love shown around him. He was all I could see. My life began as he walked towards me. He was everything I lived for from this moment on.

I bowed my head and handed him the flowers. He waved them away and said, "Coffee."

We walked a few feet to the coffee cart and sat at a table. The coffee was warm and good; I paid. He told me about the train burning. He laughed. He said the blaze was huge.

When we got up to leave, I sadly slid the welcome bouquet off the table. "I picked these out special to welcome you. Why don't you want them?"

"Flowers are for women. You take them. Save the ribbons."

We headed for my truck, he rolled his suitcase along behind him. I wasn't trained well enough yet to know he was doing women's work. I should have taken his bag and walked behind him. Me, a 5'4", 112 pound, small built female should always serve the tall, broad shouldered, strong man.

Chief wasn't as strong as I thought, though. He stopped halfway down the street, wheezing. "Go. I will wait."

The rain came. I found him shelter under an awning of a closed store. I left him there, leaning on the handle of his suitcase, trying his best to look noble, almost losing the battle to stand up straight. I asked if he would be alright. He said, "*Tunkashila* will protect me. Go."

I walked towards what I believed to be the direction of my

truck, but I was tired from the long day and dizzy with his spell. Walking turned to jogging, jogging became running around in circles as the rain came down harder and harder. I had no umbrella or raincoat, just the bouquet of bright, wet flowers trailing soggy ribbons that almost touched the ground. I was soaked to the bone and crying for *Tunkashila* to help me. Amazingly, as I am typing this, a sudden flood of summer rain has begun to cascade outside my window. Perhaps *Tunkashila* remembers me, the lost little white girl. I will listen to this rain and see where it takes me. I open my kitchen door and watch as the rain comes down at a harsh angle, huge lines pelt the ground faster than the eye can distinguish drop from drop. Storms like this would suddenly boom from the summer skies in South Dakota, oftentimes the rain would turn rapidly into a hail storm. Burnt, dead lawns covered in ice. Hot pavement cooled by piles of white. Fire burning through windows made of ice.

One of the worst hail storms came while I was sitting in a diner with Big Biker in Hot Springs, South Dakota, about an hour from the reservation. August road dirt mixed with sweat from the 115 degree afternoon made a grimy film on our faces, necks, and arms while the world outside suddenly turned to winter.

It began with the bright blue, sunny summer sky turning black in the span of a few seconds. It was like entering a tunnel with your sunglasses still on. People inside the small diner gasped as thunder cracked directly overhead. It was the loudest sound I have ever heard; it even shook fear into the locals who became still and alert like the four-leggeds, wide-eyed with expectation of the danger about to strike.

The rain fell fast and hard; the streets became rivers of impassible choppy rapids flowing with rain water. Then, the ice began to fall.

I ran outside and threw myself over the purple and silver Harley, letting my back and thick leather jacket take the beating from the golf ball sized hail instead of the bike. Locals, strangers I had never even spoken to previously, ran to the door and yelled for me to get back inside.

Perhaps I was a stupid tourist, but I was also a crazy, devoted biker. I kept my head down to protect myself the best I could from a concussion as I used my body as a shield for the custom painted gas tanks. I could hear the dents being pounded into all the other bikes in the parking lot by these balls of ice that struck like fist-sized metal cannonballs.

The Harley survived with only a shattered mirror. When the ice stopped falling, other bikers ran outside to mourn the carnage of their crushed machines. Locals quoted in the newspaper called that summer storm of 2005 "brutal" as it did millions of dollars worth of damage to roofs, buildings, and property.

Ice would remain in knee-high piles along the edges of our hotel building even when the day turned hot and sunny again. I remember having a snow/hail ball fight with Big Biker outside our hotel that evening.

The rain here in Connecticut rarely turns to hail. The storm outside now takes my memory back to the night at the Amtrak station. The hard, pelting streams of rain. So cold. So lost. Helpless. I remember praying, "*Tunkashila*, help me. Please help me find my truck. I am trying to help your people as the Ancestors asked of me. I am trying to help a great elder of your Nation, whom I have left standing back there in the rain. Please, help me."

Running around in circles in the rain, I only became more lost in darkness. An hour had passed and I still could not find my truck. I wailed up to the black sky, the rain mixing with the tears on my cheeks, long wet hair sticking to my neck and back, "*Tunkashila*, I am here! I want to help your people. You are real, right? You hear me, right? Well, I am real, too! I am here, asking for your help. Please, answer me, help me now. You are the god of my new people and I am praying for your help, why won't you answer me? Show me you want me to help the Lakota. Please, help me find my truck!" Darkness closed around me as time slipped away.

In desperation, I cried, "Ok, God, *Tunkashila* is not listening to me. I think I'm doing good things here with a big heart, but if you think this whole reservation thing is a bad idea, please let me know by helping me find my tr—" There was my truck! I dug through my pockets, "Oh no! God, please help me find my keys!"

Drenched and shivering in the October rain, I started the truck. Now I needed to find my way back to Chief. He was only three streets away and I found him easily. He was cold to the bone and I could see his teeth chatter. Even after all this time, his pride made his bones stand tall in the doorway where I had left him hours ago. I told him I was sorry I got lost; he waved a shaky hand for my silence.

Inside my truck, the heat was on and it felt good. He reached into his bag and pulled out some music. Without saying anything, he put the discs into my truck's CD player. A buffalo drum's heartbeat echoed through my body. The wails of traditional Lakota singing sounded like screams from the mass grave. Shrill, their voices shattered the night.

As I drove, Chief Two Bear Paws told me stories of the Ancestors and the Lakota way of life. He talked of the Tree of Life and the Sacred Hoop; he told the story of White Buffalo Calf Woman who brought the *chanupa*, the sacred pipe, to his people. He spoke of the mindset of the elders like himself and the traditional ways he wants to bring back to his people. He spoke in his quiet, soft, hypnotic voice all the way to Portland, Maine. Those two hours driving were a trance that felt like twenty minutes.

I cannot repeat what words he said for my ears did not hear them. I listened with my heart and felt the energy, the bittersweet pain. Behind his soft words, I heard the songs of his People. I felt the wails of the Lakota and the beat of the buffalo skin drum. It was the first time I ever heard their music. It awakened the wind within my veins and swirled the dry leaves of the Ancestor's voices inside me. I heard the song call *Tunkashila*'s name, they sang in their traditional tongue.

Their voices warbled in a high-pitched, haunting way, the Ancestors within me answered. I was transported, possessed, and all I saw was darkness. Yet, I believed it was light. Light of the path of what is Right. I had found my purpose in life. My spirit was united with my new people. I heard their voices, they called to me, telling me it was time to come home to the reservation; the Lakota were my family now. I believed them. I threw myself upon the rocks as their song enchanted my soul. I was swallowed by a sea of darkness.

The darkness was broken only by the red and blue lights of the Maine State Trooper in my rear view mirror. He said he had been chasing me for miles and I never slowed down. I had been driving 25 miles over the speed limit which is driving to endanger. He dropped it down to only a three hundred dollar fine.

I barely noticed anything. I was slightly aware Chief had disappeared into the shadows of the passenger seat, recoiling and setting his teeth against the White Man authority figure. He stared straight ahead and clenched his jaw the entire time I dealt with the officer, who seemed to never notice or ask about him.

When we were safely back on the road, Chief said he does not trust white cops. He spoke of how the White Man has wronged his people as we drove up 95 north for two more hours in the rain, all the way to Bangor. Then we went a little past Bangor, up to Old Town, where I lived.

We climbed the stairs to my second floor apartment; it was an old house in a rural neighborhood and stairs were the only option. It must have been three in the morning but all time was lost to me. I was in a trance.

I lay down on my mattress. Chief was in the bathroom,

then all was dark as the lights went out and he climbed on top of me. Without a word or invitation, sex seemed expected even though we had not touched before this. No hug, no kiss, no pat on the shoulder, no brush of fingertips on coffee cups, nothing but this rough, insistent, awkward sex.

We slept.

CHAPTER EIGHT:

Daybreak

When I got up the next morning, I noticed an alcohol prep pad in the trash can beside the toilet. It sent a chill through me. I pictured him wiping his manhood down in my bathroom with alcohol, perhaps thinking it would prevent STDs. I was clean, but now I wondered what I might have. I pushed these worries away, it did not matter. I was in this for the long haul.

Which might not be that long, considering Chief had already outlived the average life expectancy for men on the Pine Ridge Reservation. His doctor told him ten years ago he wouldn't make it this far. Due to poor diet, disease, and lack of access to proper health care, he was worse off than other fifty-something year olds I knew in the U.S. However, perhaps due to his faith, he was better off than most on the reservation. It's all in what you compare it to.

The list of things not perfect with his body was long; I only learned some of them upon his arrival.

Like others past 50, he was in need of eyeglasses, but he did not have a pair. I got him an eye test and bought him two pairs at LensCrafters in the Bangor Mall for four hundred dollars.

However, unlike most people I knew in their 50s, he arrived with his own set of complete false teeth and a pacemaker. The defibrillator made a large, raised square on his chest; a deep scar carved a valley in his flesh next to it. There was always some drool trapped in the deep lines of his face, tracing his chin with a glisten of spittle.

I was not bothered by any of this. I looked past these things for they were elements of the body which he could not help. I always saw the strong warrior within. I truly loved him for it. He was noble, a respected elder, and nothing about his body could ever change that for me; I loved his spirit.

Chief was in the kitchen standing by the vase of flowers. These were the same purple and blue velvet daisies I had presented him at the train station, embarrassing him with gifts that should have been given to a woman instead of a great chief and warrior of the Lakota nation. He was gently touching a single purple daisy petal between his thumb and forefinger. He turned to me and smiled with the beauty of a child, "How did they do that? The purple?"

I used to work at a florist, so I told him the trick I knew. "They dye the water purple and the white daisies drink it up. They become purple like the water."

Chief grunted, he sounded impressed. A dried turkey wing on the wall caught his eye. He went over to it and took it down as if it were something I was not allowed to have. He put it in his suitcase without a word. He would end up keeping it on the dash of his pickup truck, as many Indians on the rez did, until somebody stole it.

A hunter friend of mine in New Hampshire had killed that turkey a few years before. I actually cooked the bird for him since he was a step away from homeless and living off the land—and out of his car. Ironically, his "home" was the accidental weapon he had used to kill the turkey. In return for cooking something I would not eat, I asked for a wing. I did not know wings or feathers had anything to do with Indian ceremonies, I just liked the way it looked. My friend taught me how to dry it and shape it so it remained open like a fan. I would later learn the shape lends itself nicely to Indian traditions where sacred smoke is fanned with special bird wings such as this.

Chief may have had a need for it, but so did I. It reminded me of a friend I had not seen in a while. It was special to me and I was insulted he would take it down and keep it without asking, without comment. But I said nothing.

He did ask, however, to use my phone. I gave him my tracfone but told him it wasn't a real phone, the minutes were very expensive so don't use it too long. I fed the birds, made the bed, took a shower, got dressed, minutes were still ticking away dollars on my tracfone. He spoke in Lakota. He sounded passionate. I doubted he was talking about purple flowers.

In between calls, I explained to him again that it was not a real phone, it was intended to be used only in emergencies. He waved his hand and said, "This is important work." He kept my phone in his pocket and used up a hundred dollars worth of minutes in two days, calling relatives and friends across the country until the time ran out. Then he handed it back to me and said, "Make it work." I had to buy more minutes.

While he was talking on my phone our first morning together, he started opening all my kitchen cupboards. He pulled things out and threw them on the counter. He took a bite of something and tossed it back. In the middle cupboard, he discovered a dark green glass bottle of lemon juice. He drank the whole bottle in a few fast gulps. My lips puckered with empathy as I shivered with the imagined taste of pure lemon kiss.

In the time I knew him, Two Bear Paws never drank alcohol. In fact, I never saw any Indian drink or do drugs on the rez. If others might have done these things on their own time, nobody would dare disrespect Chief by using alcohol or drugs in his presence.

Chief was outspokenly against alcohol. He said alcohol poisoned his people. His life is the path of the old ways, which does not include alcohol. He told me the Lakota never even had a word for alcohol until the White Man gave him whiskey. He does not drink because alcohol has destroyed his people, made them numb, and made them forget the old ways.

Alcohol is prohibited on his reservation. Yet, alcoholism

consumes over 80% of the population in Pine Ridge.

White Clay, Nebraska is two miles south of the reservation. Its sole purpose is selling alcohol to Indians. White Clay has less than fifteen full time residents; yet, it has four liquor stores. It's only a four minute drive from the town of Pine Ridge to White Clay, but few people have vehicles on the reservation. So, nine Indians pile into an old jalopy to buy booze, while dozens without cars walk across the border for alcohol every day. For certain celebrations, such as the 40th anniversary of WKII, the 1973 Wounded Knee, protestors from the rez stopped cars going to White Clay and searched cars coming into the reservation for alcohol. Their goal is to close these border town liquor stores permanently.

While I was witness to the struggle others had with alcohol on the reservation, the Lakota I lived with never drank anything stronger than coffee.

Chief was not after alcohol in my cupboards, he just loved lemon juice.

Without a word, he continued to ransack my kitchen. After his current phone call ended, I told him I had baked him an apple pie. It was right here on the table. Come eat. He told me, "Baking a pie is good and right. You should bake pies." He threw his arms towards my cupboards and suddenly got angry. He slammed my cupboard doors and yelled, "It is wrong for a woman to live this way, alone and independent! It is wrong for a woman to have an apartment and go to work! This is not the right way! You need to get on the right path and come home with me now! I will show you how a Lakota woman is supposed to live."

I made coffee. He seemed soothed by the smell. He sat down and relaxed with the first sip. "Mmmm. *Wakalapi*, that is how we say 'coffee' in Lakota. My people also call it *pejuta sapa* which means 'Black Medicine.'" He took another sip as I served him a slice of fresh apple pie.

I knew he would be satisfied with the pie. When I was a

child, my mother taught me how to make an excellent homemade crust and apple pie was my specialty. I had inherited a love of making desserts from scratch. . . which wasn't the kindest thing to do on the rez, I would later learn, since Pine Ridge's diabetes rate is 800% higher than the U.S. national average.

That's not a type-o: diabetes is *eight hundred* percent higher. They really don't need me to bake them sweets as their diet is so poor already. And it's not their fault. When they used to follow the old ways and live off the land and hunt, they were healthy with no disease. Now, contained on the reservation, the food rations the U.S. government delivers do nothing to improve their health.

The government rations only encourage malnutrition, diabetes, weakness, sickness, and death. But it is all they have to eat.

Alarmingly, tuberculosis on the Pine Ridge Reservation is also 800% higher than the U.S. national average. Most non-reservation people I have shared that statistic with are shocked, it seems people think tuberculosis has been cured or something. But it is a common way to die on the rez. Cervical cancer is 500% higher; I never saw a condom anywhere on the rez. Infant mortality is thee times higher, many women never see a doctor their entire pregnancy. When there is a complication, another Indian life, or two, will be lost.

According to the 2012 census, the median life expectancy in the United States is 78. The Pine Ridge Reservation has its own statistic, with the average life expectancy for men at 48, women, 52. The lowest life expectancy in the Western Hemisphere is thought to be Haiti; however, 2012 statistics show Haiti's average life span as 62.

If the Lakota Nation was truly seen as its own country as some on the reservation desire, it would dominate this sad statistic with an average lifespan of 50. Out of 194 countries, it would fall into the bottom twenty for the lowest life expectancies in the *entire world*.

Tribal Government records show approximately 40,000 people live on the Pine Ridge Reservation, which covers a land area about the size of Connecticut. Connecticut, by comparison, has a population of three million five hundred and eighty thousand and growing rapidly. As I write this, internet statistics currently show the unemployment rate in Connecticut fluctuates around 8.9% and the median income is $64,500. On the Pine Ridge Reservation, unemployment is between 85-98%. Some statistics say the yearly median income on the rez is 2,600 dollars. I never saw anyone have that much. They seemed lucky to have one crumpled dollar to their name.

These statistics are the dark side of the reservation; this is what they have become because of White Man's greed. It is our shame to bear, yet White Man turns his back on what he has done and admires his war medals of honor. The Lakota still have true honor, their spirit will live on long after every White Man is dead. Which would be soon, according to Chief.

Over apple pie and coffee, Chief Two Bear Paws spoke of the Black Hills of South Dakota and the end times at hand. "The Black Hills belong to my people. The Lakota have been tricked and lied to by the White Man. Every treaty made has been broken. All White Man has done is tell lies. My grandfather spoke words still true today, he said, 'The only truth White Man ever told and the only promise he ever kept was the promise to take our land.'

"A great flood is coming. It will rain down and drown the White Man. The Lakota know the time of the flood is near. *Tunkashila* has told us to go to high ground. We will reclaim the Black Hills. The Lakota will stand in our sacred Black Hills and watch the White Man drown. *Tunkashila* has spoken. *Tunkashila* is the Red Man's God. *Tunkashila* is not White Man's God. He does not listen to White Man. *Tunkashila* is here for the Red Man. *Tunkashila* will save us, his chosen people, the Lakota."

I had chills running down my spine. I thought, "So, that's why *Tunkashila* didn't help me find my truck in Boston."

"I have spoken the Truth. You have heard the words *Tunkashila* has given to my People. You can be spared. Stay with me and you will not drown in the great flood. It is coming soon. You will live, if you go with me. We will go to the Black Hills. Stand strong with the Lakota Nation, we will not drown."

I believed him. He talked about the Ghost Dance, how White Man was afraid when he saw the Ancestors dancing. He said Ghost Shirts protected the dancers from White Man's bullets. He told a story of how Crazy Horse was bulletproof, riding through a line of American soldiers who were firing at him. Crazy Horse laughed as he passed safely by them; the bullets hit his shirt and fell away.

I was amazed at this story of Crazy Horse. I wanted to bond with Chief; I told him my own personal story of light, a palpable and undeniably visual experience with energy I had when meditating the prior year; there was even an amazed witness in the room who could verify the experience. I hoped sharing my story would bring Chief and me closer together. Instead, he waved his hand and looked away, disgusted.

"Baaah! Women have no powers! A *winkte (wink-teh)* is a man who dresses and acts like a woman, he is of two souls. He is respected in Lakota culture and has many powers. But a woman, no, women have no powers. Women have babies. Women cook."

The look he gave was firm instruction never to speak on the topic again. I recalled a transgender relationship from my past. I had always been looking for love, magic—something more than the average life held for the average person. I believed Chief and the life he promised on the reservation were my answer.

He continued, "Red Man will overcome, rise above, survive. He cannot be kept down by White Man." This spirit was the essence of the Ghost Dance, forbidden by White Man before the 1890 massacre. White Man outlawed what made him afraid, which was the Lakota's strong will to survive. Today, the Lakota still hold the sacred ceremony of the Sun Dance. They pray and pierce their skin, they make flesh offerings, they dance and become one with the Tree of Life. Chief Two Bear Paws wore his Sundance scars with pride. He knew I was learning, so he pointed to a few of the larger scars which looked quite severe, smiled and said, "Sundance."

He told me there is a sacred spot he knows, a hidden place with huge ancient arbors, far away from the eyes of White Man, a secret place where only the Lakota go to dance and pray. He said two years ago in 2003, his People passed a law which prohibits non-Native blood from attending sacred Indian ceremonies. "If you are with me, you will be allowed inside. It is the only way. I will take you there. You will see real Lakota ceremonies. You will become Lakota. You will sing and dance with us and learn our ways. My People are now your People. You will be saved from the flood. Let us go, now."

I wanted everything he promised. I felt White Man's world closing in around me, suffocating me. The only way I could breathe again was to get back to the reservation and live the Lakota way. I must follow the path of the Ancestors; I must listen to the wisdom of this Lakota man, my elder. I had to go now or I would die. But first, I had to go to work. Chief commanded me to stay and gather things for our journey. "We leave now. Get ready."

"My boss is counting on me to come in today."

"Forget him." He waved his hand in a dismissing gesture. "We must go. Now."

"Soon," I said. "Just give me one more day at work. Let me respect my boss who is my friend. Let me say to his face that I quit today."

He went to his suitcase and unpacked a stitched, white cotton blanket; it had been folded backside out. He shook it open and held up the most beautiful, colorful quilt. It was a single giant star composed of many overlapping large, bright triangles, laced with intricate stitching. "This is the star quilt of my People. Lakota women make this. It is Lakota tradition. This one is made in the style used for weddings. My mother made this for us. It is our wedding gift."

My heart soared at his indirect proposal and raced with joy at his automatic assumption of my acceptance. The single, giant star on the quilt became a million little stars glittering in my eyes for him. I wanted to give him a kiss but I moved into his space too quickly, he recoiled, I got his cheek. He wiped it. I was floating on air. And late for work.

I went to the bookstore and told my boss I was moving to South Dakota. In my heart, I was ready to be married again. Enough time had passed; I was not naive, I had thought it through. I knew I could be a good wife. There would be plenty of adventure on the reservation, so much to do and learn. I would never be bored and life would not become commonplace and dull. I would live with honor, passion, and Spirit. I was eager to commit my heart and life to this new path of the old ways; I looked with joy and respect upon the rest of my days as wife to Chief Two Bear Paws.

Of course, it sounded crazy to tell my boss the part about getting married, so I told him half the truth. I said I was going out there to help plan a motorcycle ride from Sturgis to the reservation. I would create it so the Indians could make some money for many years to come from this event, as it would only get bigger every year. My boss was supportive of my happiness and goals. He wished me luck.

I finished out the day, then went to the hair salon and got my hair dyed Elvis black. I told my hair dresser I was marrying a "Native American" and moving to the reservation in South Dakota to help plan a motorcycle event. She thought it was a great idea and clasped her hands to her heart with delight as she wished me all good things in my marriage.

I told her Chief Two Bear Paws had traveled over two thousand miles to claim me as his wife. He was waiting for me now at my apartment; we were leaving together for the reservation soon. She squealed and said it was so romantic. I gave her a good tip; I always liked her and I knew I would never see her again.

My hair was now raven black like the hair of my chief and the hair of the Lakota, my family. I was excited; I would be with my people soon. I loved them all so much already.

CHAPTER NINE:

Darkness

I went home and opened the front door to my apartment. I was met with a wall of heat. The inside temperature was over ninety degrees. Chief had turned the thermostat as high as it would go, making my three room apartment a suffocating oven. I ran to the bedroom where I kept my two parrots, fearing they had died in the extreme temperature change. They both seemed fine.

Chief, however, was not so fine. He was buried under every blanket I had, plus the star quilt he had brought with him. My husband-to-be seemed dead. I went over to him, he was shivering and hot at the same time. Weak, bloated, a little delirious, his voice was dry and raspy. "I need my medicine. Take me to V.A."

I did not know anything about this, so I called my recent ex-boss who was like a dad to me. He understood. "He means the Veteran's clinic. It's on Washington Street. Take your cell with you and I'll talk you through how to get there." Being my "Maine Dad," he knew how lost I always got.

Chief struggled to get out of bed. The day had turned rainy and cold. I wrapped a blanket around him. As we walked into the veteran's clinic, the rain turned into a light slush of early fall snow.

The older woman behind the window at the V.A. gave me a bit of a hassle, even though Chief Two Bear Paws was a Korean War veteran. The problem was his out of state ID was extremely out of state. Her long, silver eyeglass chains hit her shoulders as she held his identification cards and shook her head side to side.

"I do not understand why you are here. I do not know what you think I can do for you. I cannot help you. I suggest you contact South Dakota and discuss this matter with them. Perhaps they can mail you some medications. Or, better yet, perhaps he should just go home to South Dakota and get help there."

I did not know if her words were policy, prejudice, or good old-fashioned Maine charm. I leaned in as close as the glass would allow and locked eyes with her. "He is *dying*. Look at him. Just look." She shifted her gaze over to the left and jumped a bit at the sight of Chief. He was leaning on the counter, barely able to stand, eyes closed, drool running down his chin, head rolled to the side. He started to cough a deep, wet cough. The slush was melting on his blanket. He shivered.

"Please help him," I begged. "Can't you call South Dakota and get his medical records faxed over? Find out what prescription he needs and fill it here? It's a real emergency. He won't live long enough for the mail to get here from South Dakota. He told me he needs his water pills. Without them, he can't breathe. I don't think he'll make it another day."

She looked very concerned now that she had assessed his fading condition with her own eyes. She nodded, her eyeglass chains bounced off her chest. "Yes, I can help." With urgency to her actions, she made the call. It worked out very easily after that. Within minutes, faxes were sent and we had a short term supply of the three medications Chief needed most.

He spent the next few days in my bed, coughing up phlegm. He insisted the blinds be closed. I even had to pull down the blackout shades so no light came in whatsoever. He had me drape towels over the curtains and stuff clothes into the cracks to block out any light from the sides of the shades. He demanded the heat remain cranked up as high as it would go with no fresh air or circulation.

The darkness, stale air, and heat drove me crazy, but I sat

diligently by his side for hours giving him or buying him whatever he said he needed. I handed him tissues when he began to have coughing spells. He ignored them and insisted on spewing directly into my trash can. It was a disgusting, unnecessary mess to clean up. I could not figure out why the tissues were rejected.

I nicely suggested he could spit into them, just in case he wasn't sure what they were for. I was trying to be kind. I thought, "Perhaps they don't have the luxury of tissues on the reservation." I explained tissues are proper and polite and their use makes it easier for me to clean the trash can. I reassured him it was okay, I had plenty, it was not an extra expense for me. He shook his head no and spit his own way.

"Maybe it's easier for him," I thought. "After all, he looks really sick. It's okay, I can handle it." I would wash out the trash can in the shower and bring it back warm, clean, and dry.

He had so much fluid built up in his lungs he was drowning on air. The fluid poured out of him with phlegm and sweat. By the end of the week, his cough became drier. The swelling in his legs had gone down somewhat, but his calves were still almost double the size they should have been due to water retention.

Chief said what he needed to get better was McDonald's. I brought him what he asked for. He wolfed down two burgers, relishing this food considered a rare treat on the reservation. Cash to buy fast food is a hindrance for the residents of Pine Ridge, so is having a car and gas to get there.

The nearest McDonald's within South Dakota is two hours away from Wounded Knee. There's no Dunkin' Donuts nearby, either, which was shocking to me. In New England, there's a Dunkin' Donuts and golden arches on every street corner. It seems Dunkin' Donuts fades away around Chicago and Starbucks takes its place, that is until you get too far out into the country, then everything fades away. I guess you're supposed to make your own coffee at home when you've gone that far. There are a lot of simple things taken for granted in the city.

Chief wanted more McDonald's. I went back out, but stopped at a payphone first to call a friend. I told her how Chief Two Bear Paws suddenly showed up and how sick he was. I wanted my friend's opinion on his curt, single word commands, dismissive hand gestures, and lack of respect for my pets, belongings, money, space, time, job, apartment, beliefs, and self.

With hope tucked under my arm, I suggested what I wanted to hear, "Maybe he's suffering, you know, maybe he's just uncomfortable being sick in new surroundings? I mean, I'm being really, really nice to him, he can't keep treating me like this. His attitude will improve with his health, right?"

My friend sighed. Her tone said she was shaking her head at me over the phone. "His behavior will not improve with his health. If anything, it will only get worse. You are making excuses for ingrained poor behavior and innate lack of respect. Seriously, you should just pack him up and send him on his way as soon as possible. This whole situation sounds very bad. And whatever you do, *don't* move to South Dakota with him!" My friend's words echoed in my head. I wondered if she was right. Or if she was just white.

When Chief could walk without being supported by my shoulder, I decided he needed some fresh air. God knows I did. Typical for New England weather, the slush from a few days ago was now replaced by a sunny and rather warm day for autumn. I drove him a block away to the Old Town Public Library. We sat down at a table in front of a computer. I clicked onto a cheap airline ticket website. "Which airport is closest to your home? Now that you are feeling better, I think it's best if you fly back to South Dakota. Go see your real doctor. Get on with your life. Thank you for visiting me, we can still write and be friends."

He looked surprised. He played it cool, though, and said,

"Rapid City." I looked up one way flights; the ticket was six hundred dollars. I recalled biker friends saying it was expensive to fly into Rapid City for the Sturgis rally because it is a smaller airport in the middle of nowhere. It's pricey, but it's the only major airport for at least a four hour drive. Rapid City is two hour's north of Wounded Knee, where Chief lived. Driving down to the rez is the only option, and, as I later discovered, no bus or taxi will take you there . . . or out of there.

"I don't have money," Chief stated. "I spent all the money on train ticket here. I will get a check in a week and have money later."

I had made a decision and it could not wait another week. "That's okay. I'll pay for it. I have my credit card right here," I pulled out my wallet. "Let's buy this ticket online right now. How many days will it take before you feel up to flying home?"

"Let me think."

He got up to think while I sat at the computer, feeling stronger than I'd felt in days. I would wait a few minutes for the date to be chosen and then my life could get back to normal for me and my parrots.

He came back to the table with a handful of books. One of them was a large photography book designed to teach children about Indian culture. "Look," he turned to a glossy photo, "these are my people." Smiling up from the page was a beautiful Lakota girl about ten years old dressed for a dance. Her red dress was decorated with fringe and beadwork. The girl in the photo twirled a shawl of many colors with trailing ribbons. She was spinning, her bright ribbons and fringe flowing with her loose, long hair. The endless grassy plains stretched out behind her. She was remarkably beautiful with smiling eyes, black hair, and medium brown skin. My heart leapt with her dance.

"This book is good," Chief said. "Many true things." He

told me about the women's Fancy Shawl Dance and the Jingle Dress Dance. He then turned to another photo. "This is the Hoop Dance. My people dance this traditional Lakota dance. Some men can dance with seven hoops moving at once."

As he turned the pages and told stories, I saw so much color in their powwow clothing, so much life in their hopeful, shining eyes. He explained every page of the photo book to me, it was stunning. My heart cried out to see more.

Chief tapped the page twice with his fingertip and looked into my face. "Come home with me."

I was swept away by his gaze and the photos of his people. My friend's words of caution slipped from my mind. I clicked the red 'x' in the upper corner of the airline ticket website, closing the page and the door to common sense.

My mind was made up. These people were my new family; my new home was by his side with his people. Our people. The Ancestors had called to me. I could hear their voices again, beckoning me home to the reservation. I was needed. And I had a motorcycle ride to plan. This was going to work. I was sure of it.

CHAPTER TEN:

Departure

When we got home from the library, I opened the shades and let in some fresh air. The birds cooed with delight. Usually, they spent five hours a day outside their cages. Since Chief had been around, they remained cooped up for days. Two Bear Paws got sick almost as soon as he arrived; I knew he wanted healing quiet. I did not know how the birds would react to him, if they would bite him or be too loud. He hadn't had a chance to meet them yet. Also, I didn't want the birds to get crushed if he rolled over, not knowing there was a bird in the bed.

Parrots are what I know the most about. My nickname and I were famous in high school for how much I loved them; I always talked about them and wore parrot earrings. I have loved parrots almost as long as motorcycles. I spent my youth studying parrot psychology, learning all I could. When I was finally ready to have my first birds, I made the decision responsibly, seriously considering all things as if I were deciding to have children. I adopted "second hand" parrots and I was overjoyed to get them.

Snickers and R.D. had both been with me for nine years, longer than any marriage or boyfriend. Their average lifespan would give them each another nine years, making it my longest relationship, even longer than the time I spent with my family growing up.

The room had been midnight dark for days, so my parrots always thought it was nighttime. Birds don't usually squawk in the dark for fear predators will know their location when they are at a sight disadvantage to escape. Even though I knew they needed sunlight to stay healthy and I felt bad about it, this is how the situation had to be for Chief to heal.

Somehow, deep inside, I knew Chief would not treat my birds with respect, probably because he wasn't treating me with any. I wanted to believe this was a phase due to his illness. Time after time, I kept forgiving him almost instantly, wanting to believe things would improve between us as he got to know me better and saw my good heart.

In the endless darkness, I knew my feathered kids were still alive because I could hear their feet and beaks softly clinking on perches, toys, and cage bars as they made their way in the dark to their food and water bowls.

My parrots were my pampered kids. Non-bird people are always amazed at how much my parrots love to be cuddled, how they climb beak-feet-beak up the covers, or up my pant leg. To some, my birds seem a lot like cats, as they hop into bed with me, walk on the soft covers, and snuggle up under my chin while I watch TV or read a book. Sometimes, they sneak a bite out of my book and nibble on the pages until a proper bird toy is offered instead.

Like many parents who try not to admit one of their children is their favorite, it was obvious Snickers was my baby. He would spend evening hours cuddled up, cooing and purring while being scratched. I'd gently preen the feathers on his head and pet his beak, he enjoyed this bonding time as much as I did. Every ten minutes or so, I'd say, "Step up" and he'd step easily onto my hand. I'd lift him up and set him down on the handle of a wicker basket I lined with newspaper. He'd do his business there and never poop on me.

We had a good thing going, a mutual affection and respect. Snickers had some emotional scars from the nine years he spent with his first owner before I met him. It took a while to earn his trust. I promised him we would be together for all his days; I was his forever home.

He used to say some words and phrases in English until his previous owners sucked him up the vacuum cleaner while chasing him around on the floor with the nozzle end. They thought it was funny to watch him scream and run. After that trauma, he never spoke a human word again. So, I learned how to speak parrot. His every cluck, whisper, and screech I understood. His every head tilt, wing flap, and tail flip was communication he trained me to read. I find it amazing to watch birds in the wild, like a crow on a telephone line, because I see a lot of the same expressions in their movements, too.

Snickers was about the size of a small crow head to tail, mostly all tail. He was the type of green parrot in the movie *Paulie,* a Blue Crown Conure. Ring Ding, R.D. for short, was a Normal Grey Cockatiel with a fun, yellow crest he could raise and lower to express his ever-changing moods. My parrots received new names when they began their new life with me, it helped show them things were different now and they would be safe, as they had both been abused previously. I named them after snack foods because it helped me remember parrots are prey animals and I should always respect their needs and fears as such.

Parrots don't like things coming at them from above; it reminds them of a hawk swooping down on their back, catching them for a meal. Nothing should be hung from the ceiling above their cages, as something above their head can feel like shadows from a bird of prey. If we went outside, the birds were always looking up from their travel cages, one eye peeking around the towel, head tilted sideways to the sky, watching for bigger things that might come down from above and eat them.

R.D. was smaller than Snickers, so their out of cage time was always supervised. I did not want there to be a tousle and risk R.D. getting a toe bit off by his jealous, bigger, older brother. R.D. could fly a lot better than Snickers, so he always got away before any trouble started brewing.

Now that some light was making the room more cheerful,

the birds were waking up, flapping, they wanted to get out and play. Chief didn't give the birds a thought as he settled into the bed and turned on the TV. I decided this would be a great time to let the birds out of their cooped up nest holes known as cages. I opened their cage doors; they stepped out onto their perches, stretched their wings and flapped rapidly for exercise while holding onto the perch with their feet. I picked up Snickers and lay down on the bed next to Two Bear Paws. The parrot seemed calm; he walked around on the covers and decided to approach this new person.

Snickers walked right up and put his forehead on Chief's thigh and begged to be petted. I was amazed how much trust and love this little bird showed a stranger so quickly. Snickers was smart. He knew what he needed to do to remain safe; kissing up to Chief was a good move.

I said, "This is my parrot, Snickers. He wants to say hi. You can pet his head with a fingertip if you want. I think he likes you."

Chief looked down at the bird. One side of his mouth curled into a strange, toothy snarl which I did not understand. He reached down with his huge, leathery hand and grabbed Snickers from above. The poor bird's head was between his first two fingers, his body paralyzed, his wings constrained by his palm and fingers. His little orange feet kicked out as he was lifted off the bed and turned upside down.

Chief held the captured parrot to his face and laughed as it struggled. I was horrified. I thought of screaming and telling him to get out, leave, but no sound would come out of me. I couldn't even move. There was no compassion or love in his eyes; he looked like a predator that just caught dinner. It was the emotionless expression the lion wears while it waits for the antelope in its mouth to kick a few more times before it dies. The way his face looked still horrifies me to this day.

"I have broken many chicken necks. This bird would be easy to kill. Its feathers would look good in my headdress."

My eyes flashed like the mother buffalo protecting her calf. I was about to snap, but then he set Snickers on his shoulder. The parrot snuggled up to his neck and purred. Shocked, my anger dissolved. My last chance to send Chief on his way, my last clear thought of kicking him out, was gone as my parrot adored him.

He pressed a button on the remote control and calmly flipped the station. He said my parrots will be the first ones ever to live in Wounded Knee. He said they do not have pets on the reservation and the children will enjoy playing with my birds. I said, "Well, if there are no pets, that is good. Then there will be no cats to chase and eat my birds. I'll go with you as long as there are no cats living in your house." He agreed.

In addition to no cats, I requested two more things. First, to say goodbye to my family in Connecticut before I left with him, and second, I wanted us to have lunch with my close friend, Reverend Johnston. Chief flat out refused to have lunch with a reverend from the Episcopal Church. He would not give any more details on his decision, no further explanation than a hard stare into the distance, like he was standing to die, and a loud, firm "No."

I loved and admired Reverend Rose Johnston. We had a close bond. I started attending the Episcopal Church when I moved to Maine to go to college. I chose it simply because it was the pretty church at the end of my street. And, maybe just a little bit because its traditions were so far removed from those of my Baptist parents'.

It is Baptist custom not to baptize infants, they wait until you are older so you can make the conscious choice and commitment for yourself; I had not yet done this.

Rose was retiring without performing the ceremony she had always dreamed of: a lake baptism. This had proven to be a challenging desire for her, since Episcopalians traditionally get baptized as babies with water poured over their foreheads from the elaborate fountain by the main entrance.

Rose and I were a perfect match. I said I would gladly receive a lake baptism, that is how Jesus would do it. I loved the old fashioned idea and the earthy romance. It was a beautiful ceremony. She was a special friend to me and a very important person in my life. If Rose didn't try to stop me, then I'd know my South Dakota plans weren't so crazy.

I think Chief knew what was at stake, for I held my ground and refused to leave without having lunch with Rose first. I was serious. Perhaps because we were so far off the reservation and on White Man's land, he yielded. Giving in was not his thing. He normally had trouble even listening to another viewpoint besides his own.

Rose met us at a quaint, local restaurant not too far from the church. The windows were covered in local-made suncatchers, displayed for sale. Old furniture, heirloom china tableware, checkered tablecloths, and flowers as real as the cloth napkins gave the place a grandma's kitchen feel. In fact, grandma herself cooked every meal and every pie from scratch right there. The sandwiches and soups tasted like the food did when you were a kid playing outside and mom called you in the house for lunch during summer vacation. It was my favorite place to eat.

As soon as Chief Two Bear Paws walked in, Rose stood to meet him. Confident and tall, she spoke the Truth. She apologized for how the Episcopal Church went onto reservations out West and forced Indians to convert to Christianity. She apologized for how the Church took Indian children away from their parents and brain-washed them in schools that did not teach Indian faith, culture, or traditions. She apologized for the tipis and sweat lodges that were torn down so churches could be built in their place, she apologized for how the Indians were forced to attend. Her words shocked me, but impressed him. Chief shook her hand, thanked her, and said some words in Lakota.

No wonder he had bucked so strongly at meeting an

Episcopal reverend. I felt embarrassed I did not know the facts, ashamed I had pushed so hard, not knowing the truth. And I loved Chief even more for the courage he showed in meeting her.

At one point, Rose and I were alone for a few minutes while Chief used the washroom. She looked at me seriously and asked, "Are you okay? Do you know what you are doing?"

"I'm fine. We are in love and I'm moving to South Dakota with him. We are leaving in a few days. You are important to me and I love you, that's why I just had to see you. I would not leave without saying goodbye to you."

"Well, alright. If you believe you know what you want, then go after it. Just be careful and don't try to push your views on them. Keep quiet more than you talk. They have been hurt and wronged enough by the Episcopal Church. White Man has gone on crusades to reservations, trying to make Indians become Christians. Don't try to change them or make them believe in what you believe. Remember, you are not going there as a missionary, so don't act like one." Her points were well said and well taken.

She softened and leaned in to whisper, "And a little tip from a missionary friend: keep your birth control pills in a metal tin. I heard cockroaches are drawn to them. A metal box is the only reliable deterrent. Without it, the roaches will chew through the contraceptive's foil packaging and eat the sweet pills inside."

Chief sat back down and the conversation between the two of them continued splendidly. As dessert was coming to an end, Rose said, "I think every church should have a sweat lodge on its front lawn." He beamed. He stood up first and extended his hand. He eagerly shook hers with a genuine smile.

Chief Two Bear Paws faced Rose as a warrior and friend. His words were clear and strong. "You are a good person. You are welcome on Lakota land. Come, sit, eat, stay with us whenever you want. Stay with us for as long as you want. Our homes and our hearts will always be open to you."

She nodded, said thank you, and smiled. I was amazed.

My other meeting request was denied. Chief would not let me say goodbye to my family. I said if I could not see my family, then I would not pack all my things and leave for good in one swoop. I struck a compromise. We would take a bus south to Portland, Maine, then hop on an Amtrak train heading west. I would see the reservation, meet his people, then come back for my things. And I would be sure to visit my family upon my departure next time around.

He agreed. Anything to get me out there, I realize now. I also realize that if he would have "allowed" me to see my family and say goodbye, my bond to him, his people, the spirit of the rez, the hills, sky, and land would not have been as strong. Seeing my family most likely would have broken his hold on me and I would have revoked my decision to go with him, even to visit. He had to shield me from any power but his own in order to keep me under his spell.

However, I could not leave my birds alone. It was unfair to ask my friends to care for them at my apartment for an unspecified amount of time. It could be a handful of days, a few weeks, it might be a month. My "Maine Mom and Dad" agreed to take the birds into their home and help me out. I packed up their food, cages, toys, and perches. Chief insisted on going with me to their house to keep watch on me, but he would not get out of the truck to meet my close friends when I asked. He simply said no and remained in the passenger seat, reading the newspaper. I figured he must be feeling ill again, as his legs were swollen and he still had a touch of cough. I let him be.

It was hard to leave my babies, but I knew they would be in good hands, as they had watched my parrots before when Big Biker and I went out to Sturgis for fifteen days. They knew how to take care of my birds and the little feathered guys liked them in return. They would get lots of out of cage time and head scratches. They were also feeding Blue Fish, my blue Siamese fighting fish. He lived in a tall, thick, glass bowl that held about three gallons of water.

Chief insisted I pack my computer and printer and bring it with us on our trip. It was the only thing he asked me to bring. I padded it up into suitcases so we could safely transport it across the miles. We headed for the bus station in Bangor. At the counter, I asked for a round trip ticket to Portland. Chief waved his hand. I looked at him. "One way," he stated.

"Why? I have to come back for my birds and things, I might as well buy the cheaper ticket now."

"No. We do not know what will be. Maybe you will fly back."

Okay, I thought, that makes sense. So I asked for a one way ticket for myself. He smacked the counter, then motioned me closer. I whispered, "Well, you're going to buy your own tickets, right?" He walked away from the counter and stood near a long row of empty chairs. I followed.

"I am getting a check tomorrow or the next day. You pay for this. I will have money soon."

It sounded fishy, but it wasn't that much money, so I agreed.

Once in Portland, we went to the Amtrak station. Chief reminded me he would get some money soon, so I should buy both our tickets one way to Omaha, Nebraska. He said Strong Bear, his oldest son, would borrow his truck and meet us in Omaha.

I took comfort in this because I kept waiting for things to turn out okay just around the next corner. The way I imagined it, meeting up with Strong Bear was a good sign. I thought his son was traveling through Omaha on business. I figured he was meeting us for lunch so he could pass his dad the check which had recently arrived in the mail. I thought Chief would cash it and pay me back on the spot, then pay the rest of our way to the reservation. I did not realize there is no train service across

South Dakota. Omaha is the last stop on the rail, a stranded seven hours from Wounded Knee.

Two tickets from Portland to Omaha ran over six hundred dollars and this was just the beginning. I felt sick at the cash register and I had to step away from the counter without buying the tickets. I needed to breathe some air outside the train station.

I called my father. I asked him his advice at spending so much money and going out to South Dakota with Chief Two Bear Paws. It was the first he'd heard I was leaving; he thought I was crazy. He told me to buy Chief a one way ticket back home and to get the hell out of there as fast as possible. I got angry and told my dad he was just another white man against the Indians. I said he did not understand, I could not leave this man, I love him. It was my life and I wanted to go live in Wounded Knee.

Two Bear Paws stood behind me, glaring. My dad told me to give the phone to Chief. A minute passed. Chief listened. All he said was "Yes" at the end of my father's words, then Chief hung up and put my phone in his pocket.

I ran after him and begged for my phone back. He shook his head no and held up his palm in a "stop" gesture to end the discussion. I ran to the other side of the waiting area and dumped some quarters into the payphone. He didn't see that one coming; Chief wasn't used to women having money as a way out of his controlling decisions.

My father answered on the first ring. Before he could even say hello, I demanded, "What did you say to him?"

"I told him if you decide, at any time, you want to go, he has to let you leave. I asked him to promise me he will let you leave unharmed." My dad's voice broke as he held back emotions.

I was annoyed by his precautions. I did not know it at the time, but this promise was one of the things that saved my life. Two Bear Paws had said, "Yes." That was the only word he needed. He was a Lakota chief and he took pride in keeping his promises, although he made them seldom. He would not be like the White Man and break a promise. Even to a White Man.

I said goodbye to my dad and dropped six hundred dollars on two one way tickets to Omaha. The trip would take about forty hours.

On the train, I cuddled up to Chief. He did not put his arm around me, but he allowed me to adore him. I took it as a sign he loved me.

Other passengers smiled at us and asked if I was his daughter. I said no, we are getting married. Chief quietly corrected me, "Start saying you are my wife when people ask. Things will go better for us this way." From this point on, Chief referred to me as his wife; I followed suit. Such a simple ceremony.

Chief assured me there would be more to our union than just these self-adorned titles. "We will have wedding ceremony as soon as we get to Wounded Knee. Our first day back, we will get married."

I thought about this for a second. I was pleased, although it did seem rather rushed. "That sounds lovely, Chief. Hey, wouldn't it be something if we got married on Thanksgiving Day? How about that for a reason to celebrate Thanksgiving every year? The white girl and the Indian get married."

Chief chuckled, appreciating the irony. "*Ohan*. Yes. I like that. Sounds good." He had agreed. It was set. I really liked the idea of Thanksgiving better than a random early November date; also, somewhere in the back of my mind, I think I knew I needed more time.

When I started to answer in the way Chief instructed, people looked pleased and happy we were married. That is because these people do not know Indians the way they do in South Dakota. In the Midwest, there is much prejudice; we were met with quite different stares and reactions there.

For now, all was peaceful. There was an African-American

woman about my age in the seat next to me, across the aisle. We were soon talking about pineapples and Halloween candy and becoming fast friends. Chief made a gesture in front of my face. When I looked at him, he told me to stop talking to her. "She is not one of us." My new friendship faded instantly.

We ate tortellini in the dining car, small portions for an exorbitant price. But it was delicious. In the dining car, a young man approached Chief; it was obvious he was in awe. The young man appeared to be from India; I was curious as to how Chief would handle this because, like the African-American woman I was not allowed to befriend, this man was not Lakota.

I learned this situation was different because this person was male and his warmth was directed towards Chief, not me. Plus, Chief could charm him with Indian stories, whereas the woman and I were speaking of silly things like how delicious pineapple is with chocolate. Conversation like that did not enhance the constant, stoic, native image Chief required from us both at all times. If we always remained properly Lakota it honored our culture and invited outsiders to ask questions and learn, perhaps even write a news article quoting Chief about the Black Hills or another topic close to home and help our cause.

Two Bear Paws invited the young man to sit with us. He took photos and asked many questions. Chief offered him dinner, but he had already eaten. He accepted a cup of coffee and pastry on my tab and sat with us for more than an hour as Chief told stories and we finished our meal.

The young man's admiration grew with Chief's every word and he promised he would share Chief's message with many people on his journey. Most of Chief's concerns, complaints, and stories I had already heard quite a few times by this point; I was beginning to notice a pattern.

At breakfast the next day, Chief told me his favorite joke. This humorous side of him was new. I never saw him reveal it to anyone else, not strangers nor Indians.

A young white woman fell in love with an Indian boy. He kept asking her to ride with him on his horse. The young girl's mother said no. The daughter begged her mother, but her mother would not let her ride with the Indian boy.

One day, the young girl snuck away and called to the boy. She got on his horse and they rode all around the Indian village with the boy hooting and hollering the whole way. They had a grand time.

He dropped her off back home. She walked into the house and her mother was very upset that she had been riding with the Indian boy.

"See mother, I am fine. I did not fall off the horse like you thought I would. I held onto the saddle horn."

The girl's mother frowned. "Indians ride bareback. They do not use saddles."

Chief laughed hard at his own joke. It was difficult for me to understand it at first, because he spoke such choppy English. But I eventually figured it out and chuckled to make him feel good. Honestly, I was embarrassed by the joke. I think I still admired him too much as an Indian stereotype instead of seeing him as a human man.

Back in our seats, I started to doze off while mentally calculating how much money I had spent so far. I woke up, startled, and grabbed paper and pen. I wrote down all my expenses since Chief had stepped into my life to claim me. I started with gas for my truck down to Boston, my three hundred dollar speeding ticket, the rent I paid in advance on my apartment in anticipation of being gone and not earning money at the job I just quit, my hundred dollar hair salon appointment so I would look more Lakota, his eyeglasses, our food, bus tickets, train tickets . . . I was shocked. I had spent over eighteen hundred dollars in about ten days. And we didn't even get there yet.

I was having second thoughts. I explained my concern to

Chief. I couldn't afford this. I was thinking of getting off the train at the next stop, turning around, and letting him go onward by himself.

He opened one eye and said, "Do not worry about it. *Tunkashila* will provide. You will be safe on the reservation."

Chief took my pen and paper and drew a medicine wheel, next to it a black tipped eagle feather with Indian flair, and a mountain. He told me another traditional Lakota story. His voice put me into a trance. I forgot my worries and fell asleep as if his spoken words were the magic spell of a lullaby.

I would most likely have been awakened by a nightmare had I known I would end up spending over fifty thousand dollars in five months. My grandmother had passed away right before I met Chief and left me a decent amount of money. Also, I had been working since I was sixteen and had a nice savings account. I blew through my savings and inheritance fast and the rest I charged on credit cards which still haunt me today. The way my life is now, I usually have about eight dollars in my account until next pay day.

But I did not know these things then, and I slept for a long while.

When I woke, Chief pulled up his pant legs and showed me his calves. The skin looked about to rip; it was purple and pulled tight with water retention. "Sit too long," he said. I got up to help him stand.

He winced and could not walk. "Blanket," he said as he collapsed down into the seat. I asked the attendant for a blanket. He slept the rest of the way, waking up only to cough.

He was getting worse again, despite the medication.

NOVEMBER

CHAPTER ELEVEN:

Delays

We arrived at the Amtrak station in Omaha; it was late. We got a motel room nearby. It was good for Chief to put his feet up in bed and sleep. The next morning, I asked him how we were getting to Wounded Knee. He pulled my cell out of his pocket and made a few calls, he spoke Lakota.

He dropped the phone onto the bed and closed his eyes. "Nobody can help."

"What about your son, you said he would meet us in your truck?"

"He can't come."

"What are we going to do? We are stuck out here! And you're sick, you need help!" I dug the phone book out of the drawer. No trains, no planes, no busses, there was no way to get to Wounded Knee. I even crazily called a taxi cab. For no amount of money would he drive us to the reservation. Frustrated and out of ideas, I called a rental car place.

Chief nodded. "It is the only way."

Irritated he didn't tell me that sooner, I kept my comments to myself and made a car reservation for the next day. Since things had gone so badly with the taxi company when I mentioned the reservation, I decided to tell the rental car place I was from Maine and I wanted to sightsee, maybe even drive down to Texas if I had time. I wanted the car for three weeks. They thought that was great.

The car rental place was near the motel. Everything was near the motel. It seemed a gas station/convenience store was the only other business in town. I walked with the suitcases, Chief limped beside me. He said he would wait around back in the rental car parking garage, I could pick him up there. I wasn't sure why he suggested this. I told him I was proud to be seen with him and he should come inside with me. He insisted on disappearing and waiting around back.

I went into the rental office. The people were well-dressed in casual suits and very nice to me. There were no other customers, just three employees, a woman and two men. They gathered around me to socialize, offering bottled water and smiles. They looked at my Maine license, said it was great I was visiting the Midwest. Everyone was polite, full of kind conversation and small talk questions. They wanted to hear all about Maine, nobody had been there before. They loved my New England fall foliage and lobster stories, they were tickled at the way I could draw up a Maine accent upon request.

What can I say—they were white and easily entertained by simple stereotypes of Maine, America's "Vacationland." I didn't mind participating in white culture small talk formalities, as reverting to my professional business world pleasantries was actually refreshing after all the quiet, stoic Indian ways Chief had been teaching me. I had a great car and the price wasn't bad for almost a month's worth of time. I even got a AAA discount.

All three shook my hand and I followed one man out a large door into the parking garage. He asked me to wait a minute while he pulled the car out of line. He parked the car near me and got out. Chief silently emerged from the shadows and slipped into the passenger seat. The employee had been walking up to me with keys and handshake extended, but he saw Chief out of the corner of his eye and revoked both offers.

"He's with *you?*" he accused. "Well, that changes everything! You need to come back inside. And tell . . . *him* . . . to get out of the car and come in with you." The pause around the word "him" was filled with disdain.

Chief walked in with me. The associate announced to the room, "Look at *this!*" he jerked his thumb towards Chief. The two other associates looked up and audibly gasped at the savage sight. One agent ran to shred the paperwork I had signed while the other put the keys safely into the far back of the desk drawer. They refused to rent to me and asked us to leave.

I had tears in my eyes. I got a little loud and said, "This is prejudice! You are all racists! This man is a respected Lakota elder and chief. His name is Chief Two Bear Paws. You should be honored to meet him and show him respect! I am paying for this and I will be the one driving. I was fine to rent to before you saw him. Let's be fair here."

They told me I lied about where I was going and if I was going to the reservation, that changes everything. They said they don't rent to people from the reservation. I said I was from Maine.

They discussed the situation away from us behind a closed door and came back with a decision. "The only way we will let you leave with *him* and a car is if you downgrade the car to the lowest end model we have. There will be a thousand dollar deposit on the car until it is returned. And you cannot rent the car for as long as you've requested. We can only rent it to you for two weeks. If the car is not returned by the end of that second week, we will charge your credit card six thousand dollars and call the police."

They were the only rental place around and there was no other transportation. We were stranded, backed into a corner. Chief was sick. I had no choice. They made me sign many documents, they photocopied just about everything in my wallet; it felt like I had to offer my life in exchange for the rental car. They took out an ink pad and made me put my fingerprints next to my signed name.

Violated, Chief and I now had a car. And a little less than two weeks to spend in Wounded Knee before we had to figure out how to get it back to Racist Rentals. It's a seven hour drive to Omaha. I really hadn't thought returning the car through, but

I had faith Chief would work something out.

We stopped at a diner to eat. Surprised and delighted, I saw Indian tacos on the menu. Chief wanted a huge double hamburger and fries. I ordered my taco with extra beans, no beef. Chief recoiled and stared at me. "No meat?"

"No, I don't eat meat. I'm a vegetarian. I have been one since I was seven years old. It's not a big deal."

He grunted and ordered his burgers rare.

The meal was good. I couldn't help but gaze at Chief the whole time with love in my eyes. He ate like he was starving.

When the waitress came to refill our coffee, she asked if we'd like anything else. I asked for the check. She said, "Don't worry about that, dear. That couple over there thought you two were adorable and paid for your meal."

I looked towards the couple, but they had left. "Were they Indian?"

"No, it was a white couple." She smiled sweetly and went on her way to refill other coffee cups.

I thought they must have been tourists.

As we stood up to leave, I slipped two dollars under my empty coffee mug. Chief swiftly snapped up the cash, it disappeared into the pocket of his jeans.

"What are you doing?" I asked. "That's the waitress's tip money."

Chief replied, "I have worked hard all my life. Had many jobs. Nobody ever gave me a tip. Nobody deserves tips if I never got one."

I thought back to my waitressing days and had to argue this one a bit further. "Chief, sometimes these girls make only two dollars an hour. They don't even get minimum wage. They depend on tips to make up the difference. Tips are how they survive."

He waved his hand, telling me my viewpoint wasn't worth his time. "Go."

From that day on, any tip money I left Chief would

confiscate. I tried to outsmart him, but he would always run back to the table and tip himself for being a great patron. I had to start paying all dining bills by credit card so I could write the waitress's gratuity onto the receipt.

We got back into the car. I drove, as Chief told me I should. He would grunt a direction or command every so often to keep me on the right path. I thought we were headed for Wounded Knee, but I think we went past it, drove through the bigger town of Pine Ridge, and ended up in Hot Springs.

I recognized this town where Big Biker and I had stayed not so long ago. I was hoping Chief and I could stretch our legs and visit some of the downtown shops. It had been about nine hours of driving so far, broken only by two fuel stops and one meal. I knew there were some cute prairie dogs around here, I had taken some photos of them with Big Biker. Tourists like to toss them potato chips and watch them stand up and chew because they look so adorable eating, but people don't realize salt dries the little guys out and they die. Maybe we could stop and educate some late season tourists and save a few prairie dog lives while we were in town. Whatever we did, I was looking forward to stopping.

Chief told me to keep driving. Soon, he barked for me to turn right. I did. The street was domed in trees, I saw a white Virgin Mary statue outside a Catholic Church. I knew we couldn't be going there. "Left! Left!" Chief wheezed as he slammed his left palm against the dashboard. I turned left a little after his command, but still made the driveway.

Apparently, we were pulling into the Hot Springs V.A. medical center. Chief told me to park close and over to the left. I did as instructed.

We walked in together; he needed to lean on me the entire way. The second we got through the door, he collapsed down into an open seat. I really had no idea what to do. He waved his arm at me in disgust and fell over on his side. The back of the seat next to him caught him mid-fall, he slouched into it and became wedged into the space between the backrests so it partially held him up.

I walked up to the main counter. "My husband is very sick. He needs his medication. Water pills, especially. I think he's dying. It's an emergency."

She looked at me, glanced over at Chief, saw he was an Indian, shook her head and sighed. She slid a clipboard to me. "Here, fill these out."

I did the best I could, not knowing much about Chief. He motioned weakly for me to take his wallet out of his pocket. I never knew he had a wallet until this moment. I found his driver's license and his veteran's card. Back at the V.A. in Maine, Chief had feebly slid his driver's license and V.A. card around me to the woman behind the glass, then stepped off to the side. He always blocked my view; I never got a good look at his cards. Now that they were in my hand two thousand miles from Maine, I noticed each card had a different first and middle name. Both were different from the name Chief told me he had. I was confused. Chief said, "Do not worry about it. I have many names. Nobody knows my real name or my real birthday, it does not matter. Only my Indian given name matters."

With the potential of even more names lingering in the air, I looked at the unmatched mix of white people's names I held in my hand and went with the one on the V.A. card since we were at the V.A. Chief later told me the story of his conflicting names. He wanted to go to war but he was too young to sign up, so he used his father's name to join the fight in Korea.

He said he was about 14 years old at the time, the big Korean war was over, he saved a parachute from his jumping days; Chief was not fond of answering direct questions, so, the best I can piece together is he was a fourteen year old paratrooper stationed on U.S. soil in the Korean DMZ Conflict of 1966–1969 under an assumed name. It was one of many.

"Um, ok. Question number three . . ." Eventually a doctor

saw us in a small room. She took his pulse, shined a light in his eyes, and decided Chief needed a bed. The clinic seemed rather small and I was glad they had an opening.

I helped Chief into the bed. After a while, a nurse came in to take a blood sample. She stuck his arm ten times and could not find a vein. She was making a map of her failures, leaving a trail of bruises up and down his arm. Chief winced each time; he is a warrior and not one to make a sound for pain, she must have been sticking him quite ineptly. Frustrated, she threw down the needle, seemed to pout, and left.

A more confident woman came into the room with Miss Pouty Nurse. She arched Chief's arm and easily slid the needle into a vein without hesitation; Chief's face showed no sign of pain. Miss Pouty said, "Oh," as if she had missed an easy word in the middle school spelling bee; she might as well have scuffed the ground with the toe of her shoe and twirled her hair with her finger. The better nurse drew blood and they left together.

Much time passed, another woman came into the room with a clipboard and a stack of green papers. She told me I'd have to leave. I said, "I am his wife." She asked Chief if that was true.

He nodded and whispered, "Yes." I felt tingly inside with pride.

The woman in the white coat said, "Okay, you can stay then. These questions can get very personal, so don't be embarrassed." She asked me five pages worth of questions about Chief regarding his daily health and habits. Most of the time, Chief told me the answers.

They finally hooked him up to some IV drips and brought in a little pleated paper cup of pills. It was about ten o'clock at night. We had been here at least three hours with slow service and exceptionally unqualified help who didn't seem to care that they hadn't any skills.

A very rude, heavy, older woman with short, curly blonde-grey hair barged into the room. "You have to leave!" she yelled at me, waking Chief. "Visiting hours are over!"

"But I'm his wife."

"I don't care!" she snapped. "You have to go. Nobody is allowed in the rooms at night except patients."

"But what am I supposed to do? Where am I supposed to go?"

"Home!"

"But I just moved here. I don't know my way around. I can't find my way home in the dark without Chief's help and he's too sick to leave."

She sighed. "There is a waiting room down the hall. You can spend the night there if you have to." She pointed towards the door down the hall. "Out, now!"

I kissed Chief's hand which I had been holding and placed it gently on the bed. I kissed his cheek and said goodnight. She cleared her throat and tapped her foot.

She followed me down the hall to the waiting room. "You can see him again in the morning. Someone will come get you when he's ready. Do *not* leave this room until someone gets you in the morning." She made sure I sat on a sofa. Then she closed the door without even a "goodnite" wish. I really hated this lady.

I sat alone in the small, dark room. I turned on the TV and kept it at a low volume. The Broncos were on, I knew this was Chief's favorite team. He said everyone in South Dakota was a Denver Broncos football fan; I smiled.

The room was about the size of a closet with a sofa and a love seat. On the table in between the two sofas was a hospital telephone. I had a bright idea; I dialed Chief's room number. He answered with a raspy voice, "Hello?"

"Hey Chief, Denver's on!"

He laughed. "I am watching Denver now. It is good."

We talked a little while longer. We softly whispered together our cheers of support when Denver made a good play.

It was a sweet moment. We were both happy that I found a creative way around the mean white lady who had acted like a nun disciplining heathen school children.

In the morning, nobody came to get me. It was late. I called Chief's room. He answered the phone sounding bright and cheerful. "Breakfast time!" he said. I laughed.

The nurse heard me on the phone and came down the short hall to get me. "You can come in now," she said. She was a different woman from last night and much sweeter.

I kissed Chief's cheek. "Good morning."

He seemed in a good mood, feeling better and full of smiles. It was the best I'd seen him ever since he came to Maine.

After breakfast, I rubbed his still swollen legs gently and laid my head on the bed next to his chest. Chief tapped me on the back. He wanted to talk. I sat up.

"No surprises. I need to tell you about my family." I prepared myself for another history lesson about the Ancestors. Although my night's sleep hadn't been the best, I was still eager to learn. He said he called Deena, his daughter, this morning. She is living at his house now. She broke in while he was gone; she climbed in the bathroom window and moved in with her son and daughter.

That sounded really strange to me. Later, when I met Deena, she was wider than the window. I asked Chief about this. He said one of the grandkids climbed in, not her. That was more plausible since the smallest was his grandson, Runs Towards Hunt, "Hunter," who was nine years old. Granddaughter Skyler was about eleven, very tall and thin. She could have fit, too.

I did not like the idea of people breaking into his house when he was gone. Especially family. That sounded quite disrespectful. And now this was my home, too, although I had never been there.

When Chief was still at my apartment in Maine, I figured

he must be related to young children, although he never talked about them. I thought they'd visit, but not break in and stay.

The email I sent to all my friends before we left Maine was made simple and less crazy sounding by saying I was going out to South Dakota to watch his grandkids. I made that up. I planned on watching our own kids. "I thought it was going to be just you and me, Chief? I thought I was going to be your wife and we would have our own children and live in our house together?"

"It was to be that way. Everyone knew I had a wife coming. They should not have moved in, but I was gone and they did. They have to stay now. There is nothing that can be done to change it."

"What about your daughter's mother? Can't she and the kids live with her?"

"No. She has new husband now. Many people live in that house. No room."

"I thought you said the wife was in charge of the tipi? How can I live that way when another woman has broken in with kids that aren't mine?" I was devastated.

"It is how it will be." Chief closed his eyes to sleep.

In that moment, a nurse walked into the room and knocked on the wall. "Ok, it's time for you to go. We're sending you home." She pointed at me, "Stop by the front office on your way out, the doctor wants to talk to you. You need to pick up his medications. She wants to explain them to you before you leave."

On the way out, I told Chief I had to stop at the office. He said, "No. Forget it."

"But you heard the nurse. The doctor has your medications ready. I need to go in there and get your pills. I need to learn how to take care of you and keep you healthy."

"No. I feel good. I do not need medicine. *Tunkashila* will take care of me. He will provide the strength I need, not pills. Go." He nodded towards the door. "Leave."

I went outside with him, he was walking on his own now, but I remembered how heavily he leaned on me when we walked into this hospital. I also remembered how sick he looked at the V.A. in Maine. I put the keys in his hands. "Go, sit in the car. I will be right back." I turned around and went back inside. I found the doctor in the little front office. She was waiting for me. She opened the door, smiled, and asked me to sit down next to her. There were brown bottles of pills with Chief's name on them lined up across her desk. Well, one of his names anyway.

"Your husband was very sick. It is good you brought him in when you did. He would not have lived through the night if you had not brought him in."

Chills ran through me. I listened with wide eyes; I had no idea.

"He has not been taking his medications for a very long time. He needs his pills. He needs to take them every day. Do you have a container like this at home?" She showed me a segmented plastic box with little snapping lids.

"No." I had never even seen one before.

"Well, you will need one. Here, let me give you this," she reached in the drawer and took out a larger pill organizer box, it was seven compartments wide for the week day and four color coded rows down: Morning, Noon, Evening, Bed. "Here, this one will work better for you. You have quite a few pills to sort out. I'll help get you started."

She told me what each pill was for and filled the Sunday row. Chief needed to take about 20 different types of pills a day, all colors, sizes, combinations, and quantities. The right number of pills at the right time of day was important. A little blue/green pill was only once a day at bedtime, but the large oval pills were four pills, four times a day.

"Ok, that will get you started. You can finish the rest of the rows at home, but use that one as a guide. To double-check, compare the pill color and size to the ones in the bottle. They are all labeled on the bottle—see?—right here—with the time of day and quantity. That should help you keep things straight. Ok, you got that part?"

I nodded.

"Well, here is the next part. Your husband is diabetic. Severely diabetic. Do you have one of these at home?" I shook my head no. "This?" No. "How about one of these?" Never seen one. "Alright, I'm going to get you all set up here. We'll start from scratch."

She must have given me five hundred dollars worth of equipment. She took a box out of the cupboard and gave it to me, then said no, put it back and dug until she found the newest technology in skin pricking devices with a special blue light and an adjustable pre-measured needle depth. "Here, this is the latest thing, it just came in. I think you will find it easier to use."

She gave me a blood pressure cuff, blood test strips, alcohol prep pads, a digital monitor to read glucose levels, insulin, three or four other things and all sorts of information and charts. I listened closely and learned how to do everything right. She was very patient. I must have sat with her for forty minutes; she was thorough and kind.

"Ok, you got it?" I nodded. "Good. We have something else to talk about." She unzipped a black pouch and showed me a small glass bottle filled with clear liquid strapped next to a row of needles. "This is for your husband's erectile dysfunction. He takes one of these needles right before sex, fills it with some of the fluid from this bottle, and then injects it into his penis. He probably knows how to use this one on his own, but I just wanted you to know what everything is for."

I hoped I didn't appear too shocked. At least now I knew what the alcohol prep pad was doing in my bathroom trashcan back in Maine. This was the one and only medicine he was sure to always carry with him. I had seen the zippered black pouch just like this one in his luggage.

The doctor's eyes were serious. "There is one last thing I need to tell you. Because of his heart medicine, he has to use this kind of sexual enhancement. Never give him Viagra. If you combine this pill right here for heart pain with Viagra, he will die." She showed me a sample pack of Viagra and also held up the tiny white pill for his heart pain. "Do you understand? He will die. Very fast."

She looked into my eyes as if someday I might need this information to help save my life. It was so obvious I was uncomfortable. Her words were not incriminating in any way, but her motherly gaze was, as well as the sample of Viagra she casually collected into the bag for me with all his other medications and supplies. She could claim in any court it was an oversight, or that I read into her good intentions. But I think she knew what she was doing. I always kept the knowledge in the back of my mind and kept the Viagra pill sample pack at the bottom of my bag in the tin with my birth control pills. I felt ashamed about it, and I never planned on using it. I just wanted to feel like I had some secret control over his life instead of Chief always controlling everything in my life. I loved him too much to use it, anyway.

I fully expected he took off with the car. But there he was, in the spot where I had parked, waiting for me. He actually seemed a little grateful I cared enough about him to spend so much time learning how to properly take care of him. He didn't say so with words. But his absence of anger let me know he was pleased.

I showed him a few things from the bag. He was especially interested in the machine with the blue light, he said he had never seen one of those before. I told him the doctor said it was new and it just came in. Chief said, "The doctor never would give an Indian all the things in your bag. You cleaned out the house! It is only because you are white why you got it. You got special treatment. They experiment on Indians and veterans here. They have no skills. They use us like guinea pigs."

He held his inner arms out to me. Both were covered in about twenty large bruises each, wrist to elbow and above. Deep purple bruises and red blood spots stood out severely even on his dark skin tone. I was horrified. "That is what they do. White doctors. They use us to learn. They don't care. We are not people to them. But this place is better than the one in Pine Ridge. I would have died there. That is why we go to Hot Springs. Always take me here if I have problem. We take you here, too. Babies die all the time in Pine Ridge hospital. Nobody cares. Drive."

At his sudden direction, I started the engine and got back on the road. We stopped at a feed store. He told me to buy some things he placed on the counter. One of them was a tube of antibiotics; I did not ask questions.

Outside Hot Springs, we headed for the rez; it was nothing but grass, just endless grass. Sometimes the grace of a worn, dusty path made the steering easier for a bit as the tires fell into the grooves, but otherwise, it was only more grass.

CHAPTER TWELVE:

Home Together in Pine Ridge

We finally went past a sign that welcomed us to the reservation. We drove by the round building/museum and my heart leapt at the sight. "Oh! There it is!" I happily exclaimed. "Do you live near this place where we first met?" Chief nodded. "Wow. Well, I am sure we will stop by the museum again some day soon. Before we do, can you please let me know when we are about to go there? I would like to prepare myself mentally and spiritually before I touch that ground again. It means so much to me."

Chief pressed his lips together and waved his hand forward without comment. We headed down the road, farther than Big Biker and I had gone before. I saw a few rundown trailers and piles of trash many call home. Chief barked for me to turn right. I went right passed it. He hit the dashboard with his right hand, as if that would help me. "No! Go right! RIGHT!" His spit flew with his command. I had to turn around in a field and go back. He was so angry at me. "When I say 'right,' you go right!" Now I had to make a left. I hoped that logic was okay. I didn't dare ask, I just turned into the long, dirt driveway.

Halfway up, we encountered a worn, rustic gate with a homemade fence on either side; everything was made from cut trees and branches woven and tied together. The gate kept animals in, intruders out, it also supported the huge wooden arch that spanned across the driveway. The name of his ranch was burned into the sign that hung from the middle of the arch.

"Get the gate."

I got out and undid the gate. Got back in and drove the car through.

"Stop. Close the gate."

I put it in park, jumped back out, closed the gate, and got back in to drive the rest of the way up the driveway. This would be standard procedure every time we came home, the same every time we left. And it wasn't the driver's duty to get the gate; it was mine no matter where I sat.

A crowd waited at the top of the driveway, eager for his arrival. There must have been fifteen people, all relatives. They gathered around the car. Chief got out and demanded, "Keys!" I handed them over, but I didn't want to, as my fingerprints were the ones on file for this rental. I needed to keep track of things to get it back on time. I couldn't risk the keys going the way of my cell phone.

Chief took the keys and unlocked the doors I had just locked. Everyone climbed inside or on top of the car. There were "ooohs" and "ahhs" from the crowd. "You have a car!" they said. I was not introduced.

The crowd kept playing with the lights and horn, making driving sounds and turning the wheel, seeing how many Indians they could stuff into the back seat. There were kids and adults alike, having a grand old time with my rental.

"Water the horses," Chief instructed. We left the crowd alone to play with the car. Blessedly, it was not running and I prayed Chief still had the keys.

I followed him down to a small, three-sided shelter that housed hay. "You have horses?" I asked.

Chief was proud. "Five. My ranch is the only one with horses." I remembered reading this in his letters, now that he said it. Currently, as I type this book, the August 2012 issue of *National Geographic* has a cover story on my area of the Pine Ridge Reservation. The photos bring back memories of the endless sky, the gloom mixed with hope, and the horses. Those photos are moving pictures in my mind; they are my life and my dreams. Now long gone.

I looked around and saw there was a trough beside the

shelter. He pointed away to the hose alongside the house. I dragged it over, untangled it, it was leaking in several places but I could avoid getting wet by standing in between the two streams closest to me. I filled the trough with water. Chief walked over and wrapped the most threadbare part of hose with his hand and the flow went much faster. I thought, "At least it seems he has running water, that's a good start."

I did not see the horses, they had a lot of room to roam in the four hundred acre field; I couldn't even see the other side of the fence. There was hay strewn around the shelter, and there sure was plenty enough grass to eat. Chief said, "In winter we put a heater in the water so they can drink. We drive out in the snow and throw hay bales for the horses. The rest of the time, they eat grass."

Chief shut the hose off and walked around to the open side of the three sided, crude shelter. I put the hose back alongside the house and followed him. Inside the shelter, I was surprised to find a medium sized paint horse. He looked weak and cold. Chief held him by his head and pulled the tube of antibiotics out of his shirt pocket. He squeezed the entire tube out behind the horse's back teeth. The horse's tongue came out as he licked at the bitter taste in the back of his throat, swallowing the clear gel.

"Horse sick for long time." He pointed at the horse's right front leg. The fur was rubbed off, the pink skin inflamed, bloody, and scabbed. "Got leg stuck in barbed wire fence last winter. Horse stuck in fence a few days before we found him. We cut fence. Horse got free, but wire still wrapped around leg. Horse kept running. Nobody could catch it. I could not afford medicine."

After a year of suffering, the horse was too weak to run anymore. He now stood helpless and hurting inside the hay shelter, eyes and nose oozing, holding his swollen leg up off the ground. The barbs were still imbedded in his wound. I looked closer and saw how skin had grown over the metal burrs while other parts of the wire still wrapped around his leg. It was too late to remove the wire now without ripping deep holes into the horse's flesh. Chief hoped the antibiotics would work; he could finally afford them now that I was here to buy. The tube of antibiotics cost about twelve dollars.

We left the horse and headed up the worn walkway towards home. I stepped over animal skulls, antlers, bones, a rusty bucket, a clump of feathers, dirty water in a plastic margarine container, rusty tin cans, snack wrappers, empty cardboard cake mix boxes, and general household trash in order to follow him to the front door, where Chief stood, unlocking a series of padlocks.

The most beautiful bird landed beside me on the bundle of sticks which were woven into a fence along the sides of the walkway. I froze in my tracks. I had never seen such a gorgeous wild bird before. It had a black beak, black head, but its wings were a glorious mirrored blue. The tail captured some of this iridescence; I had never seen a tail so long and graceful. Bright white patches stood out on its chest and wings, each pure white wing feather was outlined with crisp black edges. I could have cried at its beauty. I whispered to Chief, "What is it?"

He turned from the door, glanced at the bird and said, "Magpie." It took off. I was dazzled by the flashes of white on its wingtips as they contrasted with the black when it flapped. I caught just a glimpse of Chief smiling at my wonder before he turned back to the door. I suppose black billed magpies are a common sight out West, which is their habitat, but this was a new bird to me and I was enchanted.

My toe absently ran into an empty tin can. I looked down and thought how nice it would be to see magpies dancing above my vegetable garden, which I could plant once I cleaned up all the trash.

By now, Chief had undone three padlocks on his front door, as well as the deadbolt. These safety measures seemed overkill since everyone had just been using the bathroom window to climb inside the house.

It was dark inside, but Chief flicked on the lights. I thought, "Bonus, there is electricity! This is looking good." What didn't look good was the set of eyes peering out from the pile of dirty dishes on the counter. The eyes were green. I looked at Chief, thinking of my parrots which I would soon bring here. "What's that? I thought you had no cats?"

"I don't." Chief grabbed a metal pot and spoon. He opened the kitchen door and yelled, "Baaaaah!" as he banged the pot. The cat high-tailed it out of there, allowing Chief to make good on his promise of no cats. I didn't expect that, I felt bad. We could have talked about it and made some other arrangement. It was the only cat I ever saw on the reservation. I am sure it got eaten by the emaciated feral dogs that roam in packs around the reservation, starving.

The house was humble but I loved it. I was so happy he had a real house, too, and not a shelter made from scraps or a cold, dilapidated trailer. Even if he had lived in a place like that, I would have still been with him, working to make it better. I was in love and I was here for life; a house just made it nicer.

The same global charity organization who had built the round building/museum had also built Chief Two Bear Paws and his previous wife this house only a few years earlier. It was the only real house I saw in Wounded Knee. Used hard by many as it was large by comparison, secure, and had indoor plumbing, it gave the haggard impression it had been standing for fifty, even a hundred years.

There were many photos of ancestors and great leaders taped to the walls and a few very old photos in frames. One photo was Two Bear Paws at five years old, wearing dance regalia and a huge war bonnet with eagle feathers. He looked noble and stern, even as a young boy his high place in Lakota society was known and honored.

A large wooden table was the heart of the kitchen, it was

covered by a thick pile of trash and used dishes; it would take me a solid day to clean the mess up. But it was a nice table with nine wooden chairs, extra folding chairs stood in the corner. The kitchen had a refrigerator and blue counters somewhere underneath more of the same garbage.

There was a sink piled high with what seemed like a year's worth of dirty dishes and a gas cooktop propped a few inches off the floor with cinder blocks. It was directly hooked up to a small propane tank which leaned against it, at the same level as the cooking flames. I freaked out. "No!" I pointed. "That is not safe! This whole house could blow up. Chief, I will buy you a real stove. One that has an oven. I will bake pies. Please, get that out of this house right now!" Some of the men who had followed us inside the house looked to Chief, he nodded. They disassembled the death trap and took it outside, I thanked Chief.

He went down the hallway, I followed. We passed by a sofa and a wall tapestry, I guessed that had been the living room. I peeked through the next door; it could be called a bedroom only because it had a mattress up on wood blocks next to piles of clothes. Both grandkids were sleeping in the room with their mother. Deena must have been working on some crafts because there was leather and beadwork strewn across the bed. The room had no dresser or closet, just piles of rags and blankets in the corners, which were being used as children's beds.

Dreamcatchers hung everywhere, ready for sale at the museum. I thought about the teardrop ones made with slack blue string. The ones Deena made were of a fine quality, they were so different from anything I had seen in my life. No stores carried treasures like these. Everything she made was the real thing; I admired her work, as I was always seeking Truth.

Deena would later tell me the dreamcatcher weaving is made with sinew, which is deer or elk leg tendons pounded and pressed into a thick, strong cord. When finished, it hardens into something that looks like heavy gauge fishing line coated in animal fat. A willow branch circle holds the tightly woven design, there is a hole left in the center of the pattern to allow the bad dreams to pass through. The webbing catches the good dreams so they remain with you. There are three strips of the softest, natural, white leather hanging from the bottom of the circle, threaded with some colored glass pony beads. Real horse hair and a few feathers are the finishing touches. True Lakota dreamcatchers are not gaudy like the purple and hot pink Made in China knock-offs for sale at gas stations. The genuine ones are simple, natural, elegant, and exquisite.

The traditional way Deena made them and the story to accompany them are Lakota, other dreamcatcher designs, beliefs, and craftsmanship are unique to their tribe's history and traditions. A belief different from the Lakota is that bad dreams get stuck in the web and burn off in the morning sunlight, so there is no need for a hole in the middle. I like the Lakota way better, their ways were the only ones I wanted to learn and make my own.

Every Indian tribe has a different culture and belief system for every little thing. The Lakota are the plains Indians most associated with Indian stereotypes. These are the people who lived in tipis and built domed sweat lodges. Not all Indians lived in tipis, many lived in longhouses built from wooden poles. The Lakota Chiefs still wear horseshoe shaped war bonnets with many black tipped eagle feathers framing their faces. A lot of people think all Indians wore this type of "hat." For special occasions, the women still wear buckskin dresses with fringe edges like their ancestors. Chief told me I would wear a white buckskin dress on our wedding day, as was tradition. All Indians do not dress this way, and all Indians do not hunt buffalo. Sadly, this includes even the modern day Lakota.

Sitting Bull and Crazy Horse are Indians most thought of in popular American culture, they are Lakota, with Crazy Horse being from the Oglala band. If a non-Indian child were to draw a picture of what he thought were "Native Americans," most things incorporated into the drawing would belong to the Lakota way of life and culture, such as their elaborately feathered war bonnets. The child and his parents would think this was how all "Native Americans" lived and looked. The stereotypes commonly associated with all "Native Americans" are often things belonging to the Lakota, or, what the school teacher would tell the child, the "Sioux." We can't even get their name right.

All their beliefs and customs, old ways and traditions were the ones I wanted to adopt for my own way of life, for the rest of my life. I did not care about the ways of other tribes or bands. The Oglala Lakota were my people. What I saw was a mix of tragedy and beauty. Their crafts held such skill, such fine beadwork, intricate dyed porcupine quillwork, star quilts, moccasins, such talent in the patters and use of the most fascinating natural materials. In contrast were the rags on the floor used as children's beds, the heart-wrenching trash and corrugated sheet metal shelters many called "home." The shameful horrors imposed upon these proud, beautiful people, every home filled with excessive trash and mounds of dishes with dried food smears. But this last thing was something I could fix in a day. This was my house now.

I walked into the bathroom across the hall from Deena's bedroom and looked around. "Shower, sink, toilet, window. Yeah, kids could crawl through that window and then open the larger window in the laundry room for the adults." I saw the crates on the ground beneath the windows. I understood how people broke in, knowing Chief was gone and wanting to live in his larger, more solid, warm, dry house.

Chief was behind me now; he quickly grabbed a box from the long, black table in the bathroom. There was a litter of rubber bands, shampoo, combs, flattened toothpaste tubes, dried toothpaste globs, a mirror, and lots of hair in clumps all over the table. Even though there was a lot to notice, it did not escape my attention that the box chief had crushed with disgust was Rid-X. I recognized that box with horror because catching lice has always been a great fear for this long-haired girl.

Chief stood tall in the hallway and commanded his daughter: "DEENA!" She jumped out of bed and came running, as was the custom around Chief Two Bear Paws. They were almost out of earshot, but I could piece together their words. Chief was angry she left the box out. He asked who had the bugs. Skyler did, she brought lice home from school yesterday. They did the treatment today, just before we got here. She was washing all her laundry now in hot water. I swallowed hard.

Brighter moments would be had in that laundry room, as I washed clothes for the entire family. I also washed rugs, many rugs. Chief showed me how to take them outside and beat them with a broom; he even taught me how to hang them over the fence rails and scrub them clean. We had a good time together, scrubbing rugs, bubbles all over the ground and sunshine in our smiles.

"*Wash'te*," Chief said.

"Yes," I agreed, "it's wash day."

Chief laughed. He and I would often pun each other about the word *wash'te*, Lakota for "good," which sounds a lot like "wash day" in English. Some Lakota spell this word *was'te*, or simply *waste*, but Chief said he likes to spell Lakota words how they sound so the oral language lives on. Just as he spells the sacred pipe *chanupa*, there are written variations depending on band and family dialect. I write, speak, and believe only as Chief has taught me. It is his legacy I share.

I would do the laundry and say, "Wash day is *wash'te*."

He would flash a big grin like a prankster little boy and say, "Wash day *wash'te*" back.

Indian humor seems to have a lot of double meanings. *Wash'te* was our standard joke, as well as word play involving "dear," our pet nickname for each other. When times were good and everything was nice, we would often greet each other by saying, "Hello Dear Deer" and laughing together.

As we joked this wash day, I noticed two little faces peeking around the edge of the kitchen door, watching us clean the rugs. Hunter and Skyler were wide-eyed watching Chief do woman's work. He told them it was okay this once, there was no woman around to show me and that made it alright for him to teach me. As Chief's big hands became covered in fresh suds, the grandkids could no longer suppress their giggles, which made Chief laugh even more. That memory is a sunny one full of bubbles and happiness.

Chief passed by the bathroom now on his way to the door at the end of the hall. I followed. More padlocks. This was his bedroom, to be shared with me. This room hid all the valuables while he was away. If he had left them in the main part of the house, they would have been stolen and sold while he was away on his journey.

There were clothesline cords strung across the length of the room and a big woodstove in the corner with piles of wood beside it, soot and splinters on the floor. A bucket of ash. Tonight was not cold enough for a fire yet. I hoped it was the perfect temperature for cuddling up to each other, as Chief had not touched me in so long.

If it grew colder, lighting a fire was not a problem. I learned how to chop, haul and stack wood, start a fire and tend a woodstove in New Hampshire, as wood was the main source of heat with my second husband. In my experience, tending the woodstove was the husband's job. If the wife got up in the night, it was polite but not required she stoke the stove.

Perhaps my second husband had just been a nice guy, but that's how I viewed the operation of a woodstove. Lakota traditions would teach me otherwise.

There was a table near the head and foot of the bed and a shelf along the inside wall. They were clutter free except for a drinking glass half filled with water, placed next to a digital clock radio. On the other side of the clock was a photo of me in a frame. I was standing in front of the badlands wearing my hair in two long braids. It was a photo Big Biker had taken on our Sturgis trip, I had mailed it to Chief in one of our letters. It touched me he kept it and placed it in such a prominent location.

Near the bed, I saw some big Western saddles sitting on a sawhorse. Padded cotton cloth, woven horse blankets, bridles, reigns, ropes, and general horse tack were thrown on top.

There was a big bookshelf that reached the ceiling. It was filled, not with books, but Lakota cultural items. They were special, some sacred, but almost all were treated as normal things expected to be used. I thought about how much a stuffy New York art collector would pay for that handmade, hand painted, authentic buffalo skin drum sitting on shelf number three next to the folded T-shirts and balled up socks with holes.

It was amazing how things were made from butter-soft buckskin naturally brain-tanned by neighbors who shot and skinned the animal, tanned, worked, and smoked the hide themselves. The leather ranged from white to golden, it felt like flannel yet it was stretchable and strong and did not smell like chemicals or dyes. I had a Coach purse and enjoyed browsing their store, but I had never seen such soft, pure, nice leather in all my life. Every craft was a treasure.

Chief showed me his traditional War Bonnet, he informed me only men can wear this type of headdress. It was complete with countless real eagle feathers. I saw both Bald and Golden Eagles on the reservation. Some eagles were flying, some rested nearby on fences. By far, the most magnificent is the Golden Eagle; it is bigger than the Bald Eagle and somehow looks more fierce. Chief said his headdress was a special kind, made exceptionally grand to honor his high warrior and Chief status. The feathers were gorgeous, they were wide and thick, each one stood easily over a foot long. Some appeared even longer due to their colorfully wrapped bases, which extended the quill.

There was no way these feathers just fell off a bird. Many eagles must have contributed their lives to make such a masterpiece. Each feather had a long trail of horse hair attached to the end. The band of the war bonnet, which went from ear to ear across the forehead, was intricately beaded. The sides of the band close to the wearer's ears had beaded leather discs, near these hung several white ermine fur pelts. I told Chief I knew what that long white animal was, it was a weasel in his winter coat, I could tell by the black-tipped tail. He corrected me, "Not weasel. Ermine."

There was a "Sioux" war bonnet similar to this inside a glass case at the Peabody Museum in New Haven, CT. Next to it lay a sacred pipe. I remember seeing the display on a field trip. As I stood there, nose pressed to the glass, I should have been sadly wondering if the Indians would like to have their sacred artifacts back. Instead, my young mind was admiring the genuine eagle feathers. I yearned to have just one.

According to U.S. law, the common person cannot possess even a single raptor feather, even if it was honestly found on the ground. It would mean prison time and a huge fine if the person got caught. It takes a special permit to have these feathers; the permit is not given freely to the average person. These birds are protected. Even Indians must jump through government hoops to legally have these feathers for their religious ceremonies.

Simply being an Indian does not automatically allow one to have eagle and hawk feathers, according to U.S. government law at the time. An Indian must have documents proving his or her blood belongs to a federally recognized tribe, apply in writing, and receive a permit. At that point, one can finally legally request feathers. The U.S. government will then mail the Indian feathers it has on file. Collecting one's own feathers is still not permitted, even with the permit.

I mentioned this process to Chief and he laughed bitterly, saying the law is humiliating and disgraceful to the Indian Nation. It is an infringement on their religious rights; they do not answer to the U.S. government about what is sacred to them.

"Do you know what I had to do to earn each feather? I—" he stopped himself, as if it were too big to explain. "This headdress shows I am a Chief. I am a great Warrior who has shown bravery in many battles. Do you see how many feathers there are? This headdress, my life . . ." his eyes grew distant. He shook his head and gave a sad laugh. "Nobody has a headdress like this anymore but me. Well, maybe three others, but that is all that is left. We are the last. The rest are all gone, the Chiefs, the old ways," he waved his hand over the memories and asked what I thought made the horsehair stick to the ends of the feathers.

I guessed, "Beeswax?"

He shook his head no. "Gum." He pointed to a hardened wad of pink at the end of one of the feathers, pressed into it was horsehair. "It is the old ways. We use bubblegum."

I scrunched my face with confusion. He laughed. "It was all I had when it broke at the powwow. I got the gum from Hunter who was with me. I fixed it. I danced." He chuckled over how I had believed him.

Chief stopped joking when he brought out the most precious object of all, the *chanupa*, the sacred pipe smoked in traditional Lakota ceremonies, it was inside a decorated leather pipe bag. He shared a story about how it can be buried in the ground. The only items locked away in a secret place were the *chanupa* and a large handmade drum.

A tall staff stood beside the door, it leaned against the inside wall of the bedroom, nearly touching the ceiling. It would be carried during important events. The staff was adorned with beads, ribbons, and feathers. It displayed a long, narrow flag embroidered with his family name.

The bookshelf next to it held many crafts and supplies. Among these were hand painted buffalo shields, dreamcatchers, porcupine quill hat bands with intricate colored patterns, dyed quill necklaces and earrings, beaded moccasins and jewelry.

I noticed small circle hoops with crosses inside. Chief said these are medicine wheels, powerful spiritual totems for health and protection, made with porcupine quills dyed in the Lakota colors of black, red, white, and yellow. He said only men make these. Women make most of the other crafts, especially beadwork.

There were antlers, fringe, feathers, glass beads, much leather, rawhide and lacing—and a special, almost flat, thick, pink abalone shell circle about the size of the palm of my hand. It had two small holes an inch apart in the center. A thin strip of pure white buckskin created a loop between the holes, the long leather ends hung loose. Chief Two Bear Paws told me it was an old ways tradition for women to wear this in their hair when they got married. He said it was very rare for his people to have a pink shell like this, since they lived so far from the ocean. He gave it to me; I was to wear it on our wedding day. Everything was gorgeous.

He took out a cardboard box and tossed it on the bed with a laugh. It was overflowing with bottles of medications, boxes of glucose monitors, finger pricking devices, alcohol pads, needles, insulin, he even had an old blood pressure cuff in there. "They give me all these things but I never use them." His pile of medications dated back five years ago, unopened. No wonder he recently had such problems. It all caught up with him.

I put the cardboard box back in the cabinet. "We'll use the new things I got today, but it's good to know these are here if we need them." I looked up, thinking it was a clock; I wanted see if it was time for his "bed" pills. Startled, I realized it was not a clock, but white bones.

I was looking at a buffalo skull, complete with large, black horns. The eye sockets and nose holes were stuffed with bunches of dried sage. The sage somehow made it more haunting to me. It felt alive. It could see me and it did not like me. It was hard to focus a steady gaze upon it. Creepy, bad vibes repelled my eyes and made the object swim and dance before me.

There was another one on the other side of the room, lying on top of a pile of folded, handmade star quilts. There must have been about ten quilts, all different colors, all the same big star Lakota pattern. Chief lifted the skull up from the pile of quilts; he carefully held it in front of him by the sides of its face and carried it out to the living room. He hung it from the strong nail in the wall over the couch where it must have lived before he left for his pilgrimage to Maine to claim his new wife.

It was haunting he could touch the skull that resonated so badly within me. But it seemed to do alright by him. I was certain if I touched it, it would shock me and I would fall to the floor with a heart attack. He never explained their meaning or magic to me, he would only say "Sacred Buffalo Skull" when I looked at it, which was enough for me. It was pure Lakota, the real deal, sealed with prayers and things I would never understand.

No matter how many times I saw the skulls, they always startled me. Whenever I tried to look at a Sacred Buffalo Skull, it would make me feel queasy inside and almost afraid. Maybe that was its intent. I could understand why the White Man was so afraid of the Ghost Dance that he outlawed it. When I looked at the skull, I knew I would never really be Lakota. The thing hated me. And no amount of love I could extend towards it would make it change its mind. My love deflected from its surface as something beneath its stature. I tried not to look directly at them anymore.

I set the computer up in our bedroom so Chief could lock

the door and protect it. I called the phone company and got a dial up connection for the house. The grandkids never touched the computer; Chief declared it for business use only so the two of us could plan the motorcycle ride.

CHAPTER THIRTEEN:

Bedtime Lessons

Chief said it was time for bed. I went to the kitchen, found a dirty, limp, blue, shredded slice of sponge I was afraid to touch but no soap. I skipped the sponge and grabbed a drinking glass. I chose the one that looked least likely to make the pile crash with its removal. I angled it over the sinkful of dishes towards the faucet and ran the hottest water I could get to clean it. After a few minutes, I realized I would be rinsing the glass with cold water. Hot water was a luxury to be used sparingly, only available for the shower. There was nothing to dry the glass with, which was a blessing in disguise, so I shook it off, then went to the fridge.

A multi-colored, crusty residue coated every shelf. I skipped digging any further. I filled the glass with tap water and went to find Chief. "Time for 'bed' pills." I handed him the small once a day blue-green pill that was my favorite in the bunch. I liked the size and the color. It was cute. There were four water pills to go along with it; he was supposed to take four of them four times a day. I thought I was in for a struggle, but to my delight he actually swallowed all the pills without a fight. I set the glass on the table so I would have something relatively clean to use for his morning pills.

I got into bed and snuggled against the comfort of the wall. Ever since I was a child, I have always slept on the inside of the bed. One day when I was at school, I think I was in fourth or fifth grade, my mother rearranged my room. She put my bed stark in the middle of the room. She had bought new curtains, a bedspread, and a fancy, white, eyelet lace dust ruffle which hid the bed frame and gracefully stood a centimeter away from touching the floor with its scalloped edge. She was proud of her classy décor and thought I would be happy. I came home, saw my room and panicked. I begged her to put one side of the bed back against the wall. She told me I was nicking the wall paint with my elbows and feet, but she gave in and moved it back when she saw the terror on my face at the thought of sleeping in an open-sided bed.

I feel safe and secure with the wall along my back, always have. As I nestled in and closed my eyes, Chief said, "No!" He grabbed me by the shoulders, scooped me out to the middle of the bed, climbed over me, and wedged his own back against the wall. He put his knee in my lower back and pushed me an inch from the outside edge of the bed. I teetered and reached out in the darkness for the table to steady myself.

I closed my eyes and tried to center my thoughts so I could feel okay again. Through the open window next to my head, I could hear the horses walking around in the shelter outside, they would snort softly as they munched hay. I found their sounds delightful and comforting, although I wondered how they could see and why they were up so late. There were no street lights, no city lights, not even a moon or stars tonight. Just cave-dark blackness. I slid my fingertips along the headboard until I found Chief, I kissed him goodnight. He grunted and pulled away. He put his teeth in the glass near my photo, using the dim green light of the clock radio for guidance. There were no cuddles to keep us warm. There never had been. Despite sleeping on the edge of the drop off, I fell asleep instantly; I needed it.

I awoke to a sudden, violent shaking. It must have been two in the morning. "Whaaaa—?" I muttered, blinking, it not mattering since there was nothing for my eyes to adjust to. I couldn't figure out why Chief wasn't yelling "Fire!" if I was being shaken awake so roughly. He had grabbed me by both shoulders, my head tossed side to side.

Chief was in my face. Sternly, he demanded: "Get the

juice!"

I had no idea what he meant. He shook me again, this time increasing the volume but not the clarity, "GET THE JUICE!" I was better at understanding his body movements than his words; it was too dark to see what he meant. I got out of bed only to stop the aggressive shaking.

I stood in the darkness and thought about it for a few seconds. I figured his mouth must be dry and, considering his parched state, he would be pleased if I did him the favor of procuring a glass of refreshing beverage from the kitchen, preferably of the squeezed fruit variety; his desire was urgent, thus, concisely stated as the command: "Get the juice!" This was my reality? I was too tired to argue. I shrugged and accepted.

Eyesight was of no help, so, I gently slid my hands along the table, feeling for the almost clean glass I had set aside for his morning pills. I took it with me as I felt along the walls in the dark, coaching myself in my head: "Bookshelf, side of bookshelf, some sticks in a bundle I don't remember, what's this? Eew, fur—dead animal—ignore, uh . . . clothes, wall . . . hinges! Good, hinges. Okay, this is the door, then. Great, you're doing great . . . doorknob, good. Alright, now focus. There are two interior locks. One like this: fwip—fwip—fwip, good, and one like this: slide-and-turn, good. Open. Okay, we're out in the hallway now. Breathe; you can do this.

"Take a step forward, good. Keep moving . . . wall, door frame on right—ah!—that's the bedroom with lice—ugh, I'll skip touching that door. . . okay, other side of the door frame, we're moving along here, doing good, yep, bathroom's over there, alright, kitchen should be coming up soon—" Crunch!

"Weird, wonder what that was?" Crunch! Another footstep. "Strange, I don't remember this floor being made of dirt; I thought it was linoleum? It feels like it's coated with pebbles and sand now. Odd. Okay, continuing forward, that's the kitchen counter, good job, and now . . . fridge!" I opened the fridge; it was like the sun burst in my face without heat. I stood there, panting from fridge-light blindness. Once my eyes adjusted, I saw the refrigerator seal that was once sort of white with stains was now solid black.

"Huh, that's sooo weird." By the light of the fridge, I could look down at the floor. It wasn't rocks and sand I had felt. I had been walking on a one inch thick sea of live cockroaches. Barefoot. And now I was standing on them. They crawled over my feet, tickling my toes. The entire floor moved in undulating waves of black shiny backs, antennae, and legs. The color of the linoleum floor could not be seen, the bugs were too thick, crawling on top of one another.

The fridge was swarming in them, too. My mind finally registered the reason the once white trim was now black. It was embedded with bugs. In every crack and crevice, they found some residue for their after-midnight snack. My mind could not handle the horror, it was in overload.

I had always been a germ freak like my dad and sisters. My mom spent her days in a kindergarten classroom, full of runny noses, coughs, and kisses, without so much as a flinch. So, we girls must have inherited this from our father. The four of us were in love with our portable hand sanitizers, pre-packaged alcohol wipes, and Lysol spray. I was working on letting that obsessive-compulsive side of me go. But this was beyond what even a normal person could handle, let alone a germ freak like me.

Instead of losing my mind, I became calm and neutral. Besides, I didn't want to wake anyone. I softly said, "Huh, fascinating." It was almost like I was observing myself outside my body, the scene was so grotesque.

The shelves inside the fridge were alive. "Oh, *that's* what he means by 'juice.' There's pineapple-orange juice in here. That's great." I shook the bugs off the outside, flicked one off the cap and poured some juice into the glass. As soon as I set the carton back on the shelf inside the fridge, it instantly teemed with life and turned black. I held the glass up to the light of the fridge one last time to make sure nothing was swimming in the juice. I closed the fridge and calmly walked back over the sea of cockroaches. Somehow, I could find my way just fine without touching the counter and walls for guidance this time. I talked a lot less to myself on the way back, too.

The roaches crunched beneath my feet and squished between my toes. "Ah, it could be sand, who cares? What does it matter anyway." I wiped my feet on the carpet outside the bedroom door and secured both locks behind me, subconsciously keeping the bugs out of the bedroom as the locks clicked with psychological safety. It really wasn't a bug deterrent, but at least the locks would kept the grandkids out if Chief ever wanted to touch me again. Bonus, I had not spilled the juice. I was a good wife.

Chief had fallen back asleep. I whispered to him, "I got the juice." He snored. I set the juice on the table. I didn't even care about wiping between my toes, I just wanted to sleep.

Chief woke up an hour later, shook me and said, "Get the juice!" I reached for it, tapped the surface with my finger, felt nothing swimming, and handed him the glass. He grunted, impressed I had it so fast. He drank it all in two large swallows. My fingers hovered in the dark near the glass, feeling for when he would release it. I caught it and set it on the table beside me as he flopped back down into bed. I learned to always put a glass of juice with a small plate on top beside the bed. Chief would never reach for it himself no matter how close it was to him. He always shook me awake and told me to get the juice for him. Having it ready saved me the first trip to the kitchen in the middle of the night. For that I was happy.

Five thirty a.m. came too early. Two Bear Paws shook me again. He was angry. I should have been up half an hour ago to help the grandkids get ready for school. Nobody had told me that. I jumped out of bed and got started right away, wondering quietly to myself why their mother couldn't do this, since these were not my kids and she lived here, too. Maybe she was at work, or maybe she was in bed not feeling well, I did not ask questions and I did not complain.

I always did as I was told no matter what the task, and quickly. I made sure the children were dressed in warm clothes; I put some snacks in their backpacks. Chief said they were late; they had missed the bus. Since I did not know my way around, he would drive them to their school in the town of Porcupine. They dashed away in a whirlwind of urgency. The kitchen had been so alive with the early morning rush, I suddenly found myself standing there alone.

I was swept away with a bit of sadness. I missed my Lakota family who went out the door without hugs or kisses. I looked around for a cockroach to keep me company, but they were gone, too, as daylight spilled across the dishes, counters, and floor.

I discovered it was only when the dishes were moved that a flurry of them would erupt. Moving the papers on the table caused the same effect. As long as nothing was disturbed, a box from the cupboard, a spoon from the drawer, then all was quiet on the Western front. I tried not to touch much until we could buy some serious roach spray at Wal-Mart.

I put jeans and a T-shirt on; I brushed my hair and teeth. Chief came home and said, "Let's go." I followed him. We got in the car and drove a few streets away to a housing development. There were packs of starving "rez dogs" running around. Their rib cages showed, skin pulled tight across bones. They were mostly medium to large sized mongrel dogs with what looked like a purebred German Shepherd thrown in the mix every once in a while; the packs were dangerous and hungry. Some would snap, some would snarl, they were kicked out of the way and not regarded as pets. There was just not enough food to go around to feed a pet.

We were in an area that seemed to consist of small, pre-fab, low income houses built by the government for some ancient work project and then forgotten. This was the nice area of town. Collapsed stairs and railings, broken front doors, shattered windows, tall clumps of grass dotted the ground which was mostly a sea of rocks and sand. A bouncy play ball was buried behind a stack of garbage so nobody would steal it and the kid could continue to play with it after school.

We parked the rental car in front of one of the better looking front stoops. We paused at the front door. Chief said, "Don't let the dog out. She has a little Chihuahua. What can I say," he shrugged, "she loves it. It sits in her lap and makes her happy. There is nothing I can do." This little dog was the only house pet I saw on the rez. I was sure to not let it out, as it would become an instant snack for the pack of feral dogs growling at our heels.

I followed Chief Two Bear Paws into the house. He spoke Lakota, so did the older woman inside the house. I gathered this was Chief's mother. The table was set for three: Chief, herself, and me. I was touched. She knew I was coming, yet I never heard him give her notice. It was amazing. Perhaps it was word of mouth, just like when the family was waiting in the driveway for his return from Maine.

Without an introduction or greeting offered for me, we sat down to a meal of fried eggs, bacon, coffee, and toast. She had clean, mismatched plates and coffee mugs, rusted metal utensils with the shiny outer coating wore off revealing probably lead underneath, and paper napkins. I was overjoyed. A place setting was something familiar from my "civilized" former life; I relaxed with its normalcy and settled in at the table.

The government issued tub of margarine was coated in about a loaf's worth of old crumbs, at least I hoped they were crumbs. I forced myself to refuse passing judgment, I dug deeper to the yellow layer and buttered my toast. I was truly trying to be good and break my old habits. I hated myself for the stuffy, high standards of cleanliness and germ control I was brought up with.

My family brings alcohol pads to restaurants so we can wipe down the establishment's silverware before eating. We don't touch doorknobs with our bare hands, that's what a tissue or elbow or foot is for. Every crumb of dirt is swept from floors and tables immediately. My mother said her home should be ready for *Better Homes and Gardens* to take a photo at any moment.

That's just us. It's the way we were brought up and the way we lived. But other people can't help being poor; it wasn't their fault or their choice to live that way. Sometimes a home gets messy and sometimes there might be cockroaches in your margarine; it's best not to look too closely at someone else's lifestyle. Everyone can't live in a perfect, classy magazine photo. Especially when one is meant to live in a tipi and is now confined to government issued housing, things can take on a heavy feel of depression.

Chief's mother spoke no English, or, if she did, she didn't waste it on me. Son and mother always spoke to each other in fluent Lakota. It was amazing to hear this almost dead language bouncing and alive across the table with their constant conversation. She was one person I wished I could have talked to, I loved her instantly and I liked her house. I was always happy when we visited her and I never wanted to leave. I wished we could live there all the time.

Her walls had both Lakota and American art, a calendar with birds in beautiful settings embraced by Christian Bible verses, small paintings of horses, and photographs of scenery. I found her interesting and lovely.

Adjacent to the eating area was a living room with a small TV and weathered, threadbare sofa improved by homemade pillows and blanket. A braided rug inches behind my chair marked the living room's boundaries, just as the small table against the wall made this the eating area. The kitchen was designated by two counters, I could almost touch them from my dining area chair. There was a fridge, a stove with oven, and the rez standard: a sink overflowing with at least a month's worth of dirty dishes. There were no walls to distinguish one room from another, except for her bedroom. Her room had a blanket for a door, piles of quilts and clear boxes of crafting supplies were organized and stacked outside her room. She had sage drying in clumps hanging from the ceiling; I could tell this woman knew what she was doing. I respected her and wanted to learn from her.

After breakfast, I said "thank you" in English because I knew no other words, but I had thought of a way to show it. I took my dishes a few steps away to the kitchen; I hoped I was doing the right thing. Chief sat at the table and read the newspaper, their ongoing conversation in Lakota continued. I loved them both, but felt awkward not being able to join the conversation. Neither had looked at me for the entire meal. I cleared my place and then the rest of the table, again, unnoticed. I took the lack of attention as a sign I was doing well and not offending. I spied her fresh looking yellow sponge on the edge of the kitchen sink and was elated to see dish soap. "We are in business!" I thought. "If I do the dishes, she will know I appreciate her and her hospitality. I hope it's not an insult, but I have no way of knowing. All I can do is my best and offer it with love. Here goes."

Being careful not to break anything, I selected items from the balanced pile. As I started to wash things, Chief's mother set her little lapdog on the sofa and ran into the kitchen to swat me with a yellow checkered dish towel. I did my best to show her my energy was one of love and help, not judgment. She grunted and huffed but began to work alongside me. Together we cleaned the kitchen until it shined and the stove, too. I wanted to believe she looked happy and that we bonded, but I was never sure she ever liked me, as hard as I always tried to show her love.

As we were cleaning the kitchen, I would glance at Chief sometimes to make sure things were okay. He calmly read the paper. After the kitchen was clean, he continued to read, but lifted a finger in my direction without looking up. I knew it was time to go. I wanted to hug his mom goodbye, but I thought it might offend her, so I didn't. Nobody was making any moves to touch me, not Chief, not the grandchildren. I didn't know if it was an insult to reach for them first. Maybe they thought I was stuck up for not reaching out to hug them. Or maybe they found my body and skin color disgusting and were relieved I did not impose my touch. I wasn't sure. I wanted to show respect for them and their feelings; I had no idea if I was doing things right or making them worse.

In the coming months, Chief would try to send me back alone in the car to his mother's to pick up some dried deer meat or fry bread, biscuits or blankets. I could never find my way back there. He got upset, he would yell at me, draw maps and point. Nothing worked. Finally, he would make one of the grandkids go with me for directions.

In my eyes, the rez has no landmarks; it's a completely flat, confusing prairie. Sometimes there's a dirt path, sometimes pavement, oftentimes no path just a guess through the grass. It all looked the same to me: flat sky, flat ground, absolute disorientation for me; I was a gerbil shook up inside a plastic ball.

Back at the house, Chief told me to get in the truck. It was crazy to watch him drive using only a screwdriver to steer. It felt unsafe, but he was good at it. He said the truck worked fine until he lost the keys last winter. Someone in his family needed wood to heat their home as there was a bad storm coming that night. If he did not supply wood, this person would die in the cold. He broke into his ignition and then tore the steering column out; he tossed the steering wheel aside and used a long handled screwdriver to steer the truck. He had ruined his truck for long distance travel, but he saved a family member's life in the process by hauling them a load of his own wood.

That is noble and I understand his efforts. However, it means he knew his truck was inoperable when we were making plans in Omaha for his son Strong Bear to make the long journey to pick us up in this truck. I never made the connection. I kept looking through the eyes of love and making excuses.

There wasn't much to talk about on the way into town. I had no idea where we were going or what we were doing, I simply trusted Chief's decisions and plans. It felt like the right thing to do, or at least what he wanted. It was interesting watching him steer with the screwdriver, twisting it just a hair this way or that to make the wheels go left or right as we went bumping down the dirt roads.

An hour through the prairie grass, we arrived in Hot Springs. We parked in front of a used appliance dealer and that's when I knew what he was up to. He flicked his fingers towards the store and sat in the truck while I picked out the stove alone. I talked the guys into a deal on a mismatched one. It had a cream colored top but a white body and oven door, it was ready for propane. They let me have it for $250. They wrapped it lightly in shrink wrap, two guys slid it up ramps into the pickup and tied it down with rope.

We bounced back through the grasslands, losing a burner cap and ring along the way. People were gathered in the driveway to see our new stove. Chief Two Bear Paws reached near celebrity status for this much admired acquisition. He had men poke holes in the wall and set the stove up so the gas line ran outside where it connected to the tank. I was happy knowing everyone was safer this way. I never checked outside to see what contraption the men must have built around the propane tank to keep others from stealing it; it must have been good because I never heard it went missing.

The new stove worked perfectly, minus a burner cap and ring. My way around it was not using that burner. But I've seen pots balanced on it every which way when festivities got high and many women were coming over to use the stove. A handful of women cooking at once had a way of leaning the pots against each other to utilize every burner and every bit of space.

Lakota women had a way of making things work when they had a need. These were seasoned wives who knew what they were doing; I admired them.

CHAPTER FOURTEEN:

Motorcycle Ride

I read somewhere the "Sioux" were a matriarchal society and women were highly respected by men. I never got that impression. Maybe it was an old tipi tradition, but the stories I heard of the old ways never expressed that value either.

This is why I try not to read too much about the Lakota on the internet or in history books. The information I find is not accurate to the life and ways I personally witnessed. Women were less than men, less than horses, really. Some women, like horses, were treated worse depending on the man they were with.

Perhaps it is because women lost their tipis why they seemed so depressed. Perhaps it is because the men no longer went off to hunt why they felt so angry. The things that gave the gender roles their value in the old traditions were no longer there in modern Lakota society.

I do not know the reasons. I did not move to the reservation as an anthropologist or reporter, I did not study the Lakota and take notes as if they were animals in a cage. They were my family. The only past I wanted to learn was the one Chief Two Bear Paws taught me himself about his own people. The only present was the world around me which held the promise of the rest of my life spent there on the reservation with those I loved. I did not care about century old observations made by racist white men who wrote biased words in history books. How could they truly understand the lives of those they murdered?

I felt this was part of why we were planning the motorcycle ride, to provide the Lakota with a way tell their own stories with their own words to the world. We decided to name our event "Wounded Knee Memorial Ride." Our tag line was "Meet me at The Knee."

I bought a domain name and designed a web page. Chief approved, he sat beside me whenever I worked at the computer. The air between us was alive with words and ideas as we created a letter of introduction together. I captured it from the air and typed as we spoke. We posted the letter on our website and plastered it all over the internet to drum up interest. We also mailed it to big companies in hopes they would become our sponsor and help with larger donations. It went something like this:

Hello Friends & Relations,

I am offering this message with a deep, sincere, and warm welcome. We are planning a gathering of people and the Spirits of our Ancestors here in "Cankpe Opi," Wounded Knee, South Dakota this summer.

Our first and foremost purpose of this gathering is to honor our Ancestors who lay buried on sacred ground. One of the most heinous crimes ever committed in history took place here in 1890 with blood spilled on this ground during the Wounded Knee Massacre. Our event will bring awareness so atrocities like this never happen again.

Today our people face many barriers which keep us oppressed. We hope this gathering will create unity by opening the doors to a new era of hope and understanding among all people, bridging a gap between two very different worlds. A Lakota Holy Man stated that The Sacred Tree died and The Sacred Hoop shattered in 1890 at Wounded Knee. He said The Sacred Tree will bloom again in the future. That time has come; the future is now at Wounded Knee. We will not let there be an end to our trail; help us make this a new beginning.

We will be conducting ceremonies at the Mass Grave with special guest speakers each day. Leonard Crow Dog, Lakota Medicine Man, will conduct the main ceremony. There will be a motorcycle ride from the Crazy Horse Monument to the Wounded Knee Massacre site. Chief Big Foot Memorial Riders will lead the way to the ceremony on horseback. Everyone is welcome.

Entertainment will include a three day non-competition powwow and we'll host a bull riders' only rodeo on Saturday with prizes. Every night, there will be live music on the center stage. Guests will include Native American performers as well as country and rock performers. There will even be a local "battle of the bands" with members of our community showcasing their talents.

We are in the planning stages of the event and are seeking support and donations from you. Sponsors have been contacted, but for now our major ones haven't been secured. Once we receive our main sponsors, this event will take off like lightening. Keep checking our website for details as they take shape.

Plenty of camping space will be available as well as ample motorcycle parking. V.I.P. tipis will be provided to our guests of honor and there will be others open for the public to rent. Horse rentals will also be available and guided tours offered during the event. There will be food from vendors and T-shirts for purchase, early bird T-shirts will be available on-line soon on our website. Food, craft, and other vendors please contact us now to reserve your space.

Anyone who would like to help by donating money, time, and supplies is welcome. We need to build a large stage for our musical performers, mow the grass, make the ground level and set up the rodeo fence. There is much work to do. All this takes funding and volunteers.

The Wounded Knee Memorial Ride is an event full of honor, respect, and love, not a money-making endeavor. After we pay the bigger name entertainers, rent the sound equipment for our local talent, set up dumpsters and portable restrooms, we will be lucky if we can break even. If there are any funds left at the end of the event, they will be directed towards maintenance of the Wounded Knee Visitor Center Museum and upkeep of the Mass Grave site.

This is our first year, it will grow into an annual event, so get onboard now. Let's work together to put Wounded Knee back on the map! Let's show them where we are and in the following years they'll know how to come back. This event will only get bigger and better.

All people and faiths are cordially invited to take part in honoring the Lakota past and healing our future. We are making history here and we need all of you to help. Do your part to mend The Sacred Hoop and "Meet me at The Knee!"

Wokiksuye Cankpe Opi

"Remember Wounded Knee"

Mitakuye Oyasin

"We Are All Related"

The Trail has no end. Only a new Beginning.
With the Spirit of Tasunke Witko (Crazy Horse),

CHIEF TWO BEAR PAWS

Bikers have big hearts and I posted the letter in forums I knew. Chief had connections in many Indian circles across the country and overseas; we asked them to post our letter in their groups, chatrooms, and on their webpages.

Since that time, the letter and our ideas have been cut and pasted, sheered and scalped, stolen by individuals and organizations. When they saw our ride wasn't happening in August 2006, they took the concept and ran with it in a dozen different directions starting the very next year. A hundred bikes showed up last year for a white man's ride that stole our concept but not the heart. None of these spin-off events give to Lakota community like the original would have. With our event, the Lakota would have benefited directly from every donation, and more importantly, shared their first hand stories with their own words. Their community would have grown stronger in every way.

I planned on setting up a metal drum for donations; we'd secure it to cement blocks and cut a slit in the top as a drop slot for the money. I sent out letters and emails trying to find a good price on meat. I ended up gaining the interest of a nearby buffalo ranch owner who talked with me on the phone. He was white, but moved by our cause. He said he would donate five of his buffalo right before the event for us to use in our feast. He asked if we wanted him to butcher them, Chief said no, send them live, his people will take care of that. The ranch owner thought that was pretty cool. He would bring the animals over to the reservation a week before the event. We invited him to the gathering with high honors.

This was our first big break! I could now put "Free Buffalo Burgers" on all the posters with a date and time; this would surely draw the crowd! Chief suggested the women could set up hide tanning demonstrations. It would take a few days to dry and work the buffalo hides, just like the women did in the old days. Chief said it would be interesting and a little gory to watch, I said bikers would love that. For the Lakota, the right path would open once again with the old stories and traditions, people would come to listen—and there would be buffalo. The buffalo would be hunted and every part would be used, just like their ancestors did. Everyone wins. It was beautiful.

There would already be 500,000 people nearby because of Sturgis Bike Week. I knew with a good concept and good food like this, the bikers would come. It was a way for the Lakota to get ahead and still keep their dignity. This event wasn't a self-esteem lowering hand out. It wasn't a charity and it wasn't White Man stealing. This was everyone giving, sharing with pride and love and getting more in return than they ever could have imagined. It would be Lakota standing proud on their land in their own culture, telling their own history as it should be told, with their own voice. They would present as strong warriors and leaders with hope for their future. Perhaps, as word spread and support was gained, they could get their stolen land back and reclaim the Black Hills. The sacred hoop would be mended.

The bikers would eat free buffalo burgers, they would donate money, and the Lakota would live through another winter better than before. Fewer would die in the cold, more could buy wood or propane for heat and perhaps the round building/museum could have plumbing installed. The bikers would carry Lakota stories to every corner of the world and more bikers would come next year, even more the year after. We would get more sponsors, bigger donations, and have better shows. The event would grow every year and the Lakota way of life would not extinguish, life could flourish while keeping the old traditions.

Bikers are veterans and warriors themselves; they would understand the Indian's plight and spirit, the pain in the past and present, the sacredness of their land. Bikers ride iron horses and many of them would pay to ride the mane and tail type, too. The Lakota could lead them on a horseback trail ride. Both bikers and Indians wear images of wolves and eagles with pride, bikers have beads and feathers on their leather jackets, they earn badges of honor for accomplishments, courage, and respect. Indians do the same things. Bikers are outcast by many in the mainstream population, written off as low-lifes and dirty troublemakers, but their heart is far from that. Indians could relate to that, too. I thought they would get along very well.

We needed help. Sponsorships. Chief suggested a big center stage with Indian musicians like Buffy Sainte-Marie, Koh-Teh, and Sheryl Crow. I suggested sending our letter to large lumber companies. Chief chose the spot on his land in Wounded Knee where the stage could be built and showed it to me. He spoke of putting V.I.P. tipis next to the stage. I pictured bikers renting these tipis and everyone, Red, White, Yellow, Black, gathered together watching the performers. I could see Indian artists singing their songs into the summer stars over Wounded Knee; my heart wept with the beauty.

Chief suggested a rodeo. I sent our letter to a big name soda company and asked for sponsorship. I asked if they would donate the fences and supplies we needed to set up the rodeo for the event. Chief wanted to offer a thousand dollar cash prize to bring in some top name riders, I mentioned that as well.

I hoped to get Jay Leno, also a fellow biker, to lead the beginning of the ride, even just a little way out of town. We wouldn't start the ride exactly in the Crazy Horse Memorial's parking lot, due to the fact it would be hypocritical to the Lakota's feelings about the monument, but we would start near there; it would give the bikers a familiar landmark as a meeting point. A local, family owned restaurant near the monument offered to let us use their parking lot as a starting point for the ride. This was great progress! I could now put the meeting place, date, and time of the ride online and on posters. I spoke with the manager of Three Dog Night, he was interested in having the band perform at our event. Things were moving along quite well.

We added more photos to the website, pictures of Chief in his war bonnet, powwow photos, motorcycle images, herds of wild horses including a photo of Chief's paint horse running with his mane and tail flying mid-stride, eagles, feathers, and wolves. The website was impressive. So was the T-shirt I designed.

I found a place who would print an original T-shirt design on high quality T-shirts for a reasonable price. We could sell them for a profit of nearly twenty dollars each. The shirt I created had a big buffalo hide shield in the middle, suspended dreamcatcher style in the center of a willow hoop. "Wounded Knee Memorial Ride—Meet me at The Knee" appeared burned into the shield. I included a Lakota medicine wheel, a traditional black tipped eagle prayer feather wound with beads and leather lacings, a bald eagle's face, a bear paw print, and a wolf howling. That should cover it. It was a good shirt, the grandkids gathered around my design in awe. They clung to me all afternoon when I was drawing and asked if they could have the draft copies and sketches. They hung everything I had done, no matter how rough or final, on the walls in their bedroom. I was deeply touched.

Adding dates, contact information, website, and ride meet up places to the design, I had an eye-catching and informative 8.5" x 11" poster to photocopy and plaster all over the area when August grew closer. Hot Springs, Rapid City, Deadwood, Sturgis, I would even mail flyers to my biker friends, dealers, and the Harley Owner's Group I belonged to in Maine. I could count on my chapter attending because at least ten of them came to Sturgis every year. I knew all the places bikers go, I would have it covered. They would come. I could feel it.

I could see no downside to the plan. The only flaw I could not foresee was Chief's later sabotage. The spin-off events that would rise from the ashes cheapened our ideas and used them as a gimmick to make profits for themselves.

Our idea was original; we would have cornered the market

because the entire concept was actually in our corner, on our land in Wounded Knee. If it could've happened that first year, it would've remained strong. As if to prove this, even though everything got cancelled, three motorcyclists still showed up to our event the first year during the dates we chose that August. They were looking for the action. There was nothing going on, so Chief gave them all my leather and bike gear as a gift. The size of my leather chaps was far too small for any woman in the group, but Chief insisted they take it. They came this far, they deserved something.

Meanwhile, having no idea things were about to change, I put a lot of hope, positive energy, and effort into planning the event and seeking sponsorships. We worked on it several times a week. In between chores and daily life, we checked email and sent out more letters.

On the Pine Ridge Reservation

Little White Bird, Chief Two Bear Paws,
and family members riding Chief's horses
Wounded Knee, SD

"Sacred Buffalo Skull"

Moving Day

LWB Leaving CT for SD rez with Chief

Snickers (top) and Ring Ding (R.D.)

inside travel cages in LWB's pick up truck

South Dakota

Wild Horses and big sky

LWB doing chores with log splitter on rez

Honeymoon

Double rainbows at Niagara Falls, NY

Chief and LWB Niagara Falls, NY

Little White Bird overlooking the Falls

Thanksgiving Day

Home for the holiday, Little White Bird

CHAPTER FIFTEEN:

Trash Day

Somehow, I'd missed the garbage truck. In my spoiled, upper middle class ignorance, I fully expected there to be a day of the week for citywide garbage pickup, even in this remote location. I was looking forward to trash day as there was so much garbage, it would be great to bag it up and send it away.

I asked Chief when trash day was. With a big grin he said, "Today is good."

"Um, okay, but isn't there a day of the week when the trash truck comes to get the garbage, say Sunday night you put the trash out on the curb and the man comes by and gets it real early Monday morning?"

Chief laughed like I was the best stand up comedian the rez had ever seen. "No."

I really could not get my brain around the concept of no trash day. "What do you do, then?"

"I will show you. Let's go." We got into Chief's white pick-up truck and headed down the road to the round building.

As we approached the museum and mass gravesite which had changed my life's direction, I softly wailed, "Oh, Chief. Are we going there? I would like to prepare myself before I step foot on that sacred ground again. I remember asking you if you'd let me know beforehand if we were coming here.

"It's the first time I've been back since this place changed my life forever. It means so much to me. I wanted to be in the right mindset, to clear my energy and come here with a pure heart. To show respect for the Ancestors who changed my life on this ground. Please, at least give me a moment to pray."

Chief pressed his lips together with dissatisfaction and

153

stepped on the gas pedal. We tore up the dirt and gravel driveway towards the museum, then turned around on the lawn in front of the mass gravesite. "Get out."

I sighed with sorrow as my feet touched the ground. I followed him to the front door of the museum, apologizing silently in my heart to the great Ancestors. I wished my presence could have shown them more respect and honor; they had done so much for me. Chief removed the padlocks from the door to the building and undid the chains. Inside, the room was filled wall to wall with bags of trash. He opened his arms in front of the rancid mess and smiled. "Trash day!"

The black writing, stark against the white interior walls, the photos of the ancestors, it all became a background for a massive pile of garbage. This is where they stored it. His neighbors and family, he let them all use the building to store their trash until he was ready to dispose of it.

He handed me bags of trash and nodded towards the bed of his pickup. We stacked it high, but it would take three more trips to clear the place out. When we got back in the truck, I felt like crying. We had not honored this sacred place in any way. I was devastated it was being used as a landfill and let down because he would not let me pay my respects to the mass grave when I asked.

Chief eyed me sideways, evaluating my sadness with his wisdom. He chose to say, "This is not the real grave sight. We brought in dirt and made this place. The real grave is a secret known only by the oldest Lakota elders. It will always be a secret from the White Man."

My head was spinning. "Do you mean nobody is buried there beside the museum?"

"No. There are bodies there. But which ones?" He laughed. It was a dark sound.

Dizzy with this news, my thoughts ran wild: Was he teasing me? Trying to frighten me? Why would he joke about such a thing? Perhaps his words were meant to comfort me so I could set foot on this ground easier in the future as it was a high traffic area in our lives. Yes, perhaps he was just saying this to soothe me and maybe the mass grave was still right there. On the other hand, what if Chief spoke the truth? If this was the real story, then whose voices were inside me? What called to me that day? Was it really the voices of the Ancestors who changed my life, or perhaps just an element of Chief's gift, his power over women, that possessed me?

I didn't dare to ask. I was afraid to know the truth.

Chief smiled in a way that reminded me of a badger. It was similar to the dangerous and cruel smile he had when he picked up my sweet, green parrot like he was a chunk of feathered meat and held him upside down, his little orange feet kicking with helplessness.

He held me the same way with his words. I was trapped in Chief's grasp. He liked it. The power to crush at his will, he continued squeezing and asked, "Remember the upside down American flag in the round building?" I swallowed and found my throat was too dry to speak. I nodded. "Do you remember what I said to you when you asked about it on the day we met?" I nodded again; for some reason I felt hot and pale, dizzy.

He barked a sarcastic laugh. At the sound of its hollowness, I became afraid of him for the first time. He spoke: "The story I told you 'stars upside down means distress' is the lie we tell tourists and journalists. Do you want to hear the Truth?"

I forced a "Yes," my voice was raspy. How could I not hear what was to come? The Truth is what I always sought, it was my quest, yet now it scared me. I faced my fear; I looked Truth in the eye and listened.

Chief Two Bear Paws peeled back the layers of lies and illusion on this particular onion of Truth for me, exposing the rotten core of true Lakota beliefs. Now that I was here on the reservation, trapped—unmasked came the real answer about the upside down U.S. flag:

"We hate the United States. The flag is upside down because we renounce our U.S. citizenship. We stand strong on sovereign Indian land. We want no part of America. On 9-11, we watched the buildings blow up in New York. We laughed and said, 'The White Man finally got what he deserves!' My people cheered, it is good." Chief smiled when he told the story, as if the attacks on 9-11 were a moment of glory in his history book. "You will be like that too. You will look at it and laugh with us. Once you are my wife, the government of the United States cannot harm you. They cannot get you. You are Lakota. You are safe."

I felt far from safe as I sat inches from him in the pickup truck. Images spun in my head, whirling: the upside down U.S. flag—the plane crashes on 9-11—the sins of my white forefathers smeared on the walls of the round building—falling to my knees with tears, pain, sorrow, and love at the fake mass grave sight which had changed my life and touched my soul.

The truths I believed in were all lies. I saw my parrot's feet kicking, his little toes reaching up, begging for mercy; the image faded into the outstretched, frozen, twisted, dead hands of the elders in the 1890 massacre. Chief's hollow laugh echoed in my head. His hand fell like an eagle's claw as he grabbed my thigh. I refused to flinch or gasp in surprise; instead, I released my negative feelings. I let go of all the images which brought me fear and anxiety.

I chose to feel only love. Love melted fear. I cuddled in closer to Chief, kissed his neck, and put my head on his shoulder. He allowed it.

We carried onward; after all, this was Trash Day. We drove off the road and onto the lawn behind his house, over a hill and down its sloping backside. He stopped on the crest of the next hill. We overlooked a valley filled with solid trash. Some of his relatives stood there, waiting to help.

"This is where the garbage man brings it." Chief laughed at his own joke. I was speechless. "We spread it out. When the snow melts and the spring rain comes, it will wash it away. All the garbage will flow downhill into White Man's river." He laughed hard at this, but his face looked truthful. "Get in the back."

Strong Bear and the grandkids climbed in the truck bed with me to help unload. The four of us worked while Chief drove across the valley at a slow pace. We shook the garbage out of the bags and onto the ground.

The image I saw in my mind was that 1970s era Keep America Beautiful ad campaign where the Indian canoes through trash-filled water then stands by the side of the highway only to get a sack of garbage spewed over his moccasins when some litterbug drives by and throws a bag out the car window. A single tear rolls down the Indian's cheek; he looks at the camera and his eyes beg you not to litter. Reality is such a contrast to fantasy and stereotypes.

That commercial had a lasting impact on me when I was a young child. Like many in America, I fell in love with Indians because of that actor. The "Indian" in the commercial was 100% Italian. He claimed he was a real Indian and people believed. He played the role in movies for sixty years; he was consumed by the fantasy even in his private life. He created a fictitious Cherokee-Cree family history, wore feathered "Sioux" war bonnets, married an Indian woman and adopted Indian children. Like me, he got swept up in a culture and cause that was not his by birth or blood. His sister outed him to the disappointed public in 1996, when he was 92 years old. So many self-created illusions make up our perceptions of reality.

Trash was waist deep in the prairie land. We worked hard to spread this new layer of garbage out evenly, so it would wash away easier in the spring. The children and I shook the bags out onto the ground, but it was landing in thick clumps. Strong Bear was about twenty-two, he sat on the side of the truck bed and waved me over to sit next to him. He showed me how to do it easier with my feet. His idea was to have the grandkids empty the garbage bags into the truck bed while he and I sat on the side and kicked it out onto reservation ground. This worked great! It was a smelly and nasty job but we had a ball tossing and kicking garbage together. Trash went flying everywhere; we had no gloves, but I was having so much fun I forgot I was a germ freak.

We laughed as the truck bounced around the prairie. We were throwing plastic jugs, cardboard boxes, Styrofoam containers, tin cans, soggy diapers, and wrappers gelled up with bottom of the bag slime. We got silly and joked around, making what could have sucked a ton of fun. Strong Bear and I talked about the song "Hollaback Girl" and shared ideas on what "hollaback" meant. It was a deeply philosophical discussion and a hoot when we started singing and dancing to our own a cappella version among the piles of garbage. The grandkids got into the fun. It was a Trash Day party in the back of the pickup truck.

By the end of the next load, Strong Bear and I were good buddies, teasing each other and laughing. There was a moment when we found ourselves out of earshot from Chief and the children. Strong Bear said to me, "You're a pretty cool chick. I like you. And that's why I'm going to tell you something. My dad better treat you right. You are too good for him. Let me warn you, he is not good to women."

His eyes turned heavy and clouded. He continued from a distant place, "I saw my dad punch my mother in the stomach. He hit her so hard she fell to her knees. While she was doubled up and begging for mercy, he kicked her front teeth out. There was so much blood on the kitchen floor, he just walked out and left her lying there. I was three years old. I hate my father. I only come here for his horses. If he ever hurts you, I will kill him. Don't you worry, I got your back, girl."

I was stunned and honored. Then, he reached out and gave me a big brother shoulder hug; I could feel the love. In this moment, I became family. But family to what? His story was horrifying.

Later, once the New Year came and went, Chief, Deena, and I stopped by the jail in the reservation town of Pine Ridge. I pieced together from their troubled faces, whispers, and racist slurs against the White Man that Strong Bear had been arrested on assault charges when he and another young man had gotten into a public disagreement. Strong Bear would be locked up for a while.

I thought of his promise and wondered who would protect me now.

CHAPTER SIXTEEN:

Hunting Stories

There were still a few more months of good memories to make with Strong Bear before he would end up behind bars.

Chief, Strong Bear, Hunter, and a few of Strong Bear's young warrior friends were gathered at the house one night soon after the Trash Day experience. The energy was high; I could tell something was coming.

Earlier that day, Chief had me buy a powerful floodlight that plugs into the cigarette lighter of a vehicle. Having lived in Maine, I knew we were about to jack us some deer. I was excited to travel with the hunting party. I think the only reason Chief brought me was because I did not eat meat and it would toughen me up to watch the men hunt. I was ready. We were only missing one thing, a gun. No problem.

Chief, Hunter, and I piled into the car. Strong Bear and his posse used the truck. We headed off-road into the endless prairie. Hunter angled the floodlight onto the field until we found a deer. It froze in the beam of light. Chief ran into it with the car. The pickup ran into it again. Everyone got out of the vehicles. Chief yelled to Strong Bear, "Slit its throat!"

"I don't have a knife!" He yelled back. "Anybody got a knife?"

"Here you go." I handed him the large hunting knife I carried in a leather sheath on my hip. I had picked it up in a pawn shop because I loved the multi-layered colors on the bone handle. I was a good tomboy. Plus, the leather sheath matched my hat.

I thought Chief would be mad at me for upstaging the boys. Instead, he smiled. "That is good. A woman always carries a knife. In the old days, a good woman would carry a knife, a stone to sharpen it, and flint in her pouch. It is tradition. It is right."

Strong Bear ran after the deer with my knife, out for blood as his father commanded. But he had not hit the deer hard enough with the vehicle. Neither had Chief. I was glad to see this, since the car was a rental. The car already had scratches from the rough, dry prairie grass scraping the doors as we off-roaded with a vehicle that did not belong to us. The last thing it needed was a deer-sized dent in the hood. The car seemed fine. So did the deer. It got up and bounced away. Strong Bear gave my knife back. One for the deer.

Chief decided we needed to buy a gun. The next day, as we traveled to a store off the reservation, he told me he always wanted a gun, but the U.S. government wouldn't let him have one. He said they were out to get him; he claimed he was on some list because of a misunderstanding. One of his many "misunderstandings" involved catching one of his past wives cheating. He shot her in the leg and shot the man she was in bed with in the shoulder. He told me this story himself, as if he was proud he did the logical thing.

Since my record was clean, it was up to me to buy the gun. I thought we'd do it up right and go for a 9mm handgun since people were his normal targets. He pointed with his chin towards the rifles. Of all things, he wanted a Savage model 22.257. Chief did not let me down, however; he also chose a professional, high powered scope that cost more than the rifle. The white men behind the counter told me the scope was ridiculous overkill considering the type of rifle chosen. Chief said, "Buy it." I did.

When I finally got to talk to my dad a few weeks later, I told him the story. He laughed and said, "The scope sounds kind of crazy, it's just a .22. Something like that is good for nothing bigger than woodchucks." Chief was out for mule deer. He loaded the rifle with hollow point rounds; they looked large, severe, and piercingly sharp-tipped to me.

I would hold the rifle butt in my lap, the muzzle up over my shoulder, the box of ammunition between my feet as Chief and I whipped through the prairie. We were far from the main road, zipping through the endless grass, searching for targets. Hunting what little was left around the reservation was the best source of healthy food and closest to the old ways of living when the Lakota did not die from diabetes.

We saw a few antelope with zebra patterns and twisty horns. They looked as if they bounced out of an African safari and hopped into the South Dakota grassland. Chief said sometimes, during a different time of year when their meat was better, they would get one of those, but the more commonly desired meat was mule deer. That is what we were after. The mule deer seemed to freeze when they saw us coming, then they'd bolt in giant leaps to escape. He'd speed after them, hooting the whole way, seldom getting close enough to take a shot.

An old west song I learned in elementary school echoed inside my head, the one about the deer and antelope playing. I was amazed it was true and happening before my eyes. Chief began to speak, which brought to my attention the catchy tune also claims words are seldom discouraging here. I was hoping Chief was about to say something nice, since the song was stuck in my head.

He surprised me today by asking out of the blue, "Why do you not eat meat? Why are you this 'vegetarian'?" I was flattered he would care enough to ask. Chief rarely asked me any questions, especially ones about myself, so this was a notable occasion. Mostly, he gave commands and didn't care how I felt or what I thought.

In my past, I have never initiated conversation on my private vegetarianism choice, not wishing to offend and not desiring to debate on something so close to my heart; few have ever asked me to elaborate.

"I believe all life has value equally. No one life means more than another. Who am I to say a life should end because I want it to? For example, look at that eagle up there," I pointed at the endless blue sky above the truck. A Golden Eagle was soaring overhead, sun beams slipped between the feathers of his wings. "That eagle is noble. He deserves to live. Who am I to take away his right to fly another day?"

Chief craned his neck to follow the path of my finger. He saw the eagle and said, "Get the gun."

Horrified, I handed him the rifle. He grabbed it with both hands and leaned out the window, the truck continued on its forward path without need for steering. He fired up at the eagle. In my mind, I could see the large bird descending in a looping spiral; I imagined what its dead feet and talons would look like when I held them in my hands. As an avid bird lover, it has always been my dream to see a Golden Eagle up close. But not this way.

Chief fired again. "Ahhhk!" he exclaimed. "Missed it! Too bad, the feathers would have looked good in my headdress."

I was pale-faced. Chief handed me back the rifle.

I reloaded and pushed my emotions away. In my numbness, the song drifted back into my head to fill the void. I could recall a stanza which spoke of the Red Man being pressed from the West, the song claimed the Red Man would likely never again return.

That sentiment, which paints Indians as extinguished legends, was written a hundred years ago in a folk song. Imagine how that belief has solidified over time. Imagine how today's culture views Indians and the old ways as faded images from the past, think about how the politicians and government agencies must view the idea of the Lakota getting their land back as an ancient topic not worth discussing.

Yet, here we are, side by side, Chief and I, hunting. This is real. The Lakota are still here. Still fighting to hold on. Still waiting for wrongs to be set right.

As we drove around looking for big game and keeping an eye to the sky for that eagle, Chief Two Bear Paws enjoyed telling me stories. He told me how his Lakota ancestors would hunt eagles. An Indian man would dig a hole deep enough to stand in, yet shallow enough to still reach his arms up over his head and outside the hole. He would pull grass and brush on top of the hole to camouflage it. He would poke a sturdy stick through a dead rabbit and secure it to the brush which covered the top of the hole.

The man would wait inside the hole for as long as it took. Eventually, an eagle would see the dead rabbit and swoop down to grab it. When the eagle reached for the rabbit, the Indian would reach up faster and seize the eagle by the legs, above its claws and feet. He would pull the large bird down into the hole and quickly snap its neck. There would now be feathers for his regalia. I actually saw an oil painting of this technique inside a dusty, South Dakota back country antique store once. Chief wasn't pulling my leg. This old ways hunting style was the truth, even if it was chilling.

He told me about the word "kimosabe." He laughed, saying it means something very far from "friend." Telling the White Man the word meant "friend" was a joke Indians played on the White Man and they laugh every time they hear it.

He put a new perspective on things I learned in history class. He told me Sacagawea is disliked by Indians. He would bare his teeth and growl her name, "Traitor!" She betrayed her people by helping Louis and Clark. He said she should have died before she showed them how to navigate Indian land. She gave away Indian secrets and kept the enemy alive on their quest to destroy Indians and take away their land.

I told Chief how, in kindergarten when I was five, we dressed up in school as pilgrims and Indians for Thanksgiving. We churned butter together, sat "Indian style" with legs folded on the rug, and enjoyed our feast of buttered bread while the white teacher told us fairytales of America's first

Thanksgiving.

The pilgrims in my class wore brown paper hats with white paper buckles. Even though I was only a few years old, I was angry I had been chosen to be a pilgrim. The Indian outfit was way better. It involved bright construction paper bands taped across the forehead with a single paper feather sticking straight up in the back. Chief truly thought the image hilarious beyond words.

He corrected another historically racist viewpoint by telling me "Sioux" is a French name for the Lakota, it means loosely "snake." The serpent is not an animal the Lakota perceive as a compliment. Their proper name is "Lakota."

Two Bear Paws told me this fact and many stories as we spent the afternoon driving around the prairie. He mentioned the Lakota do not have a concept of "hell." He suggested the closest thing to the idea would be *iktomi (ick-toh-meh)*, the spider. *Iktomi* is a trickster spirit, usually shifting into the shape of a spider. He is not to be trusted, but he is not hated.

The Lakota do not seem to have any dark, rotten evil in their stories. From what I could tell, the Lakota are a very positive-spirited people who choose to focus on the good in all things, which is how they bring up their children, who are respected highly in Lakota culture. The only devil truly to be hated by the Lakota is the enemy, the White Man.

We startled two mule deer; they rose up out of the tall grass almost under our tires. These were close enough for the rifle's range. I handed Chief the loaded gun, he parked the truck and took aim at the first deer through the open driver's window. It was leaping away fast, its giant arcs of travel covering too much ground quickly. He did not fire. The second deer stopped fleeing and turned to look back at us, dark eyes questioning, big, fluffy ears sticking out the sides of its face, ears longer than its antlers.

Chief switched focus and chose this second one. He shot; it went down. It did not get back up. We sped off in the direction of the hit, parking near the soft gray body of the deer. "Get out," Chief commanded. "Take the gun."

I got out, rifle in hand. Chief leaned out the driver's window and looked down at the animal as I walked over to it. The scope was so good Chief shot exactly where he had aimed, the hindquarters. It was just enough to cripple the animal and render its back end useless. But its front legs still worked, weakly. It was trying to get up. It pawed the earth with its front hooves; its knees were bent, trying to lift all the weight. Its front end could almost stand up, but its back legs would not cooperate. Its huge eyes got wider, straining with the effort and shock at its now dysfunctional body.

Chief's voice boomed across the prairie: "SHOOT!" Without hesitation I aimed the rifle. The mule deer's large, black eye filled the lens of the scope. I focused directly behind the eye, pulled the trigger, and drove the bullet directly into its skull. As it lodged into its brain, I saw the light leave the animal's eyes as it died at the cause of my hands. I felt nothing. I looked to Chief, still leaning out the driver's window. He smiled. "Good." At this, I felt pride.

We were forced to leave the deer as Chief hunted for men to help load the animal into his truck. Nobody could be rounded up to assist. I kept telling Chief I would do it, he kept waving his hand no. Finally, the meat at risk of being spoiled, eaten by a mountain lion, or stolen by someone else, he relented.

We traveled back, he put the tailgate down. We stood with our hands on our hips for a moment. I had never been close to a dead deer before and never shot at any living thing in my life other than this animal. I had no idea what to do. He nodded his head for me to take the back end while he reached down to take the front.

The deer's face was streamed with death's tears of blood, he grabbed the antlers. My end was also streamed with blood, but I had the bonus of a hundred flies and fresh excrement. It stunk to high heaven. I put my face right in the hot mess as I squatted down, grabbing its tail end with my left hand and its legs with my right. I had never touched a deer before; I was amazed how coarse its hair was, how hot the blood felt, and how dense the meat seemed. The legs felt like pure bone, stiff in my hand. I could feel a valley running down the bone, the legs felt fragile and I hoped I did not rip them from the carcass. I lifted from my knees, tossed with my arms; I had to give it all I had and then some. The deer weighed close to two hundred and fifty pounds, I weighed less than half that. I felt like I had most of the weight in my arms. We struggled for a minute and barely made it passed the tailgate, clearing it by an inch.

All four legs stuck stiffly out the back, its pointy black hooves never to leap again through the grasslands. Chief climbed into the truck and pulled the deer by its head, swiveling the antlers back and forth in order to drag the body forward so I could close the tailgate. Its mouth opened as Chief wrestled with its head, its tongue lolled to one side, its dead teeth flashed white in the sun. When I closed the tailgate, blood streamed out the crack where the tailgate met the bed. It ran in a river of red, covering the dry grass below. Blood painted the inside of the white truck bed with bright splashes of color. It was gory graffiti that told the story of this humble vegetarian's ruthless slaughter. I simply did as I was told. I had honored Chief. I loved him more than life itself.

We took the deer to his mother's. We sat on the sofa and watched TV. I could smell the rank hindquarters on my clothes; my hands were sticky with dried blood and fur. We watched a football game this way while the men gutted the deer in the walk out basement. I was so distracted, I could not focus on the plays. I asked if I could head down the few stairs off the living room and help with the deer. Chief said no. I protested, saying I should see it through until it is finished, to honor the animal. He forbid it. I was upset we never said a prayer of thanks to the animal's spirit. Chief's attitude was not what I expected from Indian stereotypes, he behaved like meat was just meat.

The men came upstairs and danced around the living room with the antlers. Chief's youngest son, Brings Thunder, held it proudly to his head, then tipped forward and pawed the rug. He charged Strong Bear who held his two index fingers up on his head. Having the weaker rack, he lost the imaginary battle, but, having quicker reflexes, he won the war and swiped the real rack from his brother. Now, Strong Bear wore it and strutted around the room with pride. They laughed and Chief hooted, celebrating the victory.

The antlers had been roughly hacked from the animal; there was a bloody, gnarled circle of skull at the base which held the pair together. Eight points in all, four on each side, made this a four point buck or "4x4" in Western speak by some, since this was a mule deer and not counted the same as a New England white-tailed deer. I asked Chief if I could have the antlers, since this was my kill. He said no, women don't get antlers and women don't get to hunt. This was *his* kill. His shot had taken it down. I was warned to never again say it was mine.

The meat was cut, his mother sliced it into thin strips and hung it on clothesline stretched in rows across her entire ceiling. It would dry for a while this way, turning into tough, unseasoned jerky. Chief said his mother would show me how to turn it into *wasna*, more commonly known in Indian culture as *pemmican (pem-ih-kan)*, a highly nutritious mix of dried meat pounded to a pulp along with chokecherries and fat. It roughly resembled loose tobacco when it was done.

The *pemmican* would be used in our wedding, in the sweat lodge ceremony, and for the Big Foot riders on their upcoming spirit ride, a yearly tradition for thirteen days around Christmastime. On this horseback journey through the wilderness, the hundred or so riders would follow the Spirit Trail of Chief Big Foot and his band who perished in the Wounded Knee massacre in 1890; *pemmican* would give them energy.

Chief said his mother would also teach me how to tie tobacco ties for our wedding. All the women would make colored pouches of cloth filled with tobacco and prayers and tie them into a single string which would hang around our ceremony. Chief dreamed big, he claimed it would be the longest strand ever made; women would work day and night for many days. He smiled with pride. "Everyone will come to our wedding and say they have never seen such a ceremony like this. We will make it big."

It sounded good to me. I was excited about our wedding and I was glad to learn the deer would go to such special use. I was happy I would encounter it again; I would work with the meat and make something good for the Lakota people with its gift. It would give me a chance to honor the life I took, now so secretly.

CHAPTER SEVENTEEN:

The Dark Horse Speaks

The spirit of life has always mattered deeply to me. That deer was the first thing I had ever killed, so it had great meaning to me. But the animal that seems to matter most to the Lakota is the buffalo. As much as they talk about the spirit of the buffalo, or *tatanka (tuh-tahn-kah)*, I think it is more the spirit of their past symbolized by the buffalo which they hold in high regard instead of the actual flicker of life itself inside the animal. I never saw anyone on the reservation respect and honor that essence of life the way stereotypes portray Indians should.

Chief did tell me, though, that horses have a strong spirit. They speak wisdom to those who seek it. There is a true story of a Lakota boy who caught a wild horse and led it around with his mind. He rode the horse without a saddle around the reservation. All he had to do was think it and the horse would lay down when the Indian boy wished it, so he could climb on or off with ease.

Two Bear Paws said many great Lakota leaders in the past could communicate with the Spirit of the Horse. He told me stories of ancestors, Lakota war leaders and great medicine men, who have heard the words of the Horse. Chief told me horses speak with their eyes and mind, they have great wisdom. The spirit of the animal speaks to those who open up and listen.

I decided to give it a try one afternoon when we brought the grandkids out to a movie. On the way there, Chief saw Hunter's little white horse had run off with some new, wild friends. He drove onto the grass, planning to rustle all the horses back in the other direction towards his ranch. The small

171

white horse took off in a flurry with a paint horse, while a wild big, black horse calmly held his ground. As we drove past it, the horse looked at me and became all the Ancestors combined, a dark spirit who was humored by my small existence.

As we held each other's gaze, I let my spirit carry my thoughts from my body. "Hello, Horse. The Lakota tell me you have wisdom and you will speak to those who listen. I am listening. I seek your counsel. Should I stay here on the reservation forever or go home to my mother who is sick? Stay or go? Which is right?"

The horse seemed to laugh sarcastically as he stood there on the outskirts of the Badlands. Came the reply from dark eyes, *"Either way it does not matter. Either way you die."*

The horse remained a moment longer. His darkness swallowed my soul, then spit it back out. He snorted and shook his head, as if with distaste. He tossed his huge mane into the air, then turned and galloped into the distance, leaving me with no clarity. Yet, with time, more and more I have come to understand the truth of his wisdom. When the Horse speaks, he is always right.

The grandkids loved the movie. They gorged themselves on popcorn and slushees, their eyes shone with the joys and luxuries seen only perhaps at Christmastime. On the way home Hunter, sick on sugar and fun, threw up in the back seat and never told me. When he threw up, his short-lived, sugared illness went away so he showed no signs of being ill around the house; I never gave it a thought there was blue puke in the back seat of my car.

When I discovered it, I suggested to Chief that Hunter clean it up. He should learn to ask to pull over before he got sick or, if it were possible, try to throw up in a shirt or cup instead of directly on the car's carpeted floor. At the very least, he should tell the truth and admit to someone it happened so it could be cleaned up promptly. Instead, he had been silent and now the mess had baked for three days in the sun, causing the vehicle to reek.

Chief got angry. "No! You clean it! You are the woman!"

I noticed Lakota children were highly respected, therefore never disciplined. On the whole, the Lakota children I saw were very polite and well behaved no matter how young; they were so much better than spoiled American children. But Hunter stood out; he was different. There was something wrong with him. He was just like his grandfather.

When the smell was gone, I gently suggested working out a plan to bring the rental car back.

Chief laughed and said, "Forget it."

"I can't forget it! The police are probably already looking for me!"

"The police cannot get you here. You are on Indian land. You are safe."

"But it's not right to just steal the car! They took my fingerprints! We need to give it back."

Chief did not agree. There was no way to get to Omaha. There are only about four vehicles on the reservation that run well enough to travel that far. And those people, having a way out, were not around to help us. Chief's truck worked for short distances locally, or a very necessary trip down the back roads to Hot Springs. But, with the steering column the way it was, it would not be a wise decision all the way to Omaha.

I needed to return the car. Chief really didn't care. I think he was proud to be one of the few to have a vehicle that decent. I was distressed and Chief let me suffer a while longer. Eventually, he came to me with a newspaper ad for a used car in Chadron, Nebraska. He had circled it, handed it to me, and said, "Let's go."

We took the rental car south to Chadron. There was a gold Taurus in the used car lot, he tried it, liked it, and said, "Runs good. Buy it." It cost 4,500 dollars. It was cheaper than what the rental place was going to charge me for stealing, so I bought him the car. The salesman was shocked I wanted to register it in Chief's name and he tried to convince me otherwise. I said no, I wanted him to have it; I knew it would mean a lot to him. Besides, I had a truck in Maine I was going back to get. Then we'd each have a vehicle.

After I bought the car, Chief tried to get me to buy a four wheeler for Hunter. It was seven hundred dollars. He said it would be good to drive around the reservation and get wood, he said Hunter would love it and it would impress all his friends. I said, "No, I don't have seven hundred dollars more. I just bought you a car." Chief seemed irritated. I knew it would just get stolen if I bought it. Plus, it really irked me how he favored Hunter. The boy was nine, bratty, whiney by Indian standards, and he had a cruel, mean energy that was amazingly dark for such a young child. Chief catered to him because he was a boy. Presently, Hunter is in a gang on the reservation, he wears his baggy jeans low and a black and white bandanna above his eyelids. That is not the way of the Ancestors.

Chief always ignored his granddaughter because she was a girl and girls have no potential except to get pregnant and cook. I loved Skyler's bright mind and spirit. She softly told me her Indian name and it translated to something complex and beautiful like "butterflies dance in her hands with wings of sunshine." They called her Skyler for short, it was a condensed version of one of the Lakota words in her Indian name; many in our Lakota family had one or two syllable nicknames based on this concept.

Skyler was intelligent, articulate, creative, and cheerful. She could easily have become anything she wanted. I told her I'd help her apply to college in a few years; college would be free because she was a fullblood Indian. She frowned and said, "Grandpa won't let me go to college." She told me she had wished to be a cheerleader in school, but he forbid that, too, because it was not traditional. She tried to sneak music from Beyoncé into the house, but he refused to let her sing or dance to it. He said she should only listen to traditional Lakota songs. She got pregnant at 16, the baby's father is not around, she spends her days smoking pot on the reservation.

Perhaps because I would not buy the four runner, Chief Two Bear Paws would not allow us to drive to Omaha to return the rental. I had to beg him to allow me to leave it in the shopping center parking lot next to the used auto dealer. He waved his hand high and flipped his fingers, which meant, fine, but he does not agree.

It helps Snickers taught me how to speak parrot, reading gestures and energy came in handy when I had to interpret Chief's feelings and instructions. He was a man of few words. Just like my parrot. Only my parrot had given up on his few words for good reason. Chief still found a few of them useful.

I parked the rental, kept the keys, and got in Chief's new used car. It was a very nice vehicle, much better than the rental. The ride was smooth, the engine good, the paint clean, and the interior quite large compared to the rental. On the way home, Chief had me swing into Radio Shack so we could get a CD player installed in the car; this two hundred dollar new addition delighted him. We listed to traditional Lakota music on KILI radio, the local radio station for Pine Ridge, the station also played country music. Chief thought the song "Tequila Makes Her Clothes Fall Off" was funny, we would laugh as we sang it together.

We could now play Alan Jackson and Merle Haggard CDs from my collection. His collection offered many Indian artists, as well as old country like Charley Pride. The oldest song I played for him was from 1960, "Mr. Custer" sung by Larry Verne. It's a song about a soldier serving under Mr. Custer who gets a bad feeling and begs not to fight all those Indians at Little Big Horn. Chief laughed so hard at this song; he loved it and asked me to play it over and over. He favored Indian artists heavily; we would play traditional Lakota and Plains Indian ceremonial songs, as well as modern Indian music like Buffy

Sainte-Marie and many others I never heard of as we cruised around together.

I loved having the car because we would sometimes get dressed up in our fine Western best and head up to the casino. The casino was one room and very small, nothing like the glitzy and grand reservation casinos near my family in Connecticut. Those Connecticut casinos were almost Las Vegas worthy palaces run by Indians who were millionaires. In contrast, this casino was a dull, local hang-out that hosted mainly Indian clientele. Often, I was the only white person there; heads would turn when we walked in. Men would come up to greet Chief and have to struggle to be polite to me out of respect for him. Chief and I did not go to the casino to gamble, we went for the buffet. It was my new favorite place to eat, this was my money well spent as it was the only time I really ever ate. I didn't have to cook and serve everyone, and I could eat without worrying there wouldn't be enough to feed a house full of others.

The casino was positioned barely on Indian land, closer to Hot Springs and White Man's land. In the future when I got a job in Hot Springs, Chief would sometimes drop me off at work. If I needed a ride home, the white locals would never go any farther onto reservation land than the casino. Chief would meet me there with the car and laugh as the white people turned tail and ran.

Chief's car was the nicest one I saw on the rez. Everyone was gathered when we arrived home, ready to check it out. I saw my opportunity and went inside the house to find the cell phone. I knew Chief had tossed it in the drawer when the minutes ran out. I found it, it still had some battery left, I added a few air time minutes to it with my credit card.

I dialed the rental company in Omaha. All I could do was be honest and hope they didn't call the cops. I recognized the woman who answered the phone; it was easy because only two guys and a woman worked there. She remembered me. I told her the rental car was in the supermarket parking lot under a tree in Chadron. It was about seven hours away from Omaha, but hey, at least it was on non-reservation land in Nebraska.

She said, "WHAT!"

"I am sorry, there is nothing I can do."

"How did this happen? Where are the keys?"

"I am trapped here on the reservation. I can't get out. I had to buy him a car so he'd let me return your car to you." I started to cry. "It was all I could do to beg him to let me leave the car in Nebraska, off the reservation. You were right, he wanted to steal it. I can try to mail you the keys."

The woman sighed. "No, that's okay, we have a second set. I'll send someone over to pick the car up. Good luck. And thank you." They never charged me any additional fees. They even returned the thousand dollar deposit.

I went back outside to join in the new car excitement. Everyone was eager to go for a ride. This car was much bigger and could fit fifteen Indians instead of eight like the rental. Everyone was happy.

"What happened to your other car?" Deena asked. Chief waved his hand. She was silenced.

"This is *my* car," he said. It had reservation plates. They all but applauded.

Chief's car was their gateway to adventure. We'd do pizza trips two hours north to Rapid City, his family and friends loved Little Caesar's five dollar pizzas. Sometimes we would pack as many Indians as we could into the car and go for the biggest treat, an all-you-can-eat buffet at the Golden Corral.

We would use the car to travel to real Western rodeos when they came to the bigger cities, we'd watch the bull riders and barrel racers, we also went to Indian dances.

One dance stands out from the others. I wore a form-fitting, dazzling red, knee-length dress my mother had sent me; she said I'd need it as I would be going to many Indian dances. I didn't believe her, but I thought the dainty black ankle boots she included with the dress were cute. This outfit was so unlike my normal tomboy clothes. I looked sharp and Chief was proud. My mother was once again right.

At this country style Indian dance, there was a contest for animal sounds. When the man at the microphone called for volunteers, Chief nodded for me to go up. I was shy being the only white person in a room full of Indians staring at me like I shouldn't be there, but I went up as he instructed. I took all the pain I had inside and howled like a wolf, it trailed into a note of forlorn emptiness. The room fell silent. The awkward quiet exploded into applause for my chilling, shockingly accurate portrayal. I won the prize. Chief and I two-stepped in a circle around the room and slow danced to a love song.

The car was a good thing for everyone, the grandkids loved to visit the hottest place in town, Pizza Hut in Pine Ridge. We used the car for grocery shopping at Wal-Mart in Rapid City and to pick up the commodities on the reservation.

"Commodities" is the word the Lakota use when referring to their U.S. government issued food rations. We would go to a dark and dirty building once a month to pick up our commodities. All it took was a name on a paper and a list of who lived in your household, how many kids you needed to feed, and you got your rations.

Commodities are the only source of food many have and this plays greatly into the cause of diabetes in the Lakota nation. This government food is full of starch and sugar, not vitamins. The only option for so many on the rez, they would either die without it, or die because of it. Chief used to say the White Man did this on purpose to kill the Indians with diseases.

The saddest thing I ever saw came in a special one time batch just before the holidays. The Lakota were given a small tin can shaped like Spam. It was canned buffalo meat.

Indian men would stand around the backside of the building and whisper to those entering and leaving,

"Commodities . . . commodities . . ." like they were scalping tickets to a sold out show in the parking lot before it started. They were selling their family's food ration for fifty dollars. I suggested to Chief we buy someone's rations as our family needed the extra food.

Chief looked startled and grabbed my wrist to stop me. He said in a hushed voice, "No. Do not talk to those men or buy anything from them. It is bad. They will take the money and walk across the border and buy alcohol." I was shocked a man could drink his family's life away like that and leave them starving.

Chief said, "This is what White Man has done."

White Man introduced the fire water to the Indian and broke his spirit. He forced him with murder onto the worst piece of land nobody wanted and gave him diseases. White Man took away the Dance and the Hunt and sends the Indian buffalo meat in a can.

The only time many Lakota families had milk was on commodities day. There would be a bag of government issued powdered milk. We'd mix it with water in a pitcher and the young children always got to drink first. It ran out quickly. We would then add water to the small can or two of condensed milk included in the commodities, reconstituting the thick syrup when the dry milk ran out on the first day.

We also received potatoes and bread mix, yeast, five pounds of sugar and flour, greasy government sausage, fatty bacon, and powdered eggs. And a big orange box that confused me. It was unmarked and looked like a giant cereal box. Deena saw my scrunched eyebrows and said, "Think of it as Cream of Wheat and it's not that bad."

It was customary to have a big pot of this white mush on the stove all morning. It filled empty stomachs faster than anything else; it would go further and take the edge off hunger for many guests once we ran out of all the good food. Deena showed me how to make the mush so it would have lumps, because the lumps were tasty. We agreed on that point with quiet chuckles, our foreheads close together while we sampled the lumps from the pot, waiting for the household to awaken.

Up long before the sun and cooking breakfast was the life of the Lakota woman. Often, Deena would help make breakfast, she would cook the meat and eggs which was a huge chore of its own. I would get the pot of mush ready, bake breads and biscuits, set the table, and make the coffee. We'd clean up the whole mess together when it was done. I appreciated her help. I could see the advantage of having two wives—and the advantage was to the wife!

It seemed to be permissible for women to do women's work together at times. Whenever fry bread was made it was done in large batches, often many women gathered together in the effort. While not a common family dinner item, fry bread was always made for a "feed," the gathering time after ceremonies like a sweat or during celebrations like powwows. Fry bread is a guarded secret I was not yet ready to be given. Instead, Chief's mother and daughter taught me how to make biscuits from the commodities mix, adding a little flour to make it better. Chief loved my biscuits. I enjoyed baking, I would always have a type of homemade bread to go with our breakfast. One morning it was pineapple upside down cake dotted with cherries. I wondered if it was the first one ever baked on the rez.

Today, it was cornbread. Deena was sick in bed pregnant, so I was on my own. We had nine houseguests who had spent the night to stay warm. Deep down, I still longed for a home with only Chief and our own children. This dream was unrealistic, as the few houses there were on the rez had more than twenty people crammed inside just to stay alive. It seemed instead of our life becoming more private, our home got more public. Maybe it was because when our commodities ran out, I wouldn't let my family starve. I would take out my credit card and buy groceries at Wal-Mart two hours away, or pay more and get them at the sad, nearly empty local grocery store in Pine Ridge. Our home often had different foods not seen on the rez, and more of it than other families. To accompany today's cornbread, I made meat, eggs, mush, and coffee.

After everyone was served and happy, I took a plate of food to Deena's room. She smiled weakly and asked for juice. I brought her some. She could barely manage to whisper one word, "*Wopila*," as she held it, yet, she translated for me: "Thank you." She was so much more polite than her father, even when she was pale and not feeling well. I went back to the kitchen and noticed Chief had been watching me from the corner of the room the entire morning. It had been very busy, he saw how I had been rushing around to make sure everyone was cared for.

He lifted his chin towards me and said, "Sit, eat." I was happy he noticed me, touched he spoke concern for my well-being in front of many others, showing he cared. I scooped some white mush into a cup and pulled a folding chair up to the only available space at the corner of the table. Chief said, "You need more, stay healthy. Eat." He gestured with his fork towards the eggs. I put some on top of my mush as the grandchildren watched.

I felt so guilty. No matter how much food I bought or made, there was never enough to go around for everyone. A small bowl of white mush was all I ate once a day for weeks at a time. It killed me to take food out of their mouths. I loved each Lakota person so much, even those I did not know who came to my door hungry were of more value to me than myself and my own hunger. I lost weight I could not afford to lose, making me even more unattractive to Chief.

Which was the last thing I wanted. I desired to be close to him with all my heart. He had no interest. We had been together only once and it had been in an awkward way, when we were both exhausted in my apartment after we came home from the Boston Amtrak station. Since then, there had been nothing, not even a kiss on the forehead or cheek before sleep.

He was no longer sick; I had been bringing him the proper pills at the scheduled times each day. I could see him getting much stronger. He said it was good to have a woman take care of him by bringing his medicine. Those words were nice, but I craved even a simple brush of his hand for any reason. But there was never any contact, not even with his eyes.

I asked him privately one night in our bedroom, "Why don't you touch me?"

"Too skinny."

"What? That's always been a good thing for anyone I've been with."

"You only know white men. White woman too skinny. The first time Indians saw White Man's woman, Indians say, 'What is wrong with White Man's woman? Are all the white women sick?' You look sick. You need curves. Once you have some babies you will look good. After babies, you will get some hips and thighs." He frowned. "And you dress like a college girl."

"Well, I can fix my clothes. We'll go shopping and get things you like me to wear so I can look pretty for you, ok?"

Chief picked out Western shirts, Wrangler jeans, a brown leather fringe jacket with bone beads and black trim, red cowboy boots, a concho studded belt, the black leather cowboy hat with a buffalo nickel band that my dad bought me was something I'd worn for years and the only thing I owned still fine by Chief. He shaped it right and put a feather in it. I could now properly accompany him to restaurants, dances, and shopping.

Still, he did not reach for me. He never put his arm around me, never kissed me, never even looked at me like I was a woman to him. It hurt.

"You need makeup. Do your eyes blue and skin brown."

I asked him to help me, show me what he liked, as I knew nothing about make up. He sighed and quickly tossed bronzer and blush, lipstick, blue eye shadow, mascara, and eyeliner into the cart, all the things I needed to make my face more of a woman and less of a tomboy. The colors he chose were good, they complimented my natural beauty. I put them on the way he liked every day. Still, he did not touch me.

"What is wrong with me, Chief? I try to be pretty for you but you never notice me."

"Too hairy."

"Where? I shave everywhere!"

"Indian has no hair on his body. Look at me. No hair. Indian man and Indian woman, both same, no hair. White people are too hairy. And they smell like onions."

"Onions! Do I smell like onions?"

"No, but I had another white girl who did. I would make her shower all the time. I would tell her she smelled like onions even when she did not. She would take shower and more shower and cry and I would laugh. It was funny."

"Okay . . . but, where else can I shave? Show me and I will do it."

He showed me, I took care of it. Still, nothing. I did not feel pretty or desired, but I found him attractive and I wanted to please him. He had no interest.

I suggested we fix his truck. It wasn't right to go on steering it with a screwdriver and it was of no use long distance that way. I could see how important his truck was as a tool to feed and warm his people. I felt it was important to have it working correctly.

He said, "Tomorrow."

The next day, we went off the rez to a huge barn filled with antiques, they also did vehicle repairs. The white men behind the counter said they had the part and could have the truck fixed in an hour. It would cost three hundred dollars. Chief said, "Do it."

While we waited, we walked up and down the aisles, exploring. There was old furniture, tin signs, lanterns, old crossbows, and snowshoes for sale. It was something different to do. The truck was done rather quickly and I paid them. It was so nice to watch Chief drive normally, without that awkward screwdriver. He never said thank you for the steering wheel, but he seemed pleased as he whipped through the grasslands and turned on a dime.

There was still blood from the mule deer imbedded in the grooves of his white truck bed. The blood had been red for a while until it turned a deep burgundy, then brown. In a few good rains it would be pretty well washed away. Although, in places it proved to be quite tenacious and I could still see traces of it come winter. I laughed to myself, remembering how my father goes to the car wash at least once a week to keep his vehicles spotless. And here I was, his daughter, riding around with a load of blood.

Chief asked me if I was bleeding, I looked at my hands and said no.

"No. There." He pointed between my legs.

I blushed. "No."

"Good. A man cannot touch a woman when it is her moon." My heart fluttered. I thought I must have done something right and maybe he's finally starting to find me attractive.

I was familiar with the philosophy of men avoiding a woman's cycle from anthropology class at the University of Maine. The professor said some primitive tribes believe a woman is "too powerful" during menstruation. This stuck out in my mind because it sounded really nice to me, like women finally outranked men at least one week every month. The way the professor spoke made women sound respected and magical with positive, special powers.

The way Chief explained it put a whole new spin on things that previously sounded good. "A woman steals power from a man when it is her moon. A man can lose his powers and strength around her, she must be put into a tipi with other women on their moons and not come out until it is done. This protects the men."

He made women sound like evil, energy sucking savages. That scared me so much I never had my period again while on the rez. I had a year's supply of birth control pills in a metal tin so the roaches wouldn't eat them, as my reverend had suggested, and oh, what sage advice that had been! I hid the pills from the roaches and from Chief. I took them one after another without stopping.

CHAPTER EIGHTEEN:

Sweat

Early the next morning, Chief commanded his people: "Make a Sweat."

Men scrambled down the hill to cut lodge poles for the frame and get supplies to cover the dome shaped structure. Woman began to cook for the festive "feed" that came after the sweat. Firewood and rocks needed to be gathered, a pit had to be dug outside the sweat lodge to heat up the rocks; the heating of rocks was a full day task in itself. The sweat would not be ready until nightfall, with everyone in the village pitching in, working all day together, united in a common goal. A high pitched, excited yet meditative energy hummed in the air and ran through everyone.

This was my first sweat. I had never been to any type of Indian ceremony before this in my life. I had never even read about sweat lodges, sacred Indian ceremonies, or anything else in books or on the internet. I have become aware since this time that there are many different traditions, depending on the tribe or band, their beliefs and customs, and the reason for having the sweat. I think it was best I entered this time period in my life knowing nothing. I was not distracted by preconceptions or my own arrogance that I thought I knew what to do. I was not comparing it to anything, for I knew nothing. I was a virgin ready to learn the way Chief Two Bear Paws chose to teach me.

The sweat lodge ceremony, or *inipi (ih-nee-pee)* in Lakota, is a time of thanks and reflection, prayers and hope for the present and future. It is tradition to fast the entire day of the sweat. Afterwards, later that night, there will be a big feast to celebrate. There are women who sacrifice attending because they give the gift of cooking all day. They plan it together so the food is hot and ready when the sweat is over. There are men who do not get to sweat because they are watching the grounds outside the ceremony, monitoring the heat and hosting the doorway, or tending the hot rocks as firekeeper. Women who are menstruating cannot attend or go near the sweat. This explained Chief's interest in my cycle the previous day.

In the afternoon, we went down the hill to see how the men were coming along building the lodge. There were long wooden poles bent into a dome shape and woven to form walls; they had the frame up. A pit burned a few feet away from the dome, a man had been assigned to choose rocks and heat them. It would be his duty to bring the rocks inside the lodge during the ceremony. The role of firekeeper was an honor, only given to the most experienced. Upon Chief's arrival at the pit, there was a question about a rock's integrity; a hand signal was given asking without words Chief's opinion. Two Bear Paws made a tossing away gesture. He motioned to some other rocks and moved his hands big and high meaning, he later told me, "make it hot."

I took a step forward to help gather wood for the pile. Chief stopped me by cutting the air, his gesture was undeniably a harsh "no" with an implication it would have been a great disrespect. He sliced the air around us into silence using the side of his hand. After that, I respectfully stood off to the side of the circle, or off the grounds. For the rest of the day, I walked in Chief's shadow, always a bit behind him, mute and obedient.

I noticed there was a buffalo skull on a mound outside the door to the sweat, two sticks stood up near it, with a third on top. The structure looked like a mini roasting spit made from bones and sticks. There was a circle drawn around it and some rocks positioned carefully; I felt fear, power, and awe for all that was happening. If Chief wanted me to know what it meant, he would have told me. I did not ask questions.

We left the men to work. Back in the truck together, driving towards the house, Chief said, "The men will put blankets up to cover the sweat and keep in the heat. In the old days, buffalo hides were used. But there are no buffalos here anymore and nobody has any hides left to use." I looked behind us in the rear view mirror and saw the men tying old, gray carpet scraps over the wooden frame, blankets would cover these.

"When I moved my hands like this to the firekeeper, it meant 'make it hot.' If you cannot take the heat, ask to be excused, it is alright. There is no shame in leaving a sweat." As we walked into the bedroom, Chief continued filling me in on what I needed to know. "Wear a white T-shirt with nothing on it."

My T-shirts were all black Harley T-shirts, except for the only white one I owned, which was an endangered species parrot T-shirt I got when I visited the Pennsylvania zoo. I held it up.

"Turn it inside out," he said as I flipped the shirt and put it on. "Good. Now get a skirt." I held up a denim mini skirt, thinking it was going to be hot in there. "No. Long skirt. Cotton," he gestured towards his ankles and made a flowing movement with his hands. I happened to have one like that with a black and cream zigzag pattern. It had been my sister Amandah's. I put it on.

"Good. Take your jewelry off, no underwear." I took my underwear and bra off and clipped the diamond drop earrings Amandah had given me to the hand knit, purple goat's wool cardigan my Maine Mom and Dad had bought me on their trip to Iceland. I had been wearing about six hundred dollars worth of love from my white friends and family, and now I was about to enter a sacred place with my new Lakota family that had cost nothing to build but was worth more than money could buy.

"Wear sweater, sneakers, socks down to the sweat. Take off everything except T-shirt and skirt outside the sweat lodge. Bring lots of towels."

Then, Chief gave me the most important instruction: "There will be a man at the door of the sweat. The door will only be this high," he gestured a little higher than knee level. "You will crawl into the sweat on your hands and knees. The man holding the flap will say, '*Mitakuye Oyasin*' to you, do not look at him at any time. Crawl forward, stop as you pass him. Say, '*Mitakuye Oyasin*' back to him, then crawl to the next empty spot in the circle. Fold your legs and sit. Be still. When the man lowers the flap, the ceremony will start. It will get very hot then, getting hotter each round. *Mitakuye Oyasin* has much meaning in Lakota, the words cannot be translated. The closest English meaning is 'all my relations.' *Mitakuye Oyasin*. Say it."

I stared at him, having no clue what he said. I shook my head and shrugged. I grabbed a pen and gum wrapper so I could write it down and memorize it. He slapped the gum wrapper away. "Say it! '*Mitakuye Oyasin*.'" I said it, he nodded. "Good."

I wrote it down phonetically on the gum wrapper when he wasn't looking. "Mee taco yay o yah sin." The Lakota 't' was more of a *dt* sound, just like it is in the name of their people, but 'taco' was a word I knew and it helped me remember.

"Be serious in the ceremony. Speak only when the spirits tell you to speak. Some people will sit in silence the whole time, this is ok, too. If you feel it is right to speak, do not pray for foolish things. Give thanks, pray for people you love. Now is the time to speak of your family, but do not pray for your pets. A white lady once prayed for her poodle in a sweat, she said how much she missed it and prayed for its health. That is not right, it is foolish and offensive."

He handed me a two inch circle made of flattened, dyed porcupine quills. "This is the Lakota medicine wheel. There is a man who holds sweats for tourists. He tells them the colors stand for the colors of man: red, white, black, and yellow united as one. It brings in the money. Tourists like to hear that, he gets big donations in a jar. Sometimes hundred dollar bills.

"His way is not right. The sweat is not a show, it is our way of life. There will not be a donation jar passed around the circle. This is not an act for tourists. The *inipi* is our sacred way of Lakota life, it keeps our traditions and honors them. It is given to us by our Ancestors. It is not a game."

I held the medicine wheel and looked at it quietly while he spoke. "The colors are not the races of man. They are the Four Directions. North. South. East. West. The Four Directions are important to the Lakota. We will speak to the Four Directions during the sweat lodge ceremony." Everything mattered. The direction the sweat lodge door faced, what prayers were addressed to each Direction and when; these were traditions I would make second nature in time, for now, my focus was to not offend anyone.

"You will smoke the sacred *chanupa* with us. Take the sacred pipe from the one who hands it to you, use both hands, smoke it, then pass it on to the person to your left.

"There is a story to tell you now. Long ago, there was a white man. He helped the Chief and was invited to a sweat with the Indians. These were the old Ancestors of the old ways and traditions. They invited him to smoke the sacred pipe with them. It was a high honor. The Chief smoked the sacred pipe and passed it to the white man. The white man took a rag from his pocket and wiped the mouthpiece of the pipe before he smoked it. When the white man passed the sacred pipe, the Indian next to him took it and pulled out a knife. The Indian cut the tip from the pipe and looked at the white man with disgust.

"This is a story. The Lakota would never harm the *chanupa*. Learn from the story and do not wipe the sacred pipe. It is disrespectful."

I thought of my family bringing alcohol wipes to restaurants and sterilizing the silverware. I also remembered the chalice at communion, how the congregation drank from one cup and how we all seemed to catch one flu at the same time. The sweat was my church now, *Tunkashila* protects us; everything is okay.

"There will be water. Drink from the cup when it is passed to you. It will be a cup with a long handle, a big spoon. Take it. Sip the cool water but do not drink too much or you will be sick. Pass the cup to the person on your left, the circle always moves this way. Smoke what is given, drink what is given, eat what is given. It is the Lakota way and it is right.

"If you are given dried sage, sprinkle it on the rocks, it is an honor. When you enter the sweat, there will be a smudge burning. Wave the smoke to cleanse yourself. Wave it with your hands like this, like you are taking a bath in the smoke. Do not stand directly over it and fan it like you are trying to put the fire out." He bathed in an imaginary basin filled with water to illustrate his words. "This is *wash'te*."

We rode in his truck down to the sweat. Every ratty old pickup truck on the rez seemed to be here; I loved it. The trucks formed a wide circle around the fire pit outside the sweat. The large rocks were ready and hot. A man stood there, tending them.

The air was electric, my heart raced. I felt excited but in over my head. This was very serious and I had no idea what I was doing except for Chief's quick coaching beforehand. I hoped I was ready. I never had much interest in anything "Native American" until the photos in *Lakota Woman* captured my heart and I asked Big Biker if we could visit Pine Ridge on the motorcycle trip. Now, here I was, less than three months later, honored to be living with this Truth as my reality, praying I didn't make a fool of myself during this sacred ceremony.

I placed the towels on a log next to a pile of ponchos.

Women gathered in a cluster on the far side of the hot rocks. Chief motioned for me to go be with the women. He whispered, "When you get out of the ceremony, be silent. Grab a towel and get into the truck. Start it and stay warm. I will be there soon. Now, go, stand with the women."

I walked passed the wood and rocks in the ground, the smell of fire and sage filled the air. The women nodded to me, they gave me a poncho and hugged me. I felt very welcome, more welcome here than I ever had on the reservation previously. The night was cold, the fellowship warm and serious. It felt like falling through stars.

Everyone gathered in the darkness, the men stripped down to their underpants and the woman kept their T-shirts and skirts on. A frost coated the dry grass and twigs beneath our bare feet. The cold moon and stars lit the black sky as the red rocks burned in the ground. White smoke swirled around all of us, a screen between the male and female bodies. It was time to begin the *inipi*.

I got in line and followed the women. We bathed ourselves with a purifying sage smudge, a woman held it out to us. A man held back the flap as Chief had said he would. "*Mitakuye Oyasin*," he said and I did not look at him as I crawled passed his feet, praying I didn't knock out the stick which seemed to hold up the doorway.

I paused for a moment next to him and replied, "*Mitakuye Oyasin*." I crawled to my left all the way around and sat third from the door, the circle filled in the rest of the way until there was about fifteen of us under the dome. Chief sat opposite the opening, the fire pit stretched the distance between himself and the flap to the outside.

The man at the entrance looked to Chief to see if it was time to begin, Two Bear Paws nodded. Hot rocks were brought in on a pitchfork, they glowed bright red. The man looked to Chief, he nodded, it was enough rocks for now, the flap closed. The dry heat was transformed by water from the ladle; it sizzled onto the rocks and filled the small space with warm, white steam. Faces were shrouded in darkness, highlighted only by the glow from red embers, shadows blurred again as the room grew hotter with more steam. Dried sage was sprinkled from a pouch; it glittered upon the embers, crackling.

We were welcomed to the ceremony. It was not completely spoken in Lakota because some younger people in their twenties were present who were not fluent. But everyone here was 100% Indian, except for me, and the ceremony was held as if I were not white. They gave thanks around the circle, anyone spoke when they felt moved to speak. Many people gave thanks Chief had found a wife. When Chief Two Bear Paws spoke, he thanked *Tunkashila* for me. I was shocked.

At the feed after the sweat, a Lakota woman whispered to me as she passed me more fry bread. "Didn't someone tell you the sweat was done for you?" I told her I had no idea. She smiled and said, "It was done to cleanse you and welcome you into the Lakota way of life and to give thanks for you and your marriage to Chief." I could have cried with honor.

During the sweat, an elder—a woman—spoke often. It seemed she was leading the ceremony. She spoke of each direction, said prayers, and chanted in the traditional Lakota woman's warble. Everyone joined in with song and words. Wails would break into speech as the next person felt it was time to speak.

The flap opened and let in a blessedly cool breeze while more glowing red rocks were piled into the fire pit. We took sips of cold water from a shared metal ladle, water never tasted so heavenly. I heeded Chief's caution and only sipped a little, even though my body's urge was to gulp and be greedy. More water was poured onto the red rocks from the ladle. Thick steam filled the room with the smell of sage transporting us out of our bodies, our spirits hugged the domed walls; we were transformed into one big spirit of *inipi*.

The rounds blended together with songs, prayers, and heat.

The sacred pipe was passed and more prayers were said. I was nervous when I took the sacred pipe and Bic lighter from the person next to me. I knew how sacred the *chanupa* was and how much of an honor it was to touch it. I didn't want to mess this up.

I tipped the flame down at an angle so I could draw it into the bowl of the pipe. I held the lighter on the tobacco too long as I inhaled. The next day, I saw I had a blister from the metal wheel of the lighter as it had gotten too hot against my finger. I tried to hide the blister from everyone so I wouldn't look stupid.

I smoked the *chanupa* and tended the glowing cherry ember with a thin stick; I had observed it was tradition to get the tobacco and ember set up for the next person's smoke. I thought I was doing well, but I accidentally crushed it so it did not glow.

The woman next to me was Chief's mother's sister. She was kind and did not embarrass me. I passed the *chanupa* to her and she got it going again without missing a beat. I don't think anyone else noticed my mistake; my heart was grateful for her expertise and discretion.

Thanks were given, prayers of request followed from whoever felt moved to speak. Some asked for healing from sickness, many prayed for their children, spouses, and parents. It seems the Lakota way of life each day is serious and soft spoken, nobody complains and everyone carries onward as if they do not notice any problems as there is much work to get done. During this ceremony, I could see everyone feels so much inside themselves every day, they just hold it in and wait for the proper time to let it out. Daily life is not affected by emotions, good or bad; they cannot allow feelings to get in the way of all they must do each day. Now was the time to speak and let it all out. Everyone listened respectfully to each other, some chanted soft sounds of understanding and prayer in support of the one speaking.

I was startled to hear much bitterness spoken for the White Man and his ways, both past and present. My initial thought was, "Hellooo, I'm sitting right here people! Um . . . ?" But then, as the heat grew as intense as their hate, I thought, "Wow, they accept me. I am honored they feel this comfortable to speak so harshly in front of me. They are being real; honesty is right here among us. They are speaking freely and holding nothing back because this is a *real* ceremony. They are doing this the way they always would with only the Lakota present. I am accepted as family. I am sitting with Truth."

More rocks came in, more cool water made its way around the circle, touching lips to ladle as one body. A bowl of *pemmican* was passed. I chewed the dried, shredded deer meat, it was greasy sand in my mouth soaking up all the water I had on my tongue. The *pemmican* was a little sweet due to the dried chokecherries in the mix. It was an honor to eat the meat. Even though a vegetarian, I could not refuse; I had to eat what was offered out of respect. I was touched to realize this meat was from the deer I shot. What a way to honor the life I took! I was pleased.

Pemmican from that deer would also be carried by the Big Foot riders. We sat here in the sweat, taking part in the same food that would nourish them on their spirit journey. Prayers for the riders were offered from the circle tonight, songs filled the air. Although my throat closed up and I did not speak, it meant a lot to me to chew the meat, bless the riders, Chief, our marriage, the people I loved in this circle and the hoop beyond. The hoop of love extended out to include all of Pine Ridge Reservation.

I was given the bag of dried sage. The woman on my left, Chief's mother's sister, nodded for me to put it on the hot red rocks. I took the sage from the bag, knowing this was a great honor. I sprinkled a little bit onto the rocks, not wanting to be wasteful. She nodded for me to put all the sage into the pit and burn the bag, too.

I thought I must have misunderstood her intent; there was not enough light to see what the bag looked like. I moved it between my fingers and could tell it was not leather, it felt like a thin, cotton cloth, which was good because the fumes from a burning leather bag would be too strong in this small space.

Her silent instruction danced in front of me. We were all one shadow held together in the black womb around us. Everything was darkness highlighted only by dancing red light from the pit, but somehow I understood and trusted.

It was too dark to follow its descent. The sage fell from the bag through the blackness and exploded with snaps onto the rocks that were glowing like molten lava. When it touched the hot rocks, it sizzled with blue and green fireworks. Large sparks turned into gold fire, they fused to the rocks like stars refusing to be consumed by a volcano. The space was filled with a deep Thanksgiving turkey stuffing smell that was richer and more developed than anything I had ever breathed in before. It was magic.

The fragrance took me to a higher place and made me dizzy in a good way. I was amazed. I released the empty bag. It drifted downward, got caught by a rock and burned up, leaving a hot white square outline. I saw her smile at me knowingly, understanding the awe I felt. White steam filled the room as everything blurred and the rocks grew hotter.

Chief Two Bear Paws said a prayer, gave thanks, and excused himself from the intense heat due to his bad heart. There is no shame in leaving a sweat. It is smart to know what your body can take, pay respect, show gratitude, and then excuse yourself. Chief had told me that himself and now he was gone.

I considered leaving, too. I knew there would be no shame in joining him. To leave would have been to think with my head and give the illusion of what I thought would look right, that is, to check on my husband. To stay would mean I listened to my heart and did what I was called to do. Remaining in the sweat would honor the Truth spoken by my soul. Something deep within me told me to stay for this last round.

I wanted to try harder to take the heat. Experienced, true Lakota men had built this lodge so it was breathable; I trusted them. Knowledgeable elders had carefully selected the right rocks that would not break or explode under intense heat. The flap was opened to let in air at the right times, water was given in moderation, the sweat did not go on longer than was tradition; I had nothing to fear from the lodge or the customs, they were done right with centuries of wisdom.

My body would tell me if I needed to leave for health reasons. I would listen to it. I would give time a few more minutes and see if I could adjust. I wanted to complete the sweat for myself, but also for Chief since his body would not let him stay. I wanted to do this for myself and for us, for the honor of our love, since he and I are one.

I have experienced a summer day of 115 degrees; that memory was breezy and cool compared to the sweat lodge. I imagined the room was 180 degrees, the steam made it feel even hotter.

When I was a child, my mother told us a story about frogs. She said a frog could stand in a saucepan full of cool water and adapt to the slowly rising temperature as the heat was turned up underneath the pot. The frog would stand there calmly while the water boiled, comfortable, never hopping out when it easily could have, unknowingly cooking itself until it died. I thought of this image and my heart raced with panic. Sweat soaked my T-shirt and plastered my hair against my face; it dripped a hot, tropical rain around me. I felt dizzy but it was my own fault, I was working myself up with anxiety. I was listening to my head. I needed to turn inward, listen to my heart and find strength within myself.

I closed my eyes and accepted where I was. I could feel my heart rate slow down to an easy rhythm as I trusted the sweat. I stopped being nervous and willed my body to agree with itself.

Next, I said hello to my mind and welcomed it down into the peace and calm my body felt. My mind and body now one, we looked outward and agreed with the room. We said hello to the heat and accepted it instead of fighting it, we welcomed it into the body. I hit a plateau of peace where I actually grew calm and focused and no longer felt hot.

Then, the room looked into me. It accepted me as part of its womb. I was transcended from the heat, a spirit without a body. My spirit met everyone else's in the room, we held hands, we were one blanket above the fire.

When we left the sweat, I silently grabbed a towel and went to the truck as Chief had instructed. I saw the value of towels and ponchos. Outside the calescent dome, midnight air hits hot skin like a wall of ice. I started the truck and cranked up the heat for Chief, he had been sitting by the fire pit outside the ceremony. He parted ways when the men left the ceremony and climbed inside the truck.

"Ahh, *wash'te*," he smiled and settled into the heat. He told me he could not catch a chill or else his lungs would make him sick and he would die. I would keep him warm.

We rode up to a neighbor's house where the feed was taking place. The serious atmosphere of the sweat turned festive here with much food and laughter.

Someone at the door actually mentioned the story of the boy who led the horse around with his mind. The boy was now a man and he was standing next to me, walking in the door, ready to take part in the great feast ahead. He laughed with the mention of the memory. People here asked him what ever happened to that horse; he said he did not know. Nods were shared, comments were made, many who remembered said it was impressive the connection they had. Several women continued to chatter about the man, his horse, and the man's sister as they walked into the kitchen.

The women were cooking fry bread and *wojape (wujhs-ap-ee)*. They welcomed me with big smiles and a plate of hot food. Everyone watched me eat the fry bread like it was my most favorite food in the world, it was. I raved its praises and complimented the women who beamed with joy at my words and obvious delight. No Lakota woman ever brags about herself. She never says her work is good, but she smiles at an honest compliment and gladly soaks it in. Lakota fry bread seems to take all day to make, especially for a crowd like this after a sweat. Their efforts were delicious.

I was grateful for good family and good fry bread. Things couldn't get any better, I thought, but then they gave me a bowl of warm *wojape*. I was in heaven. Men and women alike broke into kind chuckles over how much I loved this comforting, sweet, chokecherry pudding treat. It made the fry bread even better, which had seemed impossible until the moment I dipped it in the *wojape*.

Back home after the sweat lodge ceremony, Chief said he knew my Indian name. He spoke the words in Lakota: "*Zintkala Ska Chikala Win*" and I was mesmerized with honor. He smiled. "It means 'Little White Bird.'"

The irony of my new Lakota name was subtle yet beautiful, just like our wedding day chosen for Thanksgiving. "It's perfect—I love it!"

"You are a member of the *Tiospaye* now. This means you are family. We will have a naming ceremony."

"Wonderful! Yes! Thank you!"

A few days later, I woke up and could hardly move. I had not been eating right. Due to middle of the night chores, I rarely captured more than two consecutive hours of sleep. I was rundown. I caught the worst flu I ever had. I was burning up and just about passing out; Chief saw I was truly sick. This wasn't your average I-don't-feel-so-good-pity-me sick, this was the I'm-dying-take-me-to-the-hospital-or-morgue type of sick. He told me to get up. He said we were going out, the sun was shining, the day was good.

I could barely walk. I kept leaning on the counter and door

frames; I was too weak to pack us any food or drink. Chief told me to get in the truck, we traveled for a while. I thought we might be going to the hospital until he veered off the road. We were going hunting.

My head hit the unlined, metal ceiling of his truck. I was a limp rag doll, too sick to ride out the bumpy terrain properly. Chief looked at me and said, "You are not on vacation here! This is the rest of your life!" He handed me leather gloves and wire cutters. "Cut the fence."

I slid out of the pickup, my body a sack of wet sand, heavy on my feet, dizzy in the sun and staggering. I went up to the rows of barbed wire and cut them, one on top of the other. They would snap back at my face and I'd have to catch them or risk getting severely hurt by the clusters of sharp points. Sometimes there were gates and I'd cut the wire handles off them, too; those cut tougher. Despite the gloves, my hands were sore and blistered.

We tore it up across the grasslands, ruining white farmer's fields, letting their cattle out. Chief thought it was funny, perhaps in a noble way, to sabotage their fences. He said, "This is Indian land. Rich White Man is putting up fences where they do not belong. He will learn he should not take what is not his." We were completely removed from any houses, buildings, or roads; nobody would find out what we had done for months.

Sweat stood out in large beads on my forehead, it ran down my face, chest, and back. I was so sick but I never complained once, I did not even utter a groan of misery. I just kept getting out and taking instruction. Hours passed by. I was dizzy and could not see. I couldn't stand up anymore. I lay slumped against the door.

Chief gave me another command. I tried with everything I had, but I could do no more than barely lift my hand a few inches above my lap. If he would have kicked me out the door and left me to die as punishment for my disobedience, I would have fallen in a heap like the carcass of a mule deer and died motionless in the prairie.

Chief put a nectarine in my hand. I looked at it and said, "Don't you want it?"

He held up a netted bag of them and smiled. "Eat."

The orange fruit was complimented by whole peanuts and jars of water. We ate a picnic lunch in the middle of the prairie. It was romantic because packing food was not man's work. I was touched he took care of us, impressed he would do my woman's work for me when I was too sick to do things right.

The food and thoughts of his love revived me somewhat. We tossed the peels and shells and carried onward. I spent the last ounces of my energy getting in and out of the truck, almost collapsing each time I tried to stand on my feet, hovering a moment away from fainting every time I had to open or close the door.

Cutting barbed wire was a blur for endless hours until sunset. As blood from my hands stained the soft leather, I smiled. I was touched he'd given me gloves to wear. I could tell he had thought ahead and did so much planning. I truly loved him. I was completely delirious with flu.

The day finally done, we got back on the road and headed for home. Chief looked at me and said, "You did good today."

I could have cried my joy was so great at his compliment. They were few.

CHAPTER NINETEEN:

Annie Mae

I healed. Life went on.

Chief was not one to tell me where we were going or why, so when we went to see two famous Indians one day, I was surprised by the visits. Dennis Banks, co-founder of AIM, was in town for a short time. We parked in front of the house.

"Stay in," Two Bear Paws growled as he jumped out of the car. I saw Dennis in the yard. Chief spoke with him and they headed around the side of the house. I could not tell the nature of their conversation; it was beginning to drizzle and Dennis had the hood of his sweatshirt up. The encounter was short-lived. Chief said we were headed onward to visit Russell Means.

Russell Means is a respected member of the Lakota family, an influential man in Indian society, also well-known in white society. Once a U.S. Presidential candidate, he is a prominent member of AIM, also an actor from the movie *Last of the Mohicans*.

I remembered Russell's name from the few words I read in Mary's book. Considering Chief's friendships with Dennis and Russell, I asked, "Chief, were you at the 1973 occupation?"

"Yes."

I was excited to hear his firsthand stories. "Wow! Were you at the church in Wounded Knee? What was it like on the inside for 71 days?"

"No. I was not at the church. I was defending The Knee. I was a G.O.O.N." He said this acronym as if it was supposed to strike terror inside me. I had no idea what he was talking about.

"Ha! I was young, maybe 22 years old. I did not know to trust AIM then. I learned and changed. I am now a chapter leader of AIM."

I shrugged to myself, still confused over things I did not understand. Chief talked about homemade bombs and bricks thrown through windows; I did not know my history.

During the 1973 occupation, Pine Ridge Reservation was a homegrown terrorist free-for-all. Chief had started out on the side of the Wounded Knee locals, the Guardians Of the Oglala Nation, the "goons." They were a radical group who were skeptical at best, outraged and violent most other times, over this influx of many different Indian tribes, half and quarter breeds, whites and other races from all walks of life who suddenly poured into their hometown and took siege.

Then and now, racism is rampant on the reservation. Oglala tend to stick with Oglala blood, but even they argue amongst themselves as to whose blood is more pure and who is entitled to what and how much. Many of the Oglala on the Pine Ridge Reservation look down on the nearby Rosebud Reservation as a dirty place full of nasty people you wouldn't touch with a stick—and the Brulé on Rosebud are a band of Lakota, too.

It is commonly said on Pine Ridge that Rosebud is a place full of booze and drugs, a lower class poverty than itself. During the time period of the occupation, the goons terrorized Rosebud, too.

If this is how some Lakota treat their Lakota neighbors, imagine how some Lakota might feel about absolute outsiders interfering on their home turf.

Chief may have started out as a goon, but he soon learned to believe in the power of AIM and became a close, respected friend of Russell Means.

Russell's home was lovely. It had a glorious view from the large kitchen window, which was less of a window and more of a wall made from glass. He had many bookcases full of actual books; I never saw that before on the reservation. The walls were decorated tastefully with quality Indian artifacts, Lakota and others. This was the cleanest, classiest, best home I had been to in a long while. It was even better than many White Man's homes.

Unlike Chief, Russell had eyes that looked directly at me. But they made me long for the non-gaze of Chief, for Russell's eyes were piercing fire and ice.

I do not mean any disrespect to this powerful man, he always spoke well around me. He offered hospitality with cool drinks in his home, there was ice and slices of fresh lemon in the tea.

Still, I felt a dangerous energy moving like electric eels slithering through the air around us; I could not explain it, but I was filled with fear. I had no reason to think this way. He was a dignified man, well-poised, well-spoken, good looking with long leather straps tied to the ends of his black braids. The eels sizzled a warning as he looked at me. Electric blue sparks snapped through my head. I was filled with a vision of a dead woman's body. I felt it easily could have been mine—what were the chances I could be lost forever in the massive acreage behind this house?

Chief introduced me as his wife. Russell scoffed, it was a sound similar to a short bark. They spoke in Lakota. Then, they shared a strange, dark laugh. Chief got serious and said no. It seemed to me that simple "no" saved my life this day. I felt like an enemy spared only by the friendship and respect these two men shared.

I am not sure why Chief and I were there, perhaps to show off his new wife, perhaps to let me know I should stay in line, listen, and silently obey. Chief and Russell spoke; conversation was not requested from me. We left rather quickly, which was a blessing.

At this point in time, I knew nothing of Annie Mae Aquash.

Chief and I often listened to a popular Buffy Sainte-Marie

song, "Bury My Heart at Wounded Knee." Buffy's voice sounds emotional enough, it could move anyone's heart to break, but this song held a deep meaning for me since we actually lived in Wounded Knee. Our hometown's refrain overpowered my ears so much that I never heard the other lyrics. All I knew was the song seemed to put Chief into a fighting mood. The only time he would ever look directly at me was when he would threaten me with the words "Annie Mae."

He did this often when we were alone together, Buffy song or not. He would growl her name if I was doing something wrong, or talking too much. When we were singing in the truck or car he would laugh her name in the middle of a high moment and kill it. He would become darkness personified and at odd times say her name in various tones to me, especially when we were traveling through the badlands. I knew nothing about any type of Indian history. I especially did not know the name Annie Mae, or even the story of Leonard Peltier. I had moved to the reservation with my heart, not my head.

One day, I finally asked, "Chief, why do you keep saying that name to me? Is she an ex-girlfriend or something? I have no idea who she is."

Chief laughed at the mention of "ex-girlfriend." He parked the truck at the casino; we were about to have my favorite, a buffet lunch. This was one of the few times he turned to face me. He looked into my eyes skeptically, searching. "Is it true you do not know who she is?"

I did not know the story; I held no fear of him in my heart. "Honestly, Chief. I really don't know who she is."

He examined my energy. I could feel him inside me, looking for Truth. He found it, nodded, got close to my face, bared his teeth and snapped, "Annie Mae!" as if it was the word "Boo!" and he was about to bite my nose. He laughed at his own joke. "Go," he gestured with his chin towards the casino. "Time to eat."

The fact I had no clue about her identity just made him say her name more often. I never flinched. I was not scared, just confused. Once, he elaborated a little in a cryptic way by telling me, "Many foolish young women come to the reservation. They think they can help. The badlands hold many bodies. Any day, you could be next. You will be dead and nobody will tell the secret. Your body will be thrown into the badlands. The police will never find you. Even if somebody did find you, no one will be able to identify you. Your body will be a pile of bones picked clean by the vultures and bleached by the sun."

I laughed, trusting Chief was kidding. If he was not, I believed he would protect me from such a fate, not cause it. I had only love for Chief. Nothing he could say would make me fear him or his people. Perhaps that is why I remained alive.

Years later when I was long gone from the rez, I heard the old Buffy Sainte-Marie song again. But now, my head was clear and I listened with my ears instead of only my heart. I was startled when she sang the name Annie Mae. I finally looked into who she was. Chills bigger than anything I ever felt in my life crawled up my spine.

Annie Mae was Mi'kmaq from Nova Scotia, Canada, an Indian activist who traveled to Pine Ridge and became a prominent woman during the occupation at Wounded Knee in 1973. Her death has remained unsolved for decades.

Chief Two Bear Paws would tell me stories about the occupation era, laugh and say, "We only had three real guns, a .22 and two BB guns, the rest of the guns were toys." He would chuckle condescendingly and say, "Indians held the U.S. government at bay with toy guns, that is how stupid the FBI and U.S. agents are."

It wasn't a toy gun that killed two FBI agents during the 1975 Pine Ridge Shootout after the occupation. Leonard Peltier, a Turtle Mountain Chippewa from North Dakota, was controversially accused of shooting the FBI agents. He is still serving two back to back life sentences. Chief and I never spoke of Leonard Peltier or his story.

Annie Mae Aquash was rumored to be an eye-witness in the shooting of the two FBI agents; however, it is not certain whose side she was on. All that is known is that she was murdered.

When Buffy's song "Bury My Heart at Wounded Knee" refers to Annie Mae, it sounds like the lyrics imply the FBI killed her. Come to find out, Mary also supports this belief in her book *Lakota Woman*. Believing the FBI killed Annie Mae is one viewpoint. To this day, there is still controversy and sides are split, even among Indians, as to what really happened.

Contrary to her death falling on the hands of the FBI, some claim Annie Mae turned traitor to her people and became an FBI informant. Even this viewpoint has several sides. There are a few who believe she saw Leonard Peltier kill the agents and she ratted him out to the FBI.

Others believe Leonard Peltier is not to blame and Annie Mae's death protected the elite men who really committed the crime of killing the FBI agents. This viewpoint claims these elite men set Leonard up to take the fall and Annie Mae knew the truth of Leonard's innocence as well as the guilt of the men setting him up. Supporters of this idea insist the orders to kill Annie Mae came from the higher powers of AIM.

She never had a chance to set the record straight. Her body was found one winter's day in a remote corner of the reservation. She was said to have perished from the cold. Both her hands were cut from her body. Later, the bullet near her brain was discovered. She had been shot execution style from the lower base of her head through to her eye. She was thirty years old when she died. Thirty more years passed with her murder remaining a mystery.

Just recently, decades after Annie Mae's death, Russell Means identified two Indian men he claimed were involved in her murder. The last man's sentence was issued in 2010.

At the time of final edit for this book, I must add that Russell Means passed away from natural causes on October 22, 2012. At his twelve hour long service on day one of his four day ceremony, a family member told the crowd Russell always said his body was to be cremated so scientists won't be able to dig him up and have the cops put more criminal charges on him. We may never know the secrets he took with him to the spirit world.

After visiting Russell Means and Dennis Banks, Chief and I stopped by a garage belonging to another man, he looked like a white man to me. Chief asked me for a hundred and fifty dollars, I gave it to him. He went into the garage, spoke with the white man, and bought his saddle back. "I made this," he said as he set it in my lap.

It was beautiful, thick leather with detailed stitching. I held the saddle and admired his work. I was sorry he had to hoc it in the past, but happy we could buy back a bit of his pride in the present. It was a fine quality saddle and someone was sure to use it for the upcoming Big Foot ride.

CHAPTER TWENTY:

Wedding

Every day we awoke to a new adventure. We never lay around and were lazy. Chief got a government check, we had government issued food rations, we had no hourly jobs, but we worked harder than I ever have for anyone else. We worked for the family. We worked for survival.

We spent a lot of time searching for trees, splitting wood, and stacking it beside the house. Some extra money could be made by selling wood on the reservation, but we usually gave it away to older relatives who depended on it for their life but could not afford it.

Chief told me to use his log splitter; I was delighted to have such a tomboy task. I'd crack the hunks of wood with the machine and stack the stove-sized pieces into piles. My red and black wool hunting coat kept me warm against the backdrop of frosted rolling prairie hills embraced by an endless afternoon sky, a canvas of purple and pink broken by long white clouds. I was happy to work in such a beautiful setting.

I liked that the work mattered; it wasn't 9-5 in a stuffy office cubicle. This work was much harder and paid far less than a city desk job, but I welcomed it because it meant life for ourselves and for those we loved.

We were protecting our family from the cold that prowled on the edge of the horizon, stalking, waiting for the moment to move in and make its kill. It would find easy prey on the reservation each winter due to lack of proper housing and hypothermia. Fire would keep the beast at bay until the flame died out and the sparse reservation trees were no more.

Chief reminded me often that hunting and scouting for

wood were not woman's work. While he currently allowed me to accompany him on these outings, he pointed out that my activities would change once I had his baby and I would assume the full-time woman's role of keeping the home. He told me once the baby was born, I would wear a traditional Lakota cradleboard strapped to my back and my time would be spent solely in the kitchen. I found his words to be a bit overly dramatic, since I was certain he'd allow me to spend some time in the laundry room as well.

I was hesitant about having his baby if it meant less time with him. I enjoyed being by his side and I enjoyed the chores of the man's role so much more than raising children and cooking.

"You will get used to it," Chief said. "It is woman's work. It is the right way. It will happen sooner than you think." I wasn't sure how it could happen if we weren't sleeping together.

My mother laughed when I told her what Chief had said. She teased me with the image of a baby in a cradleboard hanging from the kitchen wall while I cooked for all the men returning from the hunt. She reminded me I would become used up once I had a child; I would have to listen to him and his new woman in our bedroom while I did chores, or got raped by his friends. This was the second time I heard her cautionary tale, but her words never ceased to haunt me. I needed Chief to tell me she was wrong. I wanted to hear him say he loved me. I wanted him to tell me our marriage would be sacred and monogamous.

When I told him what my mother had said, he was calm as if I had not spoken, there was nothing to reassure or comfort me. If her vision were false, he would have gotten angry, as he always did when he disagreed. He was quiet because he knew her words were too accurate to deny. He had just been called out for what he is. His solution was to hang up on my mother whenever she called the house. He would never even tell me she had called. He didn't want me hearing any more truths from her.

Chief said we should start working on the wedding. Thanksgiving Day was drawing near.

Two Bear Paws told me Leonard Crow Dog was a powerful medicine man and he would head the ceremony. He would marry us in the traditional Lakota way. A Lakota marriage is forever. Chief had been married three times before, he openly told me this himself, but he claimed they were not real because they had not been traditional Lakota weddings.

"Leonard Crow Dog will host the ceremony. We will stand before him and make a vow to *Tunkashila*. We will vow to be husband and wife. Our hands will be bound together with prayer ties, we will smoke the sacred pipe.

"A Lakota marriage is forever. There is no way out, not like White Man's way. White Man's way is only paper. White Man's paper holds only lies. This is why White Man's marriage does not last. Lakota marriage is strong.

"In our marriage we will give our heart to each other. It is a marriage of truth and spirit. It is forever. We do not need paper full of White Man's lies to be married in the Lakota way. All we need is our word of honor."

It was romantic to hear Chief speak so strongly about our union. A weak part of me still wanted that piece of paper, but I trusted his judgment. The traditional Lakota ceremony would be beautiful, it would have so much meaning. I smiled with love in my eyes. "Yes, that sounds perfect, Chief, I want that, too. Everything sounds wonderful. I like your idea about Leonard Crow Dog hosting the ceremony. That makes me happy and it feels right. Even in my white culture, I have heard of him. It would be an honor to have him marry us.

"Is he related to Mary Crow Dog?"

Chief hesitated. "Yes, she is his wife." (I learned much later they were divorced, but he spoke as if they were presently married.)

"Is she still alive?"

There was a longer pause. Chief begrudgingly said, "She is alive." (At the time, this was true. As this book was set to print, news came my way that Mary has died. February 27, 2013 marks the 40th anniversary of the 1973 Wounded Knee. A short time before this historical event, Mary moved on to the Spirit world.)

"Can we see her when we see Leonard?"

Chief pressed his lips together. "She should be around. They do not live far away. They live in Rosebud." He eyed me suspiciously, "How do you know Mary?"

"Because of her book, *Lakota Woman*. It changed my life and brought me here to the reservation. Without Mary and her book, I would not be standing here or marrying you. I never would have heard the voices of the Ancestors call to me because I never would have come to Wounded Knee.

"I appreciate my life here with you. I love you and I am proud to marry you. It would be an honor to meet Mary and thank her for bringing me here and giving me the opportunity to share this life with you."

He frowned. "Many true Lakota do not like her much anymore. After she wrote that book she forgot who she is, she changed. She needs a good beating to remember her place."

Wanting to believe he was kidding, I laughed and brushed his words away. I hadn't yet learned that some things should be treated as foreshadowing instead of dismissed as humor.

Shortly after our conversation, about two hours later, Chief told me Leonard Crow Dog was unavailable to host our wedding ceremony as he was away on a trip.

"We could wait for him to come back," I suggested. "I would prefer to wait as long as it took, even if it meant choosing a day other than Thanksgiving for our wedding day. Our wedding is forever. I would really like Leonard Crow Dog to host our ceremony. It is important to me."

"He will be away for a long time. We cannot wait. It is too

late, I already asked someone else to host the ceremony. He is a fellow *Tiospaye* member."

Tiospaye (tee-yosch-pie-yayh) denotes members of extended family lineage; it is the core structure of Lakota self-government, a tradition from the old ways. Usually the word is said in conjunction with a prominent ancestor from the family blood line.

I asked him who the man was. Chief laughed and said, "He thinks he is chief."

Thinks He Is Chief was coming over to discuss the seriousness of a Lakota marriage with me, to be sure I was ready for such a forever commitment. Chief told me how important this meeting was. He cleared everyone out of the house. He instructed me on how to be a perfect Lakota hostess. He said I should bring cool drinks with ice. I've noticed ice in a glass on the rez always brings "ooohs" and "ahhs" from the receiver, ice makes the guest feel like royalty. He told me to light a sage bundle and smudge myself and the room. I was then to lay the lit sage on the shell which sat on the table by the door. This would cleanse the room and purify us and our words.

Thinks He Is Chief entered the house and smudged himself with the sage bundle, he smudged the chair before he sat. He nodded his thanks for the cool drink and smiled at the ice, he poked it. He looked at Chief and laughed. He was impressed. He praised Chief for coaching me so well in the old ways so fast.

Thinks He Is Chief was a nice Lakota elder, big in stature, yet gentle in his energy. He spoke to me as if I were a real human being and not just a woman. This was very different from what I was used to. Chief always looked away from me when he spoke to me. This was not some Lakota form of respect for a new wife; he just didn't like looking at me. Thinks He Is Chief was different. He always met my gaze and his eyes showed he had a kind heart. The comment Chief made about this man's delusions of Chiefhood made perfect sense when I learned Thinks He Is Chief was the current husband of one of Chief's ex-wives.

The kitchen table was lit by soft candlelight; this was a quiet, formal time with no interruptions. I sat and listened with solemn sincerity. I was told a Lakota wedding is serious, it means the rest of my life with no getting out. I would need to learn many things and have many more lessons, this meeting was just an introduction.

Thinks He Is Chief said it is not customary for a woman to answer these questions in this first meeting. He said I should take time to think it over, be quiet and meditate, listen to my heart, seek counsel in the trees and sky. Could I be a good Lakota wife? Was I ready for this lifelong commitment? Would I pledge to learn all I could about the old ways and adhere to those traditions? I would have one chance to speak my answer, yes or no, at our next meeting. He would come back for my answer when Chief Two Bear Paws called for him. He left me to my thoughts.

My heart did not leap or flutter, instead I found it growing heavy. If it had been Leonard Crow Dog before me asking these questions, I know without hesitation all my answers would have been a resounding yes. But Chief had changed things that mattered to me without asking. Also, I knew it was a petty thing, but I couldn't shake the fact the man about to marry us was currently married to a wife Chief once had. That seemed like bad karma for our wedding.

Nothing against Thinks He Is Chief, I liked him; I just really wanted Leonard Crow Dog to host the ceremony with all my heart. This wedding was forever, you only get one of those. It's like when I got baptized in the lake by my friend, Reverend Rose Johnston. My baptism and my forever marriage, these are milestones in life that only happen once. They are a pledging of one's soul, to God, to Chief; yes, I wanted the hosts of these ceremonies to be the right ones.

About a month before my baptism, Rose told me the Bishop of the Diocese of Maine was going to be at our church for Easter. It would be a rare blessing to be baptized by the bishop on this holiday; Rose suggested we move the date of my baptism up. I was afraid to refuse the bishop; it was a great honor, but I did refuse, albeit gently. My heart remained with Rose. I really wanted her to host the ceremony on the lake, just as I really wanted Leonard Crow Dog for our wedding; it meant a lot to me.

I thought about everything for meditative moments in between chores the next day. I knew I had to think fast because the first meeting had been sudden. I was certain Chief would call Thinks He Is Chief back for the next meeting before the sun set tomorrow.

I felt our wedding was a situation that involved me in a very intimate and personal way. What bothered me most of all was how Chief made choices for me without discussing anything with me first. I could have made peace in my heart with not having Leonard Crow Dog host our ceremony if Chief had only talked to me first, if he would have involved me in the decision before he went out on his own and secured someone else so fast. I was not sure I wanted to be married forever to someone who could do that.

If this was forever, I should feel it in my heart without a doubt, like I used to, just the day before yesterday. I hoped there was a way to set things right. Maybe Chief could show me he valued my feelings and find a way to listen if I spoke my heart. I hoped we could get Leonard Crow Dog back, but if that was not possible, then maybe Chief could at least say he's sorry for not involving me in the plans as they were being made.

Either of these outcomes would set things right in my heart and I could say yes to forever honestly.

I decided to speak to Chief, softly and respectfully. I came to him in an official way, one that felt Lakota and right to me. I stood a few feet away from him and tipped my head, I asked if I could sit with him to speak. He nodded. We sat together in a space of peace, taking a moment to breathe and adjust to each other's energy before speaking.

Well, that's what I was doing anyway. Chief was reading the paper.

I asked if it were possible to have Leonard Crow Dog host the ceremony as we originally planned. Chief did not explode with rage at my question; it appeared we were having a real conversation.

He said he had called Leonard Crow Dog's house and learned he was back from his trip. However, it was too late to ask him now, because we already had the first meeting with Thinks He Is Chief. Chief said this meeting sealed him as our host.

The on/off situation with Leonard Crow Dog and the meeting with Thinks He is Chief had all happened within the span of a single day, and now, suddenly, Leonard Crow Dog was back from his trip. I was silent. I waited for Chief to say something else. Say, perhaps the apology that would mend things between us.

He continued reading the paper. I bowed my head to thank him for the conversation. I backed away and said no more as there was nothing else I could do. I started to make dinner.

The question I pondered into the night was not found on the list Thinks He Is Chief had given me. Could I live forever with a man who did not respect me, no matter how much I loved him?

I can honestly say, if Leonard Crow Dog had not been out of town, or if Chief hadn't resented my interest in Mary so much, I would be married to Chief, we'd have a few kids, and I'd still be on the reservation. Hopefully, I would still be alive.

We had dinner, we went to bed. The moon was almost full; I traced my fingers in the stardust patterns on the wall. I told Chief I wanted to go home and get my birds and belongings before the wedding. He said he'd come with me. I was afraid of that. I promised him if he let me go, I'd come back.

It would have been another broken promise made by White Man to the Indians because my plan was to run like hell.

CHAPTER TWENTY-ONE:

Honeymoon

Chief Two Bear Paws said he needed to stay with me; he claimed his magic and power over women only worked if he was next to them. We needed to stay together. We could take his new car. Plus, he told me his dream has always been to see Niagara Falls. He wanted to stop there on our way to Maine.

I thought about my options if we stayed right here. I could say no to the wedding or I could pretend my heart said yes and go through with it. It seemed, either way I died. Going to Niagara Falls grew in appeal. I agreed.

Before we left for the East, Chief had me rent a storage unit in the middle of some grassland in Nebraska. We stored his best saddles like the one he made himself, the rifle, hides, furs, anything of great value. I was not sure why we were doing this, but I did not ask, I just paid the bill. "Pay it all," he said and waved his hand. It was only three hundred dollars for an entire year for the large unit.

Putting his valuables into remote, locked storage ended up being a wise decision. When Chief arrived back home ten days later, he found his bedroom door kicked in. The locks had been bypassed by breaking the door free from its hinges. The Lakota way of life is one of honor, respect for self, others, nature. To the Lakota, generosity is a virtue. They share what they have, they do not steal, and they never needed locks in the old days.

Everything left of value in Chief's bedroom was gone. All the star quilts, the two lesser quality saddles not locked in the storage unit, the saddle pads, blankets, bridles, ropes, the Lakota crafts and supplies, the clock radio, CDs, it was all stolen and sold for what little cash it would bring. Chief's face looked so sad when he told me the one who broke in and took it all was his own son.

It was the saddest, most broken moment I witnessed in Chief's life. The happiest moment was when he finally lived his dream and stood at Niagara Falls. His smile rivaled the sun in the double rainbows that danced in the mist.

We had to pay quite the price to get there. I knew the best side of the falls was in Canada, I had been there a few times. I should have learned from Big Biker's failed strategy of heading up through Canada to go west, that I should not head up through Canada to go east. But I thought it was the shortest way to the best side of the Falls.

Continuing my bad luck streak with Canada, Chief and I were pulled aside at the border crossing. We had to park the car and let it be searched while we waited for interrogation in separate glass rooms. At that point in time, one did not need a passport to get into Canada, just a driver's license and a plausible story. And no suspicious criminal record. Which left only one of us not guilty.

They brought us back together in the same room for the verdict. "You can come into the country; *you* are allowed." The uppity custom's woman looked at a print-out report on my identity and handed me back my license. "However, *you*, Sir . . . you are not welcome in Canada. You have a criminal history. Additionally, your ID does not match the names you have been using. We cannot let you in."

"But I can't leave him here!" The customs agent was offended by my outburst. "We are trying to get to Niagara Falls and this is the shortest way to the best side."

"You will have to go around, then."

"But—"

The woman shook her head. "There is no discussion. Get back in your car and leave."

On the way to the car, Chief said, "We are only safe on the reservation. I do not trust White Man's police. They make up lies to trap me. It is not good here. We need to get out. Now."

There were officers in uniform surrounding our car. They saw us and yelled, "Get down on the ground!"

"What?" I said, frozen in place with confusion.

"Down, knees, now," Chief understood their orders and whispered to me. He obviously knew this procedure better than I did. I couldn't understand the officer's instructions; I was only used to obeying Chief's barked orders. Plus, I was an 'A' student who had never been in any trouble before. I dropped to my knees as Chief Two Bear Paws instructed. I copied him and put my hands behind my head.

A woman and a man in dark blue uniforms held us at gun point. The world was spinning around me so fast, I kept thinking, "I'm a good girl, this can't be happening. My dad is going to be so mad at me!"

"Look what we found here." She held out a small package, taunting. "We found drugs in your car, how about that! You both are going away for a long time. Explain *this*."

She shoved something in front of my nose, but all I could see was the silver shine of her handcuffs. I forced myself to focus on the package in her hands. Clarity came to me. I recognized it. It was the black pouch the doctor had given Chief at the V.A. hospital.

"It's medicine."

"Right, 'medicine,' that's what they all say. There are *needles* in here and vials of liquid! What are you shooting up?" She quickly turned to accuse Chief when she asked this.

The warrior within me surfaced as I went to Chief's defense. "He's not shooting up anything!" I would not allow white people to question the honor of this highly respected elder. "Don't talk to him like that! It's his medicine. The doctor gave it to him."

She laughed sarcastically and turned her attention on me. "Okay, then, if it's 'medicine,' tell me what it's for."

My shyness took away my thunder. "Um, you know, sex,"

I whispered the last word to keep it private between us women.
"What?!" She read the tiny words on the back side of the
vial. "There are needles here! Stand up."

I stood while Chief remained kneeling.

"Tell me—and him—" she gestured towards the male cop,
still in position, holding us at gun point, "tell us what it's for.
Say it loud and clear so we can understand you."

I got my strength back. In my mind I was a boy Indian,
earning my warrior's eagle feather, touching the enemy on the
field of battle with my coup stick and living to tell the tale. Or
not. Either way, I would stand tall and strong. It was a good
day to die. "It is for erectile dysfunction. He takes the needle
and shoots the liquid into his penis to make it hard so we can
have sex."

The woman nodded to the armed man. He put his gun
away. "Ok, stand up." Chief stood next to me, she got right in
his face. "You're lucky to have a girl like her." She looked at
me and waved her hand. "Get back in the car and get out of
here now, both of you."

She gave the black pouch back to me and we drove away.
It felt good to know I stood strong in my love for Chief, but I
was shaken we had come so close to being arrested. I was
humiliated for what I had to reveal about him. The words had
bounced off the cement walls around us when I spoke, their
echo still haunted me. I could not tell if Chief was proud or
offended; we never spoke of it.

Silent for much of the ride, we arrived at Niagara Falls. We
took a Maid of the Mist boat ride up close to the falls. Luckily,
there is a boat that stays on the U.S. side, so crossing the
border wasn't necessary.

We walked up a wooden, winding staircase that took us
behind the falls. I was listening to the white tour guide when
Chief disappeared. I spotted him standing with a man over in
the corner of the platform, away from the crowd. He was
talking nose to nose with an Indian employee who ranked

lower than the white tour guide. This man's job was silently pulling up the rear, watching footsteps of tourists, hardly noticed. Walks Softly and Two Bear Paws were instant buddies, arms around each other, whispering and laughing. I went up to Chief and his new friend, Chief introduced me as his wife. Walks Softly shook my hand and invited us to his home after work to have dinner with his wife and family. Chief accepted.

As we left the platform, Chief said to me, "The White Man took his land, too. Look around you, this belongs to his people."

We spent the rest of the afternoon together by the falls, wrapped in blankets and looking like quite the Indian couple. Other tourists loved us and posed beside us for photos as if we were also an attraction here at the Falls.

This was the happiest and most in love Chief and I ever were. He kissed me on the lips briefly for the first time in front of the falls, he put his arm around me once when we posed for a photo. It was the closest intimately we had been since the rough night long ago in Maine. We stood next to each other and watched the water. It felt like our honeymoon.

Like Pine Ridge, Walks Softly's reservation was also very flat and desolate; White Man had obviously taken the best part of the land here, too, the falls, for himself and left the Indian with the scraps. Unlike Pine Ridge, however, this place was not a third-world country. The Indian families here had real houses with insulated walls, heat, and running water.

Inside Walks Softly's home, dreamcatchers spun in the sunbeams, pretty, delicate china plates were displayed on shelves and lined the walls beneath the ceiling. I loved the man's wife and children; there were toys and small screams of laughter all around my knees.

Walks Softly worked for minimum wage on his sacred land, swallowing his pride and feelings every day on the job in order to support his family in this small reservation house. It must have killed him inside every day to watch yellow, white, and black man gloat over the beauty of the stolen Red Man's land. Their sacred water had become a tourist attraction like the Lakota's Black Hills had become Mount Rushmore.

Chief bonded so intently with these people, it was magic to see. The wife gave us food while Chief spun his stories, wrapping us all in his mystery. It is not often a greatly respected elder comes from two thousand miles away, even the children quieted to sit on laps and listen.

Chief admired the thick braids of sweet grass drying in the wife's kitchen. She gave him some as a gift; they were still green, fragrant, long, and gorgeous. He told her they did not have grass like this in South Dakota. She was shocked and sad when he said they could not hold their ceremonies in the proper traditions as there was no sweet grass left on the land around them. He promised to mail her some white sage in return when we arrived back home. He often reminded me we needed to send the sage, but it was one of those things that slipped through the cracks. It really tortured him when I did not follow through on his commitment to mail it.

From New York all the way to Maine, Chief would look out the window, point and say, "What is the name?" He was referring to a mountain, a valley, a river, even a small hill that seemed insignificant to me.

"I have no idea, Chief."

Nature's landmarks would capture his gaze as we passed by. He would point until each one was out of sight, acknowledging it as if deciding what name it should have, if it were up to him. Not too long after, another sight would capture his attention. "What is the name?" he would ask again.

"I don't think these things have names, Chief. People here are more interested in what the road is called. The name of the road tells us where we are or where we are going. If the mountain or river is big enough, its name will be on a sign. Like this river we are driving over now, its name is right there on that brown sign. Otherwise, I just don't know the names of the things you ask, I am sorry."

He read the sign, it was an Indian name, he spoke the name of the river as if it were a prayer. As we traveled the paved road across the river, he told me which tribe had named the water and what its Indian name meant in English. He spoke softly as he watched the water, "Everything has a name. It is up to you to ask and learn."

We got back to Old Town early one frosted morning. As we drove down the local streets, Chief suddenly had a grin wide enough to be the morning sun. "Go there." He pointed to a handwritten sign nailed to a post:

Hunter's Breakfast Today
4:00 a.m. - 7:00 a.m.
$5.00

I pulled over and paid the ten dollars.

A cold fog clung to crystallized blades of grass, it enfolded us in a cloak, then slipped from our shoulders as we entered the large, heated tent. There were eggs, biscuits, coffee, and piles of assorted meats. Chief helped himself to a big plate of food and walked over to a local man wearing a florescent orange and black camo jacket. "I am a hunter, too. A warrior of my People," Chief said. The white man really didn't care.

Maybe that's because there is racism here, too, against the Penobscot Indians. I explained this to Chief, he became eager to visit their reservation. It was within walking distance, just down the street and across the short bridge on Indian Island. I remembered driving past it last winter. I couldn't forget the animal carcasses I saw tossed onto the frozen water around the reservation, the blood seeping out into a red circle, staining the snow.

There are less than 600 Indians on this island part of the reservation, which covers about twenty square miles of land, most of it under water. More than 2,000 Penobscot live off the reservation in Maine. Chief was well met with a Penobscot elder at the museum on Indian Island who was delighted to meet Chief Two Bear Paws, a respected elder who traveled so many miles. They shared stories, he gave Chief a T-shirt adorned with a bright drawing of a turtle.

While the men talked, I examined Penobscot cultural items on display in glass cases. There were many artisan baskets, turtle shells, and bowls made from hollowed out tree burls. These items were not similar to the Lakota work I had seen; their cultures are different, as well as the fact the natural elements of Maine are almost opposite those of South Dakota. Historically, tribes made things from what was readily available in their areas. This is why wampum shells and glass beads from France and Italy were something the White Man could bargain with so easily when taking Indian land.

From my white public education, I was led to believe Indians must be dumb for thinking shells were money and they deserved to lose whatever they had lost. Now I see, shells were not money; Indians had no need for even the concept of standardized money. Shells were something sacred with different meanings, something to adorn regalia, something to be used in dance and ceremonies. Now, when I look into glass cases in White Man's museums, I see so much more than I did before. And my eye always has a tear.

We didn't stay long on Penobscot land. Our plans had a sense of urgency, I felt Chief was rushing us back to South Dakota. We had picked up my parrots and fish so quickly I hardly realized it happened. He also convinced me to spend $1,800 to rent a U-Haul truck and car trailer.

I needed to slow it down a moment and load my Harley into my pickup bed. I got two sturdy boards from the shed and braced them on the open tailgate. Chief watched me, he looked angry. I guess he thought it was wrong for his wife to have her own ideas and enjoy something outside Lakota traditions, like motorcycle riding. Or perhaps he was upset because I preferred this to being barefoot and pregnant in the kitchen. Literally. Well, to be fair, that expectation is not completely true, they might have given me some beaded moccasins to wear.

I moved the Harley into position. I started her up and feathered the clutch; we began our ascent. Chief suddenly stepped in too close, blocking my path. I think he did it just to spook me and throw me off; it worked. I had to tip the bike to avoid hitting his chest with the handlebars and I stalled it. The bike's front tire was up on the tailgate as the back tire slipped. One board fell, the engine was held up by the other board and every ounce of strength I had. I couldn't take my hands off either handlebar to reach the key start on the lower left side of the gas tank. In my mind's eye, my beautiful bike was already shattered on the pavement.

"C'mon, help me, please! I'm going to drop it!"

Chief folded his arms and watched. He smiled.

The new downstairs neighbor heard my struggles and ran outside to assist. He was a lanky, college kid hippie with no muscle tone, about 20 years old. He jumped up into the truck bed and gently pulled the bike forward. We rolled it together without dropping it, the task very easy with an extra set of hands. The boy looked over at Chief as if to say, "And what's your problem, buddy?" I thanked him and let him know he saved the day. He said sure, no problem. He gave Chief one last look, shook his head in disgust, and went back into his apartment.

I straddled the bike and held it upright with my thighs as I secured both handlebars above the front forks with ratchet strap tie downs, refusing to let go of who I am, a Harley girl. I did all the work, balancing and strapping it low, without even a finger's worth of help from Chief. All he did was stand there with his arms folded across his chest, hoping to watch me fail.

After I was done and the Harley was secure, I asked, "Why didn't you help me? I could have lost it back there."

"Bad heart. Lifting too much weight will kill me." Lifting

the dead weight of the nearly 300 pound buck we shot from the ground up into his truck felt heavier than this. That was lifting, this was rolling. Deer don't have wheels.

And it wouldn't have been heavy to help untangle a ratchet strap or hand me a hook. Perhaps Chief saw I didn't buy his story. He walked away to the U-Haul truck and sat in the driver's seat, ready to leave. I put the parrots and fish into the warm cab of my truck and we were ready to roll. I would follow Chief. He would drive the U-Haul with my stuff, trailing his car behind him.

We didn't get far that first day. I remember lying in bed that night wondering why I just wasted ninety dollars on a hotel room in Bangor, Maine when we could have stayed for free in my apartment. Chief said not to worry about it. We had to get out of there in case the landlord or someone I knew came by looking for me. I couldn't figure out what he was so afraid of; now I know he needed to keep me away from any person who might have talked some sense into me.

We had literally thrown the contents of my apartment into the U-Haul truck. It was a mess, worse than a ravaged rummage sale. Chief was excited about the big screen TV Big Biker had recently given me. It was like Chief hit the jackpot. He labeled each thing in his mind, assessed a value, and chose a future owner. He kept saying what great gifts my things would make for his family and friends at our wedding ceremony.

I'm not a Lakota expert, I can only speak from my personal experience. If Chief had communicated better with me, it would have made a huge difference in my perspective. I am sure there are other examples like this in my story; I am just unaware because he did not express himself well with words. I learned much later the Lakota celebrate a custom called the "giveaway."

The giveaway is tradition at certain powwows or marriage ceremonies, things are given away to show gratitude. The happy Lakota wedding couple does not stand there and demand "give me more" as is custom in materialistic white culture with the concept of wedding gifts. Instead, the Lakota couple says "thank you" and *they* give.

The greater the giveaway, the more appreciation they show for their life and the good that has happened. They are thankful for the blessing of their union and for the support of family and community members. It takes time to make the crafts and time to accumulate the possessions in one's life—to give them away is an honor.

I wish Chief had explained this to me, it would have shown how much he loved me and was grateful to *Tunkashila* for our love, and to our *Tiospaye* and Lakota community for their help and support. If he told me this custom, I would have changed my view and smiled with an honest heart when I gave my things away. As it was, I did not understand. To me, a white person, he seemed greedy like he'd won the lottery with all my possessions and I resented him for it.

I took comfort in knowing no matter what I lost, I would always have my parrots and fish. Some might say it was stupid to take my birds and my fish in his big, fancy jar. My commitment to my little friends must have appeared foolish and abnormal to Chief. Animals on the reservation are there for survival of man, for food, clothing, tools or work, not love and companionship. There's not enough food or money to support even human babies, a "pet" is not a concept they possess, except for the allowance Chief made for his mother's tiny dog.

Chief did not understand that my birds, even my fish, were my children to me. I made a lifelong promise that is not optional. I do not take on the responsibility of caring for a life lightly.

Before Blue Fish, I had a red Siamese fighting fish named Red Fish who outlived his species' maximum life expectancy by three years. I read all I could on their natural habitat and proper care in captivity. I even made up some of my own ideas,

I gave him toys and played games with him.

Red Fish recognized me and would come to me like a dog. Even at eight years old, he would see me coming from the other side of the room, wag his tail and jump out of the water. He would then hold still right at the surface and let me gently pet him. He would eat out of my hand. It was no gimmick or coincidence. He'd swim around and come back to my fingertip out of his own free will, peacefully enjoying the company.

Friends witnessed this and were amazed. They would try it and he would sink to the bottom and hide under a plant leaf. As soon as it was my finger in the water, he'd swim right back to the top and over to me. When he died of old age, I cried so hard I was late for work. I walked down to the river, said a prayer, and put his body on a leaf. I watched the sun sparkle on the ripples around him as he drifted away. Blue Fish was the replacement for Red Fish; I expected him to surpass his life expectancy, too.

Every night I would bring Blue Fish into the hotel with the birds so he would not get cold. Every morning I'd load them back up again. At the rest area in Connecticut, I told Chief we had to stop to meet my family for the goodbye lunch. He pressed his lips together. He let me lead the way to the buffet.

It was a painful blur. I was arrogant and certain in my choices. Chief ran the conversation at the table and I barely got a word in to anyone. My family was polite and kind to him. I was unaware their exhibit of proper manners was forced.

My mother took photos in the parking lot; she was all smiles and sweetness. The last thing she whispered to me revealed her true feelings. "No matter how hard you try, you will never be an Indian to them. They will always see you as white and you will never be accepted. *We* are your family. I love you. Don't go."

On the phone later, my father told me he did not like the way Chief looked at him. He felt Chief despised him, even wanted to kill him, because he was the White Man, the enemy.

He said Chief never spoke a direct word to him the entire time, all my father received were hateful glares. My father is a man of pure logic, he is not one to talk "hippie" about vibes and energy, what he felt from Chief must have been very strong for him to say such a thing.

Only my bravest sister showed up to face the pain and her reaction was the most heart-breaking of all. Amandah was smiling and supportive for the entire meal; she laughed softly if a joke was made and added agreement when I expected it. She excused herself to the restroom after the meal. I noticed she had been gone too long and I went to find her.

The restroom was empty. I looked around, confused as to where she had gone. The stall on the far end was closed, I heard a soft sobbing. I went into the stall next to her.

"Hey, Amandah, what's going on? You ok?" My sister was not quick with tears. I had never seen her cry.

She sniffed and tried to stifle her sadness. "I-I'm fine. You can go back and eat dessert. I'll just be a m-minute."

"Hey, come on. I can tell you're upset. What's up?"

"I don't want you to see me like this. So I won't come out. But if you really want to know, I don't want you to go. I thought you'd stay here with us. When you lived in Maine you said you were moving back home to Connecticut after college. I don't know why you are running away to South Dakota. I was looking forward to having you here as my sister and friend. I wanted to do fun things with you. And now you are gone. I will never see you again. I don't know how all this happened so fast."

"It's my right to make choices in my life how I see fit. I never make any decision thinking, 'Oh, this will really hurt so-and-so,' or 'yeah, this will make them angry.' I am not malicious in my behavior. I always work for the side of good and try to do the right thing. I need to move out to South Dakota. It is my life's calling to help these people. If you really were my sister and friend, you'd support me and stop being so selfish."

She cried harder; I walked away. Chief nodded; it was time to go.

On the road, as my parents and Amandah exited the highway, I almost thought I would follow and stay. But I loved Chief, even if he did not respect my feelings. The Lakota were my family and the rez was my home. My heart longed to be back there. Something deep inside me knew I had treated my sister rotten, but I could not tap into those emotions.

All I saw was the big sky of South Dakota. I saw myself standing on a hill overlooking the reservation, smiling as the motorcycles rolled in for our Wounded Knee Memorial Ride in August. I saw the Lakota Nation getting stronger; they were no longer starving and freezing, they were proud. They told their history with their own words. They had their honor back. They had their pride back. I could even see it working out so, someday, they would get their stolen Black Hills back.

This vision overpowered me, it was all I wanted. All I could see. I threw my birth family away so easily. I only felt a slight tugging in my heart as I watched them drift farther down their exit ramp. I continued heading straight down the highway and west towards my future.

It was my destiny to follow Chief. I would marry him and help our people help themselves with the motorcycle ride. He called me his wife, although the ceremony had not happened. He called me his wife, although he never touched me or looked at me or treated me as if I were a human being with feelings. I was still too hairy, too skinny, or too white for Chief to show me even the slightest affection.

This trip had given us the privacy we needed to work on an intimate relationship, but we made no progress. We had been alone together for seven nights and nothing had improved. I would take a shower and walk past him without a stitch on my body; he would never even take his eyes off the television.

There might be some Lakota perspective on modesty to

explain his behavior, similar to my misunderstanding of the giveaway, but he never offered me any conversation. Every time I would try to speak, no matter what the topic, no matter how sweet or neutral or nice my tone, even when my body was fully clothed, he would wave my words away, telling me to shut up. I don't believe that was a cultural misunderstanding. Like the sacred buffalo skulls that hung upon the walls at home on the reservation, he truly seemed to not like me no matter how hard I tried to show him love. Our nights together were silent; our daytime breaks from driving were the same.

The day before Thanksgiving, over coffee at a Chicago service plaza table, I finally had enough. "You treat me so badly. Why?"

Chief repeated his usual "White Man has wronged me" spiel. His passion and anger were so great it was hard to hear the facts through the pain. He spoke at length of all these things:

The Fort Laramie treaty of 1851 involved an actual fort which was built on Indian land without permission; the threat of war loomed in the air. White miners wanted to survive crossing the Oregon Trail on their way to California for gold. The Fort Laramie Treaty of 1851 was drafted, a treaty in which the Indians agreed to allow safe passage for these outsiders in return for U.S. government payments of $50,000 for fifty years. The U.S. government broke the treaty when the duration of payments was reduced to ten years, with only interest on the money being paid.

White travelers became white settlers, their presence chased away the game. The trespassers claimed land that was not theirs, set up fences for the cattle they brought with them, and, in an effort to eradicate the plains Indians through forced starvation, the whites slaughtered the buffalo to the point of near extinction. A herd of 10,000 buffalo could be eliminated in three days' time, with the whites cutting out and keeping only the choice tongue meat, the rest wastefully left to rot.

It was Indian custom to use every part of the buffalo and to roam wherever the herd went. The Indian's movements were now confined, they could not follow what few buffalo were left. With their largest food source and mainstay of life exterminated, Indians became increasingly dependant on monies promised by the U.S. government so they could buy food from the white trade merchants.

With the promised government monies falling short to non-existent, Indian chiefs became concerned for the survival of their hungry people. The U.S. government did not care, store merchants would not extend any more food on credit, it seemed everyone figured the Indians would just starve out of existence and America would be better for it.

Many local battles ensued, leading to The Dakota War of 1862, also called the Sioux Uprising. Chief Two Bear Paws used both names and explained that even though these wars involved mainly his Dakota brothers a little farther east, the Dakota wars affected the Lakota and were a contributing factor in the series of events that led up to the Wounded Knee Massacre in 1890.

The Sioux Uprising in 1862 ended with the largest mass execution in U.S. history as 38 Dakota Indians were hanged in one day under President Lincoln's orders. Three hundred and three were originally scheduled to be executed; Lincoln feared a nation wide Indian uprising would result if that number was kept, so he reduced it to 38, with plans to completely annihilate the Dakota "savages" through other means vocalized by white war leaders of the time.

The U.S. government drafted The Fort Laramie treaty of 1868 under the guise of peace, which lasted for a few years until the U.S. broke this new treaty, too. The land boundaries of the Fort Laramie treaty of 1868 included the sacred Black Hills as part of "The Great Sioux Reservation." It was stipulated in the treaty that no outsider was allowed to interfere with Indian land. This treaty allowed Indians to govern themselves and it kept the White Man out of their sacred Black Hills.

The treaty made way for White Man's roads and trains, and began the process of putting Indians onto reservations. White Man had scared away the game with their presence, cut up Indian land with roads, took away their guns and horses, interfered with the Indian's migratory hunting rights by putting boundaries on the hunt so they could no longer follow the roaming buffalo herds, and, for good measure, White Man massacred the buffalo. This treaty made Indians dependant on government food rations.

Six years later, Custer and his army dishonored and violated the treaty by illegally trespassing onto Indian land; gold was found in the Black Hills. In 1876, The Indians killed Custer, defeated his men, and captured his flag at Little Big Horn, but their battles were not over.

Eight months later, as if in retaliation for Custer's death in June, The February Act of 1877 redefined Indian territory and removed the Black Hills from Indian land.

The U.S. government said it would withdraw food rations if the Indians did not agree to the theft of their sacred Black Hills. Threatened with starvation, a few Indian leaders reluctantly signed, but this was not the three-fourths majority needed to make an agreement legal, as defined by the 1868 Fort Laramie treaty.

Indians were officially put onto reservations. Any Indians who did not willingly move to and stay within the confines of their mapped reservation areas were considered insubordinate rebels and allowed to be killed on sight. Beliefs such as this had a heavy hand in the 1890 Wounded Knee Massacre, which is noted as the final battle of the American Indian Wars.

U.S. history wipes Indian history out of its mind and puts an end to the whole mess when the bodies are dumped into the mass grave at Wounded Knee Creek in 1890. As the dirt from the mass grave is wiped from White Man's hands, the U.S.

turns its back on the sorrows and plight of the Indian.

Since The Fort Laramie treaty of 1868, Indians have declared they will reclaim their sacred Black Hills. Even government courts of the 1920s did not want to hear the Indians' appeals, it seems they were surprised the savages had lived this long. They hoped they would simply die out in time from, as Chief claims, the government's food rations sent to poison the Indian with malnutrition and disease. They held on.

White Man finally heard the case in Supreme Court and, in 1980, more than a century later, issued a verdict to make up for the illegal theft and great injustice by offering monetary compensation for the stolen Black Hills. The Indians refused the payment, stating they want their land back instead. This battle still rages on today.

My coffee now cold, Chief had said all this for about a half hour as I listened silently. It was the most I had ever heard him speak at once. While I agree his points and perspectives are valid and I will always feel sympathy for the wrongs done, I was fed up and tired of paying the price for what every white man did to his people long before I was even born.

"I hear your words, but I do not see why they are your answer for mistreating me. I have given you everything, my possessions, my money, my life as your wife. And you can't even touch me? You hate my body and my skin color, but you don't see my heart. I hate to say this to a respected elder like you, and I'm sorry, but you're an asshole and I'm out of here."

His face fell with shock. I took the keys off the table and went outside. I unlocked the padlock on the back door of the U-Haul and rolled it up. The snow was coming down now as I stepped over the fallen mess of my poorly packed possessions.

I grabbed the bird cages and wedged them against the Harley's tires. I wrapped the bags of parrot food and their perches in a blanket to protect them from road salt and threw on my white, designer winter coat Big Biker had given me last Christmas. My birds, my Harley, my truck and a warm coat to face the storm. This was all I needed and all I cared about; he could have the rest.

Chief stood on the ground and silently watched me. When I was done, door padlocked, keys back in his hands, he finally spoke.

He looked me in the eyes and said, "I don't have any money for gas."

"Alright," I sighed. We went back inside to the ATM. I gave him two hundred and sixty from the ATM, the most I could take out in a day, plus a hundred dollar bill from my wallet I kept stashed away for emergencies.

"This should get you home. Keep my stuff. Sell it or whatever. Goodbye."

He said, "Wait." I paused. "Thank you." I turned to face him, surprised at his words. "Nobody has ever treated me this good. Nobody ever put me up in hotels. Took me out to eat, bought me a car and a rifle. Gave me so much money. You have been good to me. Thank you."

Despite my anger and whirlwind to leave, I still had a tear in my eye. I knew it took a lot for him to thank me, a white person, a woman. And I could tell he was sincere, not just playing me. "Thank you for saying that. You are welcome."

I drove away without looking back.

CHAPTER TWENTY-TWO:

Thanksgiving

That night, without him next to me in the motel room, I felt very bad for how I had treated Chief. How could I have left such a respected elder alone in the snow? And I had walked out just when he had started to appreciate me!

I called information and got Chief's mother's phone number. She put someone on the phone who could speak English. (I learned much later she could speak English just fine, but she chose never to say a word to me.) I said Chief and I got separated in the snow storm. If he called to check in with them, I asked if they would please give him this phone number. I left the same message at home with Hunter and also at his Aunt's house.

I prayed it would be enough to get him back. I felt so awful for what I had done.

About three hours later, close to midnight, my hotel phone rang. I grabbed it, breathless with gratitude to *Tunkashila* and God. "Oh my gosh, Chief, I am so sorry for what I did to you! I can't believe I left such a respected leader of his people out in the snow like that. Please forgive me! Are you okay?"

He grunted. "Okay. Almost died. Much snow. Almost went off road. At hotel now. Iowa."

"I am at a hotel in Ohio."

"Spent all the money on hotel and gas. I am broke. Stuck."

I told him to check with his front desk in a little while and call me back. I wrote a letter stating Chief Two Bear Paws was allowed to use my credit card for gas, food, and hotels on his route to Wounded Knee, South Dakota. I included both sides of my driver's license and credit card. I stated, "If this note's authenticity is questioned, please call my parents' house. I will be staying with them for Thanksgiving." I listed their home phone number and my father's name. Chief said he got the fax. He laughed and said it looked good, "*Wash'te.*" We had begun to patch things up.

My parents kept Thanksgiving dinner warm for me; they held off eating for two hours as it took longer than I thought to get across Pennsylvania. When I walked in the door, we were short one person. My youngest sister, Julie, had locked herself in her bedroom, refusing to see me. We shared a long standing silence from her side since the day I left home for the woods of New Hampshire years ago. No amount of apologies or coaxing could bring her back no matter how many times I tried to speak with her.

As we began to eat the salvaged meal without her, the call came that put the final touches on this ruined day. My father answered the phone. He handed it to me with a frown. I sat at my parents' Thanksgiving table and explained to a gas station attendant more than a thousand miles away that Two Bear Paws was authorized to buy gas using my credit card. My parents were so disappointed in me. My father looked beyond disgusted I could make such an irresponsible arrangement.

After Thanksgiving, I only stayed a few awkward days with my family, never catching even a glimpse of Julie. Although Amandah came around me and tried to play nice, I could see our bond was wearing painfully thin due to the strain I had brought to everyone's lives.

I was in a deep fog that got more enchanting every night when I would finally get ahold of Chief. He told me *Tunkashila* spoke to him and said he was not treating me properly. Chief promised to kiss me and touch me if I came back. "That is the way to treat a wife. *Tunkashila* showed me the error of my ways. I was wrong and I will make it right."

Although, deep down, a voice inside me said he was already kissing and touching someone else. Whenever I would call, he would be out. I asked what he was wearing; I was told he left dressed in his finest Western hat and clothes. He only did that when we went out on the town. I knew he was seeing someone, but I pushed it away, wanting to believe he was still mine.

"Okay. Why don't we start over? I will rent a trailer in Hot Springs and live there with my birds. I'll get a job and give you money, we will go out on dates. We can start back at the beginning and do it right this time. Take it slower. Have some romance. I will still help plan the motorcycle ride, but I want to live in Hot Springs for a few months and see the changes you are making. We can get married in the spring if all continues to go well as you promise. It was all moving too fast before. Let's take it slower and enjoy the journey together. I love you. We can work this out. That's the plan I want. I will come back on those terms, okay?"

Chief led me to believe he agreed by offering me silence.

It sounded good to me. I was once again a starry-eyed school girl. I stayed in touch with Chief throughout my decisions, I told him about the trailer I found in Hot Springs. He said it was a good location right off the highway, near the feed store and the gas station. I actually knew right where that was. I rented it over the phone; I even paid a few months' rent in advance.

It hurt my mother deeply when she overheard me one night talking on the phone to a local girl friend. "Thanks for the invite, but I won't be in town long enough to do that with you. I just came home for the holiday. I'm heading back to South Dakota in a couple days. I rented my own trailer. What? Yes, I'm still with him. We're starting over and taking it slow this time. I'm really in love with this guy, I want it to work with all my heart."

My family could not believe I was leaving. My mother pleaded with me to stay. She even offered me and my birds the finished basement, which was a very nice place to live. They just wanted me to be safe. They loved me. When she saw she could not convince me, she advised, "At the very least, leave your truck and Harley here; that way you will always have them when you come back."

I never planned on coming back. I recalled the day ten years prior when a much younger me had called, begging to come home, not wanting to live in the woods of New Hampshire anymore, not wanting to get married just to stay warm. I remembered I was denied and how devastated I had been. I faintly realized how much meaning her current offer had and how much I would have loved to hear those words so long ago. It was too late. This was my destiny.

Early in the morning, I wrote them each a note and slipped out the door. I heard they all cried. My mother said her tears fell like quarters to the floor and she never truly recovered from the pain and heartbreak I caused her. She said the situation made my father old, he worried so much about me. Both my sisters were lost to me; we just couldn't heal over the scars.

My father caught me sneaking out to leave forever. He pleaded with me in early morning whispers to do as my mother suggested and leave my truck and Harley in their garage and rent a car to go back out. "You'll always have them if you leave them here." My mother's wisdom was accurate. I lost everything I had left. What I regret losing most was not my possessions.

I headed west with my Harley, parrots, fish, and truck. I kept driving, putting miles between the loss I could barely feel inside my heart and getting closer to the pull in my soul from South Dakota. When I finally stopped at a hotel late that night, I called Chief's house.

Deena answered. She told me they got everything out of the U-Haul truck. She said everybody was so excited to have my portable phone in the kitchen, it was way better than the old one-piece phone they used to have. I found it ironic I was calling my own phone that, only a week ago, used to be in my apartment in Maine, two thousand miles away from Deena.

She said they strung a hundred feet of phone line across the ceiling so they could have the phone base on the kitchen counter near the door. I knew this area was the hub of daily activity. I was happy my phone could be of such service to the family; at least something good had come from losing all my stuff.

She told me Chief was out, but I could try back in an hour. Several attempts later, my calls reaching well after midnight and just a few short hours before my wake up call was scheduled, he was home.

"I will meet you in Wall." Chief had spoken.

Yet, I still questioned. "Why? I know the way to my trailer. Remember the plan we agreed to? We said we'll take it slower and start by dating each other. I will still help plan the motorcycle ride with you. If all goes well and you really do change your attitude towards me, we will get married in the spring."

"I will meet you in Wall." A cold finger ran up my inner arms; the chill held me as I fell asleep.

DECEMBER

CHAPTER TWENTY-THREE:

Date Night

I pushed myself too hard trying to make the trip in two days instead of three. I was dangerously nodding off at the wheel.

There was still bright afternoon sunshine when I got a motel room on the outskirts of Wall, about an hour from where I was supposed to meet Chief. I just couldn't make it any farther. I called him and gave him the address of the motel. He set out to meet me in his car. Figuring I had some time to myself to relax and unwind before he arrived, I let the birds out of their modified cat carrier cages for the first time in almost two days.

I opened the curtains. The sunbeam spread across the bed and touched their play baskets. They perched quietly on the wicker handles, newspaper below them, eating a seed ball snack, hurting nothing and bothering nobody. They stretched their wings in the sun and seemed to smile. The picture window was large; my parrots could see trees, sunshine, and blue sky again. Life was good. For a minute. Then the motel phone rang. A motherly voice scolded, "Come to the front desk right now!"

This was a tiny, one story motel with eight rooms, so I made it to the front desk in a few steps. The woman who checked me in and owned the place scowled. "Do you have *birds* in there?"

I stared at her wide-eyed, too stunned to move, let alone talk. My parrots hadn't even made a peep. How could she have known?

"Pets are *not* allowed," she stated in a hoity-toity fashion, looking down at me from her perch high above her small spectacles. "You did not tell me you had *pets* when you checked in. You deceived me and just for that I should kick you out and keep your money."

White people I encountered in the Midwest seemed pretty uptight about being lied to and deceived when that's all they ever did to the Indians. Maybe it's a guilty conscience that made them so offended over such small things like parrots in a motel room or lying about my destination at the rental car office.

Chief was already on his way to meet me here, there was no way to contact him if plans changed. I could not sleep all night in my truck on the side of the road with the birds. I would run out of gas trying to keep them warm, as there was no gas station or alternate motel around for a hundred miles. I started to cry. She was so mean. I was emotionally and physically exhausted.

"Well," she huffed. "You only have one choice to make. Leave now or put your birds back in their boxes for the remainder of your time here. There will be an additional twenty dollar fee for having pets in the room."

She secured her glasses up higher on her nose and held her hand out for the twenty. I gave it to her. I stuffed the birds back into their dark crates, closed the drapes, and a sense of hopelessness came over me. I couldn't shake it for about five years.

If the old woman had been miffed about my parrots, she was really going to hate it when I let an Indian in the room in the middle of the night. Chief Two Bear Paws snuck into my room after midnight. We were up at five and out the door. The birds, fish, Harley, and I followed him in his new gold car.

We stopped at a restaurant in the middle of such a nowhere I could never find it again if I had to. To the best of my knowledge, it's somewhere between hell and the moon a hundred years ago. To say the place was rustic is a compliment. It was older than John Wayne movies, most likely

Wild Bill Hickok's father ate here when he was a boy. There were literally tumbleweeds blowing in the parking lot.

The land around the restaurant was flat and dry as far as the eye could see. I was amazed to discover I could feel claustrophobic in such an open space. The emptiness closed in around me. Endless distance became suffocating inches as I realized help was not to be found in any direction and the only building for miles was this restaurant.

The restaurant is a dark brown wooden shack. Inside, it is even darker. Animal skulls gleam in the only thin stream of light from a partially boarded up window. Perhaps the boards are weathered shutters, closing out the afternoon sun, but to me they are the lid of a coffin.

There is fur and feathers, bones and teeth. A white waitress seats us at a table in the corner. My elbows stick to the table. I cannot tell if the tablecloth is made from thick oil cloth still seeping oil, or if it has been soaked with grease from a hundred thousand lunches and dinners consumed by road weary travelers.

As the restaurant loses its John Wayne appeal and starts to feel more like a horror movie, I begin to wonder what's in the burgers. Somewhere in my head I hear a witch's cackle, "There's more than one way to pay your bill. Nobody gets out alive, dearie. Ha ha ha . . ."

"And what would you like, Miss?"

"Uh . . ." I blinked. "Um, the soup? And can you make me a grilled cheese, please?"

"The soup we got's today's beef. Do you want your burger rare, too?"

"Um, no." I couldn't bear saying the word "vegetarian" to this meat-insistent woman. If I had, I think tomorrow's soup de jour would have been "vegetarian stew" . . . with white meat. "Uh, I'm feeling a little queasy today. I really want something light. A bowl of stew's fine, but if you could sweet talk the cook into just a simple grilled cheese, I'd be ever so grateful.

Please. Thank you." This seemed to satisfy her; at least I had beef in my stew.

I ate around the meat, gagging at the strong taste of animal oil floating in my broth, choosing carrots and potatoes to accompany bites of my equally greasy grilled cheese. The butter on the outside of the bread tasted like it had been grilled in beef fat. I'm sure it had.

Chief was amused, smiling at how the meat tortured me. He said this was his favorite restaurant, but he seldom gets out this way. His burger dripped blood onto his fries. I pretended it was just his ketchup. He sopped up both with passion.

Out of the corner of my eye, I saw a black bird, wing broken, struggling on the ground. I pointed out the window. "Look at that. Do you see that black bird over there suffering? I think it's hurt."

He looked through the slit in the shutters to the parking lot, grunted, and said, "More ice tea."

I asked the waitress for his refill and paid the bill. In a moment of romantic weakness, perhaps it was the dim lighting or the fact this was his favorite restaurant, I was swept away with love for him and wanted to let him know its depth. "Chief, I love you. You are the most special man in my life, right after my dad. You mean that much to me."

Chief threw his burger down, he pounded both fists so hard on the table our glasses and utensils rattled. The three other guests looked over at us, even the stuffed elk head on the wall seemed startled by the sudden loud noise.

"No! That is wrong! No other man is more important than your husband! *I* matter more than anything! Forget your father. Forget your family. Cut your mother's apron strings! Move on. You are with *me* now. *I* am the only person who matters in your life." He got closer to my face, grabbed my eyes with his own and snarled, "*Say it.*"

"You are the most important person in my life, Chief, I love you more than anyone else."

"Good." He finished eating.

Confused as to how shame so quickly replaced my feelings of love for my family, I thought, "Is he right? Do I need to let go of my family more? I will be living at least a three days' drive away from them, can't Chief see I already put him first? I turned my back on my mother, I chose a life with Chief over my own blood, what more can he ask for? Well, maybe this is the Indian way, perhaps he is right. I need to try harder to see things his way, to become Lakota."

I was still pondering when Chief got into his car. As I reached for the door of my truck, I saw my little green parrot pressed against the travel cage bars. His precious white rimmed eye peeked out into the sunbeams, I saw him clinging to the door with his sweet birdie feet. I was overcome with guilt and compassion. I could not let the big crow suffer in the corner of the parking lot. I had to help.

Making my own decision without asking Chief, I ran over to save it. I could see a big, dark wing flapping with its struggles. It was covered in dust and dry grass. I realized my dying crow was a scrap of black garbage bag trapped in the brush, flapping in the breeze like a bird with a broken wing.

Feeling foolish, I went back to my truck. Two Bear Paws leaned out his car window and hollered my name. I ran over. "Did you get the bird?" If I had, he surely would have killed it and taken the feathers.

"No, it was just a black garbage bag."

Chief laughed so hard he had to snap his false teeth back into place. "Drive." He waved his hand onward.

I expected we'd arrive at my trailer and I'd give Chief a kiss goodbye as he headed back to the rez in his car. I grew more confused as the day wore on because the scenery never looked right. The warm day was turning into a freezing evening when we arrived at a row of storage units. He unlocked the padlock and rolled the door up. His best saddles were still here, along with the rifle, just as we had left them.

253

"Leave the motorcycle."

"What?"

"Leave the motorcycle."

"Why?"

"Winter is coming, you need to store it."

"Well, okay. That makes sense. I'll need the truck for work and I can't be driving around with my bike in the back." I looked around for some wood to make a ramp so I could get the bike down from my truck. There was nothing to be found but saddles, some reigns, and a rifle. Chief picked up the rifle and put it in his car.

I was at a loss for ideas. "There's no way to get the bike out of the truck, Chief."

"Leave the truck."

"What!"

"Let's go."

"Wait, wait. How am I supposed to get back and forth to work from my trailer if I leave my truck here?"

"Use the car."

"You mean you'd let me borrow your car?" Chief nodded once. "But, then, what will you do for a vehicle?"

"Truck."

Okay, that made sense. I had forgotten about Chief's big, old pickup. The plan sounded good. I took my birds in their carriers, their two larger cages and food, grabbed the fish, but left my Harley, my riding gear, and my truck in Chief's storage unit. Ownership shifted when he padlocked the door.

"Drive."

The night had turned exceptionally cold, it was now thirty degrees or less. A black, starless sky seemed to take away all hope of brighter days. We were traveling down winding back roads with no streetlights. I kept thinking we'd arrive at my trailer eventually. It was so late, I guessed Chief would be spending the night and I'd take him back to the reservation in the morning.

"Park." He gestured to a parking space on a small town street. "Get out."

I did as instructed; Chief took the keys from my hand. He stood there for a moment, staring majestically into the darkness, his black felt cowboy hat on his head, turquoise and silver bear claw earring in his ear. I thought he looked quite sexy and dignified. We were standing in front of a movie theater. Chief put his arm around me and smiled. "Date night."

I thought, "Wow, this is so romantic. He's really trying." I blinked back tears of gratitude to *Tunkashila* as I bought two tickets. A half hour into the movie, I whispered to Chief, "I have to start the car for a few minutes and run the heater so the birds will stay warm. Can I have the keys? I'll be right back."

"Forget it. Date night." He reached for my hand and held it. This was the first time we ever held hands; I was flooded with appreciation and love. But it was chilled by the knowledge my birds were freezing to death.

I snuggled up against him and picked the keys from his coat pocket. After a few minutes more, I gently laid his hand on his lap. I said I was going to the lobby, I'd buy us popcorn and sodas. He nodded in agreement. I went through the swinging doors, leaving the darkness of the movie theater and his sightline. I sprinted for the car. I cranked up the heater and spoke softly to my birds. I shivered in the cold. I found a blanket in the trunk and covered their travel carriers, hoping it would hold the heat against their bodies for at least an hour.

Chief's lack of concern for my birds' well being overshadowed his romantic advances. Part of me knew something wasn't right and wanted to run. I thought about driving off and leaving Chief there, but I had no idea where I was. A light was on in the parking lot nearby, but the gas station was closed. The town was as dark as the sky.

I almost put the car in reverse and took my chances, but then I thought of poor Chief, who had no cell phone, no cash, and no friends or family with a vehicle who could come pick him up. Chief had put his truck keys on his car key ring so nobody would steal his truck while he was gone; it was a great theft deterrent, but it make picking him up with his alternate vehicle an impossibility. I had no idea how far from the rez we were. I was sure it was not close enough for him to walk; besides, it had turned inhumanely cold outside. I could not be that cruel. If I ran, the only place I could go was my trailer. I was certain he would find me there and make me pay the price for leaving him in shame.

I went back to my seat with sodas and big popcorn in hand. Chief reached in for a handful. Even though his hands were all over me, his arm pulling me confidently towards him so he could kiss me in the dark, my thoughts were with my feathered babies freezing in the car. I hoped the short burst of heat was enough to help them survive. I slipped the keys back into Chief's pocket.

Looking back, I think stealing the keys from him helped break our bond. Two dead birds would have broken it as well. Either way, it does not matter. Our bond was bound to get broken. Chief most likely saw taking the keys as another theft, more lies and deceit from White Man. I saw my birds as my babies; a mother would not leave her infant alone in a car seat for an hour and a half in less than thirty degree weather. The baby might not die, the parrots might not die, but either has a great chance of getting sick or frostbit from the exposure.

About an hour later, we returned to the car. Chief eyed the blanket tucked around the cages in the back seat. He knew I had done wrong against him by stealing the keys and seeking warmth for my birds. He commanded, "Drive."

I backed out of the space and drove through the barren town, blackness surrounded us. If I would have seen just one person, I would have asked directions. There was nobody around; my only choice was to trust Chief. "Thanks for the movie, that was a great idea. I had fun. What a good date night. Which way do I turn towards Hot Springs and my trailer?"

Chief stared straight ahead and waved his hand to the left. I went left. The road went from desolate but paved to completely abandoned by time and tarmac. As the bumps got worse, the prairie grass got taller. I asked Chief if this was really the right way to my trailer. The birds chirped as we went over the next large bump. Chief waved his hand in a forward direction without comment.

I was beginning to get worried as we drove deeper into the darkness. After an hour of silence, Chief barked an order: "Right!" I was so surprised at his words, and by the fact this did not look a thing like Hot Springs or my trailer, that I missed his direction. "Right! Right!" He slammed his fist on the dashboard. I spun the car around on a random grassy patch that looked like all the other random grassy patches. I took a shot in the dark and turned right at the spot I thought he wanted. He was silent. This confirmed I had chosen correctly.

"Gate!" he demanded. Trained to respond to this command without thinking, I stepped out of the car. As soon as my feet hit the ground, fear crawled from my heels up to the backs of my knees. I knew that command. I knew this place. This is not what I had asked for. Chief misled me.

I unlocked the gate. I drove the car through it, but I broke routine and did not step back out to secure it. Instead, I flew forward and turned the car around in the dirt patch beside his house. My thoughts were spinning as fast as my wheels. "Ok, I've got my bearings, I can find Hot Springs and my trailer now. I need to get off the reservation first, and fast. That shouldn't be hard since I'm the one driving. I've always had control of the situation because I've had control of the car. It's time I started acting like it, I need to take charge. Chief won't be happy, but we can discuss our feelings on the drive. Maybe I'll drop him off at the end of the driveway or maybe somewhere along the road, but no matter what, I am going home to my trailer with my birds tonight." Decision made, adrenalin racing with the engine, the car completed its circle of retreat. I headed back for the gate and salvation.

If a bolt of lightening and a rattlesnake had a contest to see who could strike first, Chief's hand would have won. Before I even knew what happened, Chief snatched the keys out of the ignition, his other hand moved the automatic transmission through neutral into park. My fast-moving getaway vehicle was now a heavy hunk of motionless metal. I was dumbfounded by his speed and how fast the tables had turned.

"Get the gate."

"Get the gate? What's going on? We talked about this! All this time I thought you were giving me directions to my trailer, instead we end up here, back on the reservation? This was not the deal! You tricked me! I want to go to my trailer—now!"

The lightening flashed in Chief's eyes. I saw his fist strike out with an arc of speed so fast my vision could not follow. When the world shook, I thought he had split my head. It took me a moment to realize he had struck the headrest just a hair's breath from the side of my left temple.

My body had gone completely numb. I stared at him, wide-eyed like the deer I shot, awaiting the next blow. I wondered what would happen to my birds when I died. He would probably let them freeze to death in the car overnight. I closed my eyes, a tear trickled out as my final thoughts were a prayer of blessing for my mother and father. I was just beginning to pray for my sisters when Chief grabbed me by the shoulders; he shook me hard. I opened my eyes. His hand was raised. He held up the car keys and jingled them. "You stay with me. *This* is home."

Amazed to still be alive, I rolled fate's dice and attempted to bargain. "Can we talk about it with the heat on? My birds are freezing, it is so cold in here. I promise I won't drive away, let's just talk. Please, make it warm in here for them, they will die if it is cold like this much longer." I could see my breath inside the car, crystallizing on the inside of the windows.

Chief's laugh was evil as he shook the keys. "No talk. You

want them to live, you come inside with me." His lips pointed at the house. "You are my wife. Let's go to bed."

I was trapped and out of ideas. Chief won. I had sex in darkness as black as the roaches. My birds chirped from their cramped travel carriers on the dresser. Only the darkness saw me cry; we were slipping off to sleep without a sound when Chief grabbed my shoulders and pushed me out of bed. I tumbled to the floor. "Light the fire."

I made the fire and wished I could sleep in front of it, away from Chief. I went back to bed, as was proper for a wife to do, and fell into a spiral of dreams darker than the depression that had swallowed me.

This was our new nightly routine. Every two hours he would throw me out of bed so I could tend the fire. I would still "get the juice." Often, the juice shift was sporadically placed in between the fire shifts, so my already sparse sleep time dwindled greatly.

In return, Chief Two Bear Paws honored the words *Tunkashila* had spoken to him. Every night he would treat me like a wife, spit on me and take me roughly from behind, saying, "This is what the horses do. It is natural and it is right." He would never look at my face except when he bit me, inflicting as much pain as possible, enjoying the silent tear that would stream down my cheek. He would grin in a nasty way, relishing my suffering, and bite harder. I had to take all he gave. I knew he was challenging me to be silent as a sign of strength. These were tests to make me a good woman. If I made a sound, even an involuntary wince of pain, it was weakness and he would make me bleed. Perhaps that's how horses did it, too; I never watched them.

I asked Chief what he did when I was gone. He said a woman from Rosebud came to cook for him because he was hosting a talk at the round building. The visitors were from Texas, one woman promised to donate six thousand dollars in the spring; he had her under such a spell. He laughed and said he was going to buy himself four pickup trucks, one in every Lakota color, with her donation.

I knew he had women in our bed. Maybe the Rosebud woman who cooked, maybe the spellbound Texas guest. Most likely both or more. My photo was gone from the shelf by the bed; the artwork I had painted throughout my life and brought with me to the rez had been cut up and thrown onto the wood pile outside.

The only thing I asked about was my Sturgis scrapbook, full of irreplaceable photos of my not so long ago journey. He said, "Baaah! You don't need that! I burned it." He had also burned all my clothes that made me look like a college girl, including my favorite pair of jeans. Any trace of me had been extinguished, the way opened for another wife to care for him so soon.

Chief still had the U-Haul truck, it sat out in the tall grass behind the wood piles. I couldn't believe I was in this situation again.

I noticed he had torn the steering column out of his pickup truck a second time. I asked what happened; he said he'd lost the keys. Somehow that bummed me out hard. I had paid three hundred dollars to fix it so he could have something nice and he ruined it in less than a month's time. There was no sense of pride in caring for possessions on the rez, perhaps because possessions could be stolen at any time. I began to notice my belongings from Maine around the house.

My futon frame creatively stood on its side; it was positioned as a wall, separating the living room from the kitchen. Lakota crafts were tied onto the slats, it was actually ingenious and beautiful; I thought it must have been Deena's idea. My large screen TV and DVD player completed the living room. A 30"x40" double matted and framed, signed and numbered art print, a five hundred dollar gift from my Maine Mom and Dad which I treasured, hung above the sofa next to the sacred buffalo skull.

My baby blanket, the one my mother had saved for decades and given me with loving tears recently, thinking I would soon wrap my own child in its softness, was a tattered rag on the floor. It was destroyed and full of dirt where Hunter's sneakers had pushed holes through it as he kicked and pulled the too-small blanket, getting comfortable on the sofa, covering himself in my sacred things as if they were meaningless.

A parrot tapestry my mother had spent hours quilting for me hung like a prize in our bedroom; that was at least good.

The white, calf-length, three hundred dollar faux fur coat I usually wore only on Christmas day had been torn into strips; rolled up pieces were stuffed as draft dodgers under all the doors and windows to keep out the winter cold.

There was some sweet honey-almond lotion beside the bed that was not mine. I used it on my legs; they were very dry as I had been shaving them so often to please Chief. Our bed felt different the very first night. When I woke up, my legs itched something fierce. I ignored it. I kept ignoring it as it got worse each night. I broke out in huge red welts. I moisturized my legs with the sweet lotion every night, hoping they would heal.

Chief was never affected, except by laughter. My legs were a swollen, itchy disaster. Out of desperation, I went into Deena's room. She had been sleeping and sick a lot lately. I felt sorry to wake her, but this was serious. I pulled up my pant legs and asked helplessly, "What's wrong with me?"

She turned her head and opened one eye. "Looks like bedbugs."

The scabs inside the middle of the red welts were driving me insane. Chief would not let me scratch them, he would slap my hand and say no. I disobeyed him in the dark one night and ripped the scab off the worst itchy bump on my ankle bone. It was instant, pure relief. It bled like a faucet, red warmth streamed down my heel. I limped to the bathroom and turned on the light. I looked at the soft side of the scab in my hand. There was a bug imbedded in the scab, like the scab had grown around it. It was black and large; I could see its head and body. This thing had been living under my skin! There were more of them. Every scab had a bug underneath. Picking it off and bleeding it out was the only way to lessen the pressure and itch. By not allowing me to scratch, Chief had kept me suffering and enjoyed every minute of it.

The unfortunate thing for me was the source of the infestation was not remedied. I threw the cream out, the sweetness only seemed to attract them more. I never even thought of buying a new mattress. Like any other situation on the rez, I just learned to adapt. Every night, more bugs would crawl back inside me; it seemed no matter what I did, I permanently had bugs under my skin for the rest of this time on the rez. I wondered what on earth Chief had been sleeping with when I was gone.

My broken spirit registered nothing. I was pushed out of bed earlier each morning, my thoughts were, "Drag the body out of bed, cook the breakfast, clean the kitchen, nothing matters." Except, after the chores were done, I would remember I still had my birds.

I asked Chief if I could go feed and water them now that the fire was made, the children fed and cared for, the rugs taken outside and dust beaten from them with a broom, the laundry washed and hung up to dry on the folding wooden drying rack I had purchased in Vermont long ago in another life. He nodded and did me one better. He surprised me by saying, "Bring them out."

My heart got lighter when I saw my birds so happy to be free. Snickers jumped from his basket handle perch and landed on the table, interested in the remaining corn bread from breakfast. I broke off a piece and gave it to him. Chief picked the bird up by offering his finger. He eagerly stepped on and scooted up to Chief's shoulder, nestled into his neck, and purred in his ear.

The grandchildren stood mesmerized by R.D. fluttering

from his basket to the table, also chasing breadcrumbs. My birds had weak wing muscles from being cooped up, but R.D. was so light he could still fly fairly well. The children chased him around the sunlit room, laughing.

The kitchen door opened with another late breakfast guest. I had to block R.D. from flying out into the sun and cold. A small gust of wind could easily have carried him off to die. Cockatiels are migratory birds with no sense of "home" as a direction. I could relate to that. If he flew out, he would panic and be lost to me. I carried R.D. into the bedroom. People kept coming in for food; there was still white mush on the stove and cornbread to feed them until I made lunch.

Everyone who entered was startled to see a bird inside the house; they would pause and leave the door ajar to the cold. The draft was too much, so I took Snickers to the bedroom, too. My feathered kids stood on the empty clothesline like it was a telephone wire, chirping happily. I closed the door and thought they would be safe playing outside their cages for a little bit.

Chief Two Bear Paws walked into the bedroom to grab a saddle pad so one of his sons could catch a horse and ride. He saw my birds on the clothesline and said, "Put them away. No more birds." My parrot's two larger cages stood on the table in the corner. This is where they spent the rest of their time on the reservation, caged forever and never allowed out again.

It was fortunate Chief permitted me to feed them, but he was angry while I did it. Whenever I cared for my birds he would follow me; I would shake nervously as he barked orders for other "more important" things I should be doing, like caring for the grandchildren and performing the many duties of the household.

Daily, he would offer to kill my birds so it would free me up for a few more minutes of women's work. I kept being nice and I never complained, I knew my crushing punishment if I ever got out of line.

I was carrying the grandchildren's dirty clothes to the laundry room when Chief pinned me up against the wall in the hallway. His teeth were a snip away from biting my lip or nose. He snarled, "Why are you not pregnant yet? You must have pills. Where are you hiding them?"

I held my breath, his fingers dug into my upper arms as his grip tightened.

"Stop taking them or I will tear up all your things until I find them. Throw the pills away—or I will. You need to have a baby. Once you are pregnant, you can never leave. The apron strings with your family will be cut, no more phone calls, no more promises.

"The child must stay here on the reservation, he will have Lakota blood. He will learn the old ways. If you try to go, you will not be allowed to leave with your child. You will not get away, you will remain here forever." He threw me against the wall. I finished the laundry and hid my pills even deeper, making sure to take one, if not two, every day.

I shared my feelings with Amandah once, when I was alone cooking. My phone call caught her during an off-guard moment missing me; our conversation was almost like the old days before I had severed our family ties. I told her how much I wanted to get pregnant and have a family with Chief, my husband, and stay forever on the reservation. I would do this in a heartbeat if he could treat me a little bit better.

Amandah said I should call a taxi and get out of there. Just come home and be done with all of this. I tried to explain to her how there are no taxis and the way out is an hour's drive. It was impossible to walk out. I told her how AAA laughs and hangs up when you break down and call for help; it happened to me when I tried.

The desolate regions of South Dakota cannot even be imagined by those who have not seen them. I was here for life; I might as well make the best of it.

CHAPTER TWENTY FOUR:

House Guest from Germany

Chief laughed and said, "The German is a rich man, we will take him for all he has." The joke was on him when we found out later all he had was strength and ability to offer in lieu of money.

Chief told me they had never met in person, our soon to be guest had written letters from overseas and wanted to visit in order to participate in the Big Foot ride, a thirteen day horseback journey which would begin mid-December. Every year, the Big Foot Riders follow the spirit trail across the snowy plains and rocky passes, honoring the path Chief Big Foot and his band walked in 1890. Chief Big Foot was searching for freedom for his people, but they found only death in the massacre at Wounded Knee.

The ride is a journey of respect for the Ancestors. It is a trail of hope and healing for the Lakota way of life. The riders are in constant prayer and meditation, often fasting along the way, eating only *pemmican* for energy in the endless wilderness.

I prepared the sleeping area for our German guest as Chief instructed, making a bed with blankets and my old futon mattress. I created a shelf for his things and gave him his own bath towel. This little bit of living room floor near the second woodstove was now claimed as his space.

I secretly hoped he would stoke the woodstove during the night, leaving me with only the bedroom one to tend. I wasn't thrilled about having another mouth to cook for. Life was already hard enough, but I never complained, even with my face or gestures. I was a good wife, although Chief never again suggested confirming our union with a marriage ceremony.

Chief and I put on our Western best and headed to Rapid City to pick up our new houseguest. Rapid City, simply "Rapid" to the locals, is known for its rampant racism against Indians.

A white man I knew from Rapid once said to me, regarding the plight of the Indians, "This is why when a people are conquered they are exterminated. The right way to wage war is to wipe out the enemy. We made the mistake of letting the Indians live and this is why we are having so many problems with them today. They are a conquered people. They need to let it go. They should feel lucky we let them live and just get over it."

There are several "cowboys and Indians" type statues on the streets of Rapid. One statue in particular offended many: a twelve foot tall, bronze Indian hanging his head, his hands bound behind his back, symbolizing what reservations have done to the Indian, the man, his life, and spirit. New age, liberal white people—probably the same tourists who think the Crazy Horse monument is an honor to the Lakota—spoke up in defense of Indians, demanding the statue be taken down out of respect for "Native Americans."

In 2008, a more "Native American friendly" seemingly "politically correct" statue of an old Indian woman pinning an eagle plume into a young Indian girl's hair was put in its place.

What's ironic is Chief actually liked the old statue better. He felt the bound Indian was an accurate portrayal of White Man's wrongs; it spoke out against the White Man with Truth. He was only offended when they took it down. Chief was insulted by the inferior replacement because it made no statement against the White Man; the new statue pretended everything was okay with Indian life on the reservations.

For now, in our time period of memories, the powerful, larger than life-sized, bound Indian statue dominates the street corner outside an upscale trading store which sells near-museum quality Indian and non-native crafts at prices only a rich man could afford. The bronze Indian, although defeated in posture, stands tall behind our guest from Germany, who is also tall and broad shouldered; he, like the statue, has a quiet air of strength and confidence.

He saw Chief Two Bear Paws and waved, Chief pulled over, he got inside the car. "Ello, my name is Philipp," he said with a large smile. He told us his name in German means "friend to horses," which was perfect, since he also mentioned he raises horses back in Germany.

Philipp was a gentle soul, soft spoken and kind. He was genuinely interested in the Lakota people, learning, asking questions, listening more than talking. He was respectful to everyone.

We stopped by the dirty, run-down grocery store in Pine Ridge. Philipp walked next to Chief as I pushed the shopping cart. Chief tossed many supplies for the Big Foot ride inside, overfilling the cart with a feast's worth of food for a hundred riders. He turned to us, opened his arms and commanded, "Buy it," then walked out to sit in his car.

Philipp and I looked at each other in shock. "I don't have uh . . . much money," he said.

"Yeah, me too. He's always filling up the shopping cart and saying 'Buy it' to me. I've spent about fifty thousand dollars here and my credit cards are maxed out. How much do you think you can contribute if we split it?"

"Maybe . . . say . . . um . . . a hundred dollars?" He spoke with a thick German accent so unusual for the reservation.

Some Indians walked by us and smiled. They asked if we were married. We both jumped and said "No!" at the same time, then laughed. We knew it was strange to see what appeared to be a white couple shopping together on the reservation, a rugged white man with shoulder length blonde hair was especially out of place.

As I dug in my wallet for what cash I had, Philipp did the

most amazing thing. He pushed the cart! I was floored. He was doing woman's work without protest. I remembered the first tiff Chief and I had at Wal-Mart in Rapid City. I got the cart from the stack at the door and pushed it over to Chief. I let it go, thinking he'd catch it. Instead, he let it roll right past him, saying, "Women push the cart. Get it." It was early in our relationship and I was highly offended. Over time, I got used to always pushing the cart and always buying whatever he chose without suggestion as to what I might like. The looks in Rapid City were very racist towards Chief. People would glare at him and stare at me with horror as if I had been kidnapped and needed help. I was too in love at the time to realize I should have taken someone up on it.

As Philipp pushed the cart towards the check out, something inside me rustled, like a stunned bird weakly flopping around, struggling to wake up. "There *are* kind men out there," I thought. "I almost forgot." The tear in my eye was kept private. Even if I tried, I knew I could never explain how much that simple action, a man pushing a shopping cart, meant to me.

We loaded the supplies into the trunk and headed home. My favorite Dixie Chicks CD was playing on the car stereo. The little bird struggling for life inside me fluttered awake just enough to sing. Both Chief and Philipp were shocked as my high, sweet voice filled the car. I was surprised too, because singing was not one of my talents. Philipp's kindness had moved me to fill the car with sunshine on this winter's night. It was a little bit of magic we all felt. Even though women have no magic, according to Chief.

In the time before the Big Foot ride, the three of us spent our days wrangling firewood. Chief had kept his eye on a large dead tree for a while; it had been too big for the two of us to handle alone. It was good to have the extra brawn Philipp offered; he could wield a chainsaw effortlessly. The gnarled, leafless tree was situated on the corner of an abandoned barn foundation way out in the wilderness. I packed us a lunch and we set out to claim it.

There was not much I could do to help until the tree fell, so, while Philipp worked and Chief watched, I explored the area. Not too far away, I discovered an odd doorway into the ground. I walked down the square, rock stairs and entered a dark room made of stones. I assumed it was an old root cellar. Tree roots broke through the walls, the room was claustrophobic and creepy.

I headed back up the stone stairs towards what remained of the worn, wooden doors. Chief was at the top waiting for me, blocking the sun. I froze and looked up at the dark shape of his body. "This is where we put the young white girls. White girls stay here and die while the men drive away. Nobody finds their bodies down in the hole."

I was chilled by his words. I recalled a black and white photo I had seen of an ancient Lakota burial tree. Dead Indians were laid in the leafless branches, stark against the winter sky. I would not receive such an airy, sunlit burial from the oldest traditions. My death would be a forgotten place, a lost spirit in this empty, dark hole.

A shadow blocked the sun from Chief's back. He turned to see Philipp towering over him. Chief laughed at his overheard words as if they had been a joke. Philipp said the tree was down and he asked how Chief wanted the trunk cut. Chief left to give instruction; I climbed out of the cold, stone grave and into the warm, early winter sun. We loaded wood into the truck for two days and spent the rest of the week stacking it beside the house.

Philipp spoke with me after breakfast one morning. As I cleaned the kitchen, he sat and chatted. I learned we both shared that same sense of wanderlust. The feeling that life must be lived with passion and there must be something more out there, just over the next horizon. We agreed that life must be lived, experienced with every grateful breath we take.

We both had a soft spot in our vast hearts for the Lakota. Time is frozen here on the reservation; the past becomes current events as the modern day Lakota fight for the land and the spiritual rights they inherited from their grandfathers and grandmothers. Time stands still as if it were the 1970s, and sometimes even the 1870s, here on the reservation. Yet, the Lakota do not give up. Philipp and I do not give up on them. We stand and face the mistakes of our white ancestors, we join the Lakota on their journey, we support them in any way we can. We are not the first to become mesmerized by the reservation and the culture we were not born into, and we will not be the last.

Philipp understood why I was here. The same things I saw and felt moved him, too. For many years he had been visiting from Germany, spending a month with various tribes in the Midwest, offering his labor, learning and sharing with those who took him in. This was his first time with the Oglala Lakota.

Before Philipp arrived, Chief told me many Germans visit the reservation each year. He said Germans have a great interest in the Lakota and their way of life; Germans feel a connection and are somehow drawn to the reservation. Chief admitted that, in fact, one of the best Lakota dictionaries was written by a German man. It was no wonder Philipp and I were here.

Every year, Philipp worked hard in Germany to save up enough money so he could spend several thousand dollars on a plane ticket and have funds to travel for a month, living off the land with the Indians on many different reservations in the U.S. On this visit, he would be participating in the Big Foot Ride and helping out however he could. He dedicated much of his life and spirit to those here around us. He would develop a deep love, appreciation, and bond with the Lakota and he would be invited to Sundance. He would soon pledge the next four years of his life in preparation for the Dance.

After we established a trust by sharing life philosophies, Philipp translated his thoughts into carefully chosen English words to express concern for how Chief treats me. "Chief is blessed to have you. Your heart is big, you give everything you have . . . m m m . . . but he does not see it. I think you should, uh, write him a letter and tell him you love him, but also tell how you, uh . . . need more respect."

I stayed up late into the night after my woman's work was done to write a seven page, heartfelt letter. I met with Chief alone after breakfast the next morning. I handed him the folded pages. "This is a letter from my heart. I wrote it for you. I want us to have the best relationship possible. This letter shares things I am grateful for. It also suggests ways I could feel more loved and ways we can work towards getting there together."

Chief took the letter from me and immediately threw it into the woodstove, where it burned on the coals. I gasped. He said, "I do not care what you think or how you feel. I am not reading that. Make the fire." He walked away as I fell to my knees. I threw dried grass and bark on top of my scorched letter, then piled on sticks of wood, holding back tears.

I never let Chief have the satisfaction of seeing me cry. It did not cross his mind to care about my feelings on anything, even our marriage ceremony. Just as it never crossed my mind I must have humiliated him in front of his people by not marrying him on Thanksgiving Day.

Philipp frowned when he heard Chief did not read my letter, he searched for English words to express his condolences. "That is not right he burned it. At least you, um, expressed how you feel. You put your heart out there and uh . . . know his reply."

Young men spent the day chasing horses and catching them with ropes. They would lasso a horse's neck, claiming a half-tame horse from Chief's corral or taking a wild horse from the many herds that still roam free on the prairie. They would then swiftly jump on its back and ride hard, wearing the animal down. No horse ever seemed completely tame, and most of the riding was done bareback. Tack was solely a rope wrapped around the horse's nose and behind its ears, a rider rode with nothing else except, perhaps, a blanket loosely tossed on the horse's back. Saddles were in short supply. Indians are great at adapting and working with what they have, or inventing solutions when they have not. Philipp raised horses back home; he was impressed at the young men's skills. They caught him a half tame horse to ride and Chief gave him one of his good saddles to use.

Chief's youngest son Brings Thunder was very cruel to the horses. He'd catch a horse with the lasso, and then beat its head. Once on its back, he would thrash its sides with his big, heavy boots over and over. He constantly demanded the animals obey with bruising kicks to their bellies and fists to their heads and faces. This cruelty continued long after the animals submitted. Today he chose the big paint horse. He rode it hard and led the way through the prairie, followed by his older brother, some friends, and Philipp.

Late that afternoon, Chief was inside the house reading the paper while I gathered some wood. Something caught my eye. It was the large paint horse walking alone in the road near the bottom of the driveway. He was riderless. The makeshift bridle told of the struggle; it was broken, dragging on the ground. There was no sign of anyone else around. I laughed and thought, "Hooray for the horse!" I imagined he bucked the jerk and ran for it.

I had seen a dead horse on the side of the road in nicer weather, half eaten by starving rez dogs, mountain lions, and vultures. The horse carcass was full of holes, rotting. I gasped and Chief said it was nothing, he has seen a dead Indians rotting on the side of the road. I did not want a fate so harsh to come to this beautiful creature. Without thinking too much, I set the wood down and walked to the bottom of the driveway. I spoke softly to the horse the whole way and reached out with my heart.

The horse was almost out of sight, he was headed up the road, looking for greener pastures, possibly in Wyoming. I sent loving energy his way. He heard me and stopped. He turned his head to look at me. I stopped walking too, and said, "Come on, boy, let's go. I'll walk with you," I motioned with my head towards home and started to walk up the driveway.

I looked back over my shoulder, the horse turned around to follow me. He walked faster up behind me, then slowed to a gentle walk at my shoulder. I kept talking nicely, offering peace and love with my energy, as I slowly reached up to grasp the hanging rope. The horse never spooked or tried to run away, he followed me all the way to the big gate. I asked him to wait, he listened and patiently stood still as I undid the latch and walked him inside. I led him easily into the corral.

I went into the house, excited to tell Chief. "Hey, guess what? I found the big paint horse in the road. He had no rider and a broken bridle. I talked to him softly and walked him all the way up the driveway, through the gate, and into the corral. He's fenced inside now, isn't that great he followed me and you didn't lose the horse?" It felt like a true Indian thing I had done, using my spirit to guide a horse. I thought Chief would be proud.

He threw down his newspaper and glared at me. "No! That is not right! Women are *not* allowed to touch horses! You did the wrong thing. You should have left the job to the men. Now that you have done the harm, go bring the horse oats in a bucket. And then bring in the wood."

My bubble burst, I took the bucket of oats to the horse. The sunset was a smoldering deep orange, a color so intensely rich I could almost smell it. The night sky moved in on streaks of black clouds, striping the sky into tiger fire. It was beautiful, but somehow lonely. I saw the silhouette of the large paint horse in the field, his body outlined by the sunset. I set the bucket down and stepped away. He was cautious to come over.

My spirit was sad now, I had lost my confidence.

After I walked outside the gate, he carefully approached the bucket. He ate all the oats, restoring the extra energy he had expended on the rough ride from Brings Thunder. The other riders came home then, they were surrounded by a pack of starving, barking rez dogs. The curs whined and nipped at the horses' legs; the Indian boys whipped and kicked them away.

Brings Thunder rode double with another bareback rider. The young Indian men hooted to the large paint horse, they teased Brings Thunder for losing it. Philipp was quiet. At least everyone was home safe now. I brought in wood and tended the fire. I cooked.

And I cooked again in the morning. I made a special breakfast of French crêpes with fresh berries in sauce. Philipp loved it, but Two Bear Paws wrinkled his nose, tossed it aside, and demanded better food like bacon and eggs. I had sausage and quickly prepared him his own plate of alternate breakfast, in between trying not to burn the delicate crêpes in the frying pan. I never had time to eat. Chief went into the bedroom, leaving me to clean.

Philipp sat at the table and studied his Lakota/German dictionary. He looked up at me and said, "It is uh . . . amazing . . . you are, um, here on the reservation. It is . . . how you say . . . noble . . . what you have given up to be here." He talked about his life back home, his horses, the cabin he built for himself and his girlfriend.

I gave him one of my favorite Harley T-shirts to give to his girlfriend as a gift. We talked a bit more while I cleaned. Chief came in and sat with Philipp at the table. They talked man to man, then Chief went outside.

Philipp remained behind for a moment, he looked very sad. I asked what was wrong. He said, "He wants me to kill a horse." Philipp was upset the horse had been sick for a year. He felt it was wrong to let it go lame with a leg wrapped in barbed wire, untreated and infected for so long. He felt the

Indians could have tried harder to help when it happened, instead of letting the flesh grow around it, making the horse get sick. I remembered the day I watched Chief give antibiotics to this horse, a year too late.

I watched from the kitchen window now as Philipp somberly carried the rifle out to the shelter. He led the horse with a gentle hand under its nose. Although in pain, it followed his kindness willingly. I saw him pet it, speak softly, then let go. It limped behind him eagerly, not lead by rope or kicked by boots. He led it up over the hill so the other horses, who were gathered around the water and hay at the shelter, would not have to see.

I heard the rapport echo through the hills, knowing it was the sound of death. Part of me mourned—for the horse, and for Philipp. I knew how his heart must hurt to kill a horse, an animal he respected and loved so greatly.

Chief knew, too, that is why he smiled an evil grin when he heard the shot and laughed. He was upset, though, that Philipp had taken the horse so far away; he did not understand why he hadn't shot it at the shelter, close to home.

I looked up from the dishes. Through the window above the sink, I could see Philipp walking slowly over the hills, carrying the gun across his back, wearing a look of deep remorse on his face.

Chief stood up from the kitchen table and went out to meet him part way. He told him something that made Philipp even more heavy with emotional weight. Chief said, "Skin the horse." The hide would be used for decoration; it would later hang on the wall overlooking our kitchen table.

He instructed Philipp to slit the horse's body under the nose, down the middle of its throat, across the belly to its rear. The pelt hung outside the house, draped over fence rails, drying in the sun.

The mane and tail were still attached; the mane stuck up in a row down the middle of the top portion, the tail was a stiff brush off the back.

The horse's long hair looked gruesome as it flowed in the breeze, dancing around in the sunshine as if it remembered life instead of being attached to a dead, blood-stained hide.

Chief saw me looking and said, "The Lakota are not savages like some tribes. We do not eat horses."

CHAPTER TWENTY-FIVE:

Chief Big Foot Ride

It was time for the Big Foot ride. We loaded the U-Haul truck with cooking supplies, hay for the horses and bales of straw to sit on, buckets, rope, a cooler of ice filled with perishables: milk for coffee for the few who took it that way and sausage, other food in boxes and bags, a gasoline powered generator with a large electric coffee pot, sleeping bags, and warm blankets. Everyone was impressed Chief had a U-Haul truck; it was this year's model in mint condition, it had the newest style engine, heat, and air conditioning. It was perfect for transporting supplies. He laughed and said he stole it; his plan was to paint the sides white to hide the lettering. I felt sick when he voiced his intentions proudly to the others. This truck belonged back at U-Haul weeks ago.

Philipp noted my distress at Chief's braggart behavior. "You have to, uh, get that truck back to the company," he whispered. I nodded, wide eyed, knowing full well I must do that, but having no clue as to how. Chief was so proud to "own" it and always kept the keys.

The riders gathered their horses and tack. That is, what little tack they used. There was rumor a rich man on a hill was marketing the Big Foot ride to those outside the reservation. The Lakota heard he used their sacred event as a ploy to get donations of money and saddles for the ride. The Indians lamented they never saw a dollar or even one saddle from the hundreds of saddles and thousands of dollars he received for donations. Many rode with just blankets on their horses and grabbed a handful of mane. Those that had saddles did not have a good fit to their horse. Often, the saddle was too small

277

and cinched too tightly.

I thought this ride would be a man's thing, since women could not touch horses. On the morning of their departure, I held out a single white feather to Philipp. "My mother is sick. Would you carry this white feather on the Big Foot ride in prayer for her healing?" I had brought the feather with me from my home town in Connecticut.

Philipp agreed and wrapped the white feather in a piece of soft buckskin, he put it in his pouch next to his hunting knife. He later told me he took the feather out and said a prayer as the sacred journey began, then carried it in the breast pocket of his shirt the entire way, often saying a prayer for her. When I told my mother about this months later, she cried with appreciation.

The men rode away on horseback. I expected Two Bear Paws to follow with the U-Haul truck. I imagined he would be gone a few days, possibly two weeks. When he motioned for me to go with him, I suggested, "No, it's okay. You go on ahead. I will stay here."

"No, you come."

"I need to stay here and keep the house warm for you and the riders when you get back. You are taking Hunter with you and there are only two seats in the U-Haul. I will stay here and cook and care for Skyler."

"No! Take car." He handed me the keys.

"But Chief, we will be gone so long. What about my parrots?"

"Forget them! You come with me! Leave now!"

"Ok, let me get my coat and boots."

I ran into the bathroom and unplugged the space heater, as I passed by Skyler's room, I asked her to follow me. I set the heater next to the bird cages in the bedroom with a prayer nobody would steal it. I told her Chief was making me leave for a while, I asked if she would care for my birds while I was gone. She nodded. I showed her how to lift the little doors to reach the food cups, keeping her fingers safe from biting beaks.

I showed her the bags of food kept inside a metal can to keep out the rodents. I asked her to also change the water each day. She said she would do it. Their life depended on her.

There was no need to lock the bedroom, there was nothing left to steal. Besides, his sons would be on the Big Foot ride with us, almost every young man would be. I put on my coat and cowboy hat, grabbed my boots and bag, and headed out.

A line of ratty pickups and rez cars followed the Big Foot riders down the road a few miles, showing support for this great journey. Chief motioned for me to follow; I did as instructed and trailed behind the U-Haul truck as the caravan slowly drove behind those on horseback.

Women and children lined the frosty grass on the sides of the road, men who were not riding on this journey leaned over my windshield and glared at me. They stepped in so close I feared I might run over their feet. Their hate was obvious as they snarled at me, the token White Man. They shook their fists at my face through the glass as if I was not supposed to be here. I was confused by their behavior because my heart was pure. I was shocked and saddened at how mean their eye contact felt and how threatening their words sounded.

We traveled a way I had not been before; it was even more desolate than anything imaginable. I believe we went through Allen, South Dakota, which is listed as the poorest city in the United States, then headed up to Kyle, SD, which is eleven miles from the North American continental pole of inaccessibility. The riders would then head up towards Wall through the badlands.

This must have been why Chief laughed when I asked if I could take the car and go stay in a motel maybe. I really just wanted to go back home and check on the birds. Chief said I could never find the way out of here, there were no roads. He held out his hand for the car keys.

We spent the first night with a feast and ceremony in the middle of nowhere. It seemed to be a schoolhouse under the stars with no other building or sign of human life for eons in any direction. Inside the building, the lucky ones had folding chairs, the rest sprawled out on the muddy floor. There was a humble kitchen in the schoolhouse where women had cooked all day; traditional Lakota food was laid out on long folding tables. Everyone took pre-dished plates of food and ate. Philipp gave me his fry bread, he knew how much I loved it, and I gave him the meat from my plate in return.

Men sounded the buffalo drum; they called out in Lakota to Red Man's god. They marched in a circle and chanted for their Ancestors with ancient words, they wore feathered headdresses and carried giant staffs tied with eagle feathers. The atmosphere felt like somber war with a festive flair.

I closed my eyes and listened. The sound of the drum made pictures behind my eyelids. The emptiness I saw became an expanse of sky filled with oil and land turned to water.

The sound of singing turned the sky into sweet almond oil dyed purple, it swirled down as the water rose up and turned into an ocean of human blood. Then, the entire image compressed and became contained inside a clear glass jar.

Purple bubbles of oil slid through the red liquid of life, the two never mixing, the alluring combination beautiful, yet the truth of what it was horrifying.

This vision was a symbol to me for the bitter-sweet, beauty-sadness, push-pull paradox of the reservation itself and the energy here in the room tonight.

This gathering, which seemed to celebrate war, honor for the dead, and nobility of Lakota life, settled into a calm lull as a hundred people crowded onto the cold, wet, mud-soaked floor to sleep. I could hear raspy coughs coming from the young and old alike. Everyone seemed sick with the flu. I don't know what tuberculosis looks like, but I am sure it sounded like some of the men in this small room, heated only by bodies and the breath of the ill.

Chief Two Bear Paws told me to use the payphone in the

corner to call Deena at home and tell her we made it. There was a long, coughing line waiting to use the only payphone. "Sure, I can do that. Just let me go to the car first and grab my bag."

"Why?"

"I have to get coins for the phone."

That made sense to Chief, he gave me the keys. "Get a cloth for my face, too." Hunter met me at the car and said he was cold; he wanted to hang out in the car. I locked him in and went back inside with my bag.

Chief took the keys, I handed him the face towel. In front of the other men, he got angry. "No! This is wrong! Wet the cloth! You should know this by now! This is woman's work, do it right!" The towel hit me in the chest and the men looked at me with disgust.

This was the first time I had ever gotten him a cloth. I went to the kitchen to do it right and dampen the rag with warm water. Women washing dishes had heard Two Bear Paws yell, they glanced nervously at my ignorance. One brave woman whispered in my ear, "You better learn fast."

I brought the damp rag back to him, he wiped his face. I sat down in the empty folding chair between Chief and Philipp, digging in my bag for quarters for the phone. I also took my hand sanitizer out of my bag.

Chief's eyes lit with fire. "NO! Put that away!" He pushed my hand deep into my bag and was highly offended. I only wanted to wipe the phone down, as everyone had been hacking away on it. He pointed to the door. "Leave." I stood outside in the cold.

Hunter was asleep, curled up under a blanket in the back seat of the car. I gently tapped on the window and he let me in. Philipp came over and asked if he could sleep in the car, too, since the floor of the schoolhouse was a few inches of thick, cold mud. I was glad to see his love for the Lakota had not blinded him to the highly filthy and unsanitary conditions in there; I was relived I was not the only one to notice.

I pulled a blanket around me in the front seat and turned my back to Philipp. He reclined the passenger side and soon slept without a word. Since Chief had banished me to the cold outside without keys to either vehicle, I did not know what he expected me to do besides this to survive. The three of us dozed for a while until Chief was done with the gathering and came outside. He banged on the glass beside my head and yelled for me to get in the truck, he told Philipp he had to sleep inside the building on the floor like everyone else, he was not special. Philipp went back inside and spread his sleeping bag out on the mud. Hunter spent the night in the car.

Chief and I crawled into the back of the U-Haul truck. I pulled the door down against the frost, securing it with a yellow nylon rope, leaving only a few inches for air and moonlight at the bottom.

It was cold enough that exposed flesh would have fused to the metal floor. I put a layer of straw down, I gathered blankets and some clothes for pillows, enough for the both of us, side by side for warmth. I lay down and closed my eyes, glad I would not have to tend the fire or get the juice tonight. I hoped I might actually get five hours of uninterrupted sleep. I was dreaming to think that, for Chief Two Bear Paws got right into my face.

He was on his hands and knees beside me, nose to nose with mine. His teeth became fangs; no wolf could match his vicious face inside that cold, metal box that night. He growled, "You think you are better than us? You look down on us. We are dirty Indians to you. You take out your White Man's medicine as protection against touching us. White Man has always thought he is better than us, we have always been dirty Indians to him. You insult us with your presence."

He grabbed me by the throat and started choking me. Death sweat froze in prickles on my body; I could smell the deer I killed and the smell of death this time was my own.

With the last breath I had left inside me, I squeaked out, "Wait, Chief, wait, I love you, please, let me speak." Easily, they could have been my last words. I would have died there in the cold in the back of the U-Haul truck, my body tossed into the prairie. People would have said I died of exposure like Annie Mae.

Two Bear Paws held me by the neck against the floor, but his grip loosened a little to allow me to speak. He was doing me no favors by still crushing my windpipe; air whistled as I sucked it into my body.

I said in a raspy voice, "You are a great leader of your people. They look in your eyes and see a respected elder; I look in your eyes and see a legend to his people. I respect and love you and all your people. Before I moved here, I was a germ freak. I always wiped down door handles and even silverware at restaurants. It is not Indians I hate, it is germs. Even White Man's germs I wipe away. Germs make all people sick. Getting sick and dying, that is my enemy. Not Indians. I love all of you and would never hurt you." With that, he took his hands away.

As we drifted off to sleep in the freezing air, he told me a bedtime story about the 1862 Sioux Uprising. The money promised to the Indians by White Man's U.S. government had not come through, the stores refused to offer Indians any more food on credit. A goods trader commented haughtily that he did not care if the Indians starved to death, as far as he was concerned "let them eat grass." A few days later, the man was found dead with grass stuffed into his mouth and stomach.

Chief Two Bear Paws told me tales of the Indians who had killed the arrogant White Man and stuffed grass down his throat into his stomach; he was proud of them. He was deeply mournful for the starving Indians and admired his Dakota brothers for the strength their leaders showed in standing up for their people.

This incident eventually led to Chief Big Foot traveling

with his band of Miniconjou Lakota to seek counsel with Oglala Lakota war leader Chief Red Cloud on the Pine Ridge Reservation.

Chief Big Foot hoped to find a better life for his people, but their hope died at the Wounded Knee Massacre of 1890.

Naturally, all this was on Chief's mind tonight.

He told me I reminded him of the callous white man who wanted the Indians to starve, die, and "eat grass" when I brought out my hand sanitizer. He almost sounded apologetic for what darkness had come over him as he tried to kill me.

"Chief Big Foot was sick. He had pneumonia. It got worse on his journey to Wounded Knee. He surrendered because he was so sick." No wonder my talk of germs had caused Chief's grip to loosen.

I wasn't sure if it was his attempt at reconciliation or if it was simply the frigid air which made him decide to put his arm around me and hold me this night, but this was the first and only time he chose to have me so close. Somehow, as much as I had always desired it in the past, I did not find comfort in his embrace. Daybreak and the frosted morning could not come soon enough.

The next day we traveled through nothingness and roadlessness until Chief said it was the right place to set up camp. Our band of riders met up with more riders in a patch of grassy area surrounded by trees.

Chief gave me an order: "Make the fire." I gathered fallen branches, dry grass, and bark from the wooded area around us, men tied their horses to bushes on the outskirts of the growing brush pile. Philipp was the only one who came over to help. As he bent to pick up wood, my heart was grateful but my whisper sharp. "No. Thank you, but this is woman's work. Go back with the men and drink some coffee."

I carried an armful of kindling to the center of the clearing. Foregoing the old ways, I walked over to the U-Haul to get some matches and the gas can. I noticed Hunter was hunkered down beside one of the truck's tires. Something on the ground held his attention. I started to check if he was okay. Chief leaned out the back of the U-Haul, where he was pouring coffee for the riders and happily showing off his generator powered, electric coffee pot. He jumped down and stood next to me with his palm out to stop my interference.

Hunter had built a circle of rocks; in the middle he had trapped a deer mouse. As he lifted a large rock, I winced. Chief's gesture held me back as Hunter dropped the weight on top of the mouse for no apparent reason other than the joy of killing. He picked up the rock and admired his skill. Chief smiled with pride and told me to get back to work making the fire.

I headed to the other side of the gathering, looking for more wood over there. I saw a mid-twenties young man on a horse, the saddle was too small and it was cinched too tightly. The young Indian had been riding for hours this way, pushing the animal onward; there was still much ride ahead in the days to come. There was no saddle blanket or pad, just an improperly fit saddle pulling against horse flesh. The horse's skin had peeled back along the edges of the saddle. Blood was trickling down its belly and legs. The Indian kicked it onward towards the fire.

I saw many horses treated poorly, heavy boots kicked horse flesh so hard the animals were bleeding with the repeated impact; blood collected in the soles of boots and stained the snow as the men dismounted.

A horse's face is the most sensitive part of its body; ropes pulled too hard or wrapped too tight rubbed faces raw in the cold weather. A hackamore was often used. The colorful, braided reigns caught my eye, as well as the large, bright tassels that dangled from the horse's chin for weight and decoration. This type of bridle should be used with an easy hand by the most experienced for training purposes. The thick bosal over the horse's delicate nose is even more painful than an aggressively handled bit when abused; it can break fragile bones and cause sores like the ones on these horse's faces which would never heal.

Horses were punched in the head, face, neck, withers, belly and rear. They were whipped, slapped, kicked, spurred, and beaten into submission.

Like Indian women, horses learned obedience means survival.

Reality is a horse that cannot be broken. Stereotypes view Indians as gentle, kind-spirited beings in tune with nature and all living things. The Indians gathered here today for this sacred journey in no way resembled that romantic notion; their anger showed in all they touched. Yet, the horses they abused were not ferocious monsters.

Horses can be connected with by using kindness. After my time on the reservation, when I moved to Hot Springs, SD, I took a bus ride way out into wild horse country where the movie *Dances With Wolves* was filmed. People on the old blue bus watched the wild herds run and play. Horses would scatter as the bus approached. Some of these wild horses lived their entire life span without ever seeing a human. These horses were not pets, they wore no shoes, they saw no vets. They were not given treats; they were not petted, brushed, nor cooed over. If they got into fights, they bit, they bled, they healed. Their untamed manes were scraggly and long. The guide told us the wild mustangs with the zebra-striped inner leg markings were descendents of the first Spanish horses brought to America.

The driver brought us on a walking tour around the bus, he pointed to naturally growing white sage bushes identified by green leaves covered in fuzzy gray softness. All the people on the bus were white tourists; they admired the natural sage with sounds of awe. Dried versions of this sacred plant were what I sprinkled on the hot rocks during the sweat. I walked the other way.

I knelt down far from the crowd and chose a horse in the

distance. His back was to me. He was standing with many other horses. "Come." My heart called out to this one wild gray being. He heard my voice without sound and perked his ears; his spirit saw me before his eyes. He now turned his head and trotted away from the other horses towards me. He walked up and laid his head in my hand. I gently petted his nose, it was the softest velvet.

Another person approached, the gray horse startled and raced back to the protection of his herd, black mane and tail flying. A little love goes a long way. I wish Chief Two Bear Paws had learned that about me.

Flames from the fire gave warmth and light, tin cups were handed out and filled with beans and sausage from the pot. This would be the Big Foot riders' last hot meal before we parted ways; many would fast on this spirit journey.

As I watched the horses' long faces bathed in flickering firelight and saw the men warmed by food and burning timber, it felt good to be a woman. It was my place to provide and I was proud to serve.

The men headed out early the next morning. I saw Philipp ride with skill and kindness. The half wild horse listened because Philipp's confidence was clear, yet his words were soft and his spirit gentle. His horse danced circles around the others, turning this way and that up the steep hills, cantering into a gallop, then slowing to a walk, ears up and flipped backwards, listening to Philipp, a friend to horses, and trusting him.

Chief drove the truck, I followed in the car, we went home to await the riders' return.

As soon as we set foot inside the house, I ran to the bedroom to see if my parrots were still alive. The fire was out, but the space heater was on and their corner of the room was warm. They chirped with happiness to see me, they had food and fresh water in their cups. I was grateful to Skyler, who stood beside their cages and smiled. My words thanked her from my heart. She tilted her head as if to say, "watch this" and reached her finger inside the cage bars. Snickers bent his head into her hand and enjoyed being petted. Sweet Skyler, the young girl with butterflies dancing in the sunshine of her hand, had obviously spent time talking to the birds, caring for them, and earning their trust while I had been gone.

"ZINTKALA!" Chief bellowed my name from the kitchen. I came running. "What are you doing?" he demanded.

"Checking on my birds to see if they are alive."

"No!" his fist hit the table. "The first thing a woman does when she gets home is tend the fire. Then, she feeds the children if they are hungry. Make the fire, feed the children. Then, look in on the birds!"

CHAPTER TWENTY-SIX:

Christmas

Almost two weeks later, the riders would return from their journey through the wilderness. They had faced the snow and cold, found their inner strength and shown endurance while honoring the Ancestors and their People on this vision quest of solitude and dignity.

But I would not be there to see it. I screwed up and let my pride get in the way, causing me to miss the emotional day of December 29th, which is the yearly anniversary of the 1890 Massacre.

Christmas Eve day I asked if we could make a special trip to the store so I could buy everything I needed to make nine cheesecakes from scratch with various fruit toppings. Chief saw no reason to disagree with that and we got right on it. The total came to more than a hundred dollars for supplies. I knew it would be such a treat, it was my gift to everyone on this special day. I started baking and Chief gave me my space. He took the grandkids with him to help set up tables at the round building for the festivities.

The only time I was ever alone in the house for any duration was when Chief took the grandchildren to school if the snow was deep or they missed the bus, but he was always back within the hour. This time was different. I had the house to myself for about four hours. It was glorious.

The late afternoon air was warm for winter and the kitchen was hot. I opened the door and my world turned lusciously breezy. The largest expanse of endless sunset spread out before me. Forever was a blanket laid above the hills. The sunset was pink fire. Long, pink clouds burned with passion against a rich, ice blue sky. This moment is the most breathtaking of any I experienced on the rez, and it was mine alone. I played my favorite Dixie Chicks CD and sang to the fire in the clouds as I folded the sour cream and cream cheese batter.

My father called just as the desserts were done baking. I was happy to share this moment with him. I got eight cakes out of the oven just fine, but the ninth fell out of my hands and crumbled upon the open oven door. My father laughed and said, "I'll eat it! Sounds good to me!" I laughed and scooped hot cheesecake into little bowls, it would be something different for the grandchildren to try when they came home from the round building with Chief.

I used this time to set up the presents I had been secretly stashing away; I had purchased them in Connecticut during my Thanksgiving break. I wrapped the gifts and set them around the room along with the Christmas card Amandah had sent. Her card was full of silver sparkles and carried a loving blessing across the miles as if no pain had taken place between us. Her gesture tugged faintly at my heart.

But I brushed it away and chose to focus on my Lakota family. For Chief, I had bought a Denver Broncos stocking and filled it with a case of his favorite orange tangerine gum; he could never get enough of that gum. His aunt and mother were getting luxurious deep purple shawls, Skyler would receive a butterfly necklace with a blue sapphire, Deena silver dreamcatcher earrings, and Hunter a fifty dollar watch. This gift impressed Chief most of all, he later told me it was good and right his grandson got it. Hunter would be the talk of his school and the only Lakota Indian with a watch.

For Philipp, I made a white feather ornament wrapped with silver beads and wire. It was a small token of thanks for carrying my mother's feather of healing on the Big Foot ride. I wrapped the gift and laid it on his mattress beside the living room fire.

Philipp later told me he found a scrap of wrapping paper

with the tag addressed to him, he asked me about it. I told him it had been a gift. He said somebody else got into it and took it before he had a chance to see it.

A few weeks earlier, I had said to Chief, "I don't know if you already have something you are thinking of giving me for Christmas, but if I could put in a request, the thing I would like the most would be to sleep in on Christmas Day." He never made a sound. I wasn't even sure if he had heard me.

I woke up Christmas Day, feeling rested for the first time in months. I was startled Chief was not lying next to me; he was nowhere in the room and daylight shone through the window. I looked at the new bedside clock radio, it was 9:08 a.m. I could have cried. Chief loved me so much he had listened to what I asked for and gave me my wish for Christmas. He even gave me more than I asked by not waking me to get the juice or tend the fire throughout the night. He had slid out of bed without waking me for the first time ever. I was beside myself with complete joy. Then, I started to panic as I heard the women in the kitchen cooking. I should be out there helping! I hoped asking to sleep in had not been the wrong request.

Two Bear Paws walked into the bedroom and told me my father was on the phone, he handed me the portable. The fact Chief told me was another gift. I was getting showered with thoughtfulness and affection this holiday. My dad wished me a Merry Christmas and that was icing on the cake. Cake! I had to get out there and put the strawberry, blueberry, and cherry toppings on my cheesecakes. I ran out to the kitchen, everyone was in a festive mood. Deena gave me a butter soft, white deerskin bracelet she beaded in a geometric pattern with all shades of blue seed beads. She tied the straps onto my left wrist and I felt so loved. The rest of the presents would be shared at the round building later. The kitchen crew was taking off in that direction now; they would set up some food there, then gather at a neighbor's house to put the finishing touches on their gifts.

Everyone left and I was alone in the house with Chief. I went to the bedroom to change out of my slippers, T-shirt, and pajama bottoms— *"ZINTKALA!"*—but I didn't get the chance. As soon as I made it into the bedroom, Chief yelled my name from the kitchen table, where he sat reading the newspaper.

This was his way and it annoyed everyone. Most every time, Chief would be reading the paper and the party hollered for would be elbows and knees deep in household work he had already delegated. Chief would yell as if it were an emergency and once you dropped everything and arrived at his feet, he would give a seemingly insignificant order or ask for some little item closer to him than you, since you used to be across the house a few seconds ago and the little thing he wanted was almost sitting beside his wrist.

I had requested politely on several occasions if he could please come find me and tell me what was on his mind, such as the chore he wanted me to do next, or that it was time to leave for the store. If it was an object he wanted, perhaps he could simply wait until I was in the room again and then ask for the item and I would be glad to hand it to him, as I was never far from him for long. I told him the yelling startled me and was very disrespectful.

Not caring what I thought or felt, he continually boomed my name and everyone else's across the house. Even Deena and the grandkids found his habit obnoxious. They would sigh and roll their eyes from the other room where he could not see, but then they would still respectfully run full speed to Chief.

This time, I calmly walked into the kitchen and stood there, arms folded.

"Make the coffee."

I got the large, stainless steel coffee pot out from under the counter and set it up to brew. It would take about an hour. I took my eight cheesecakes out of the fridge and lined them up on the counter. My plan was to go back to the bedroom and change into daytime clothes because I would have to bring my cheesecakes down to the round building after I topped them with fruit.

As I was headed back to change, I paused by the kitchen table. I thought twice before I spoke, then decided not to listen to the small inner voice which told me to keep walking without a word. It was too late to try to salvage my inner dignity by calmly walking past him without a word, for I had already chosen to pause beside the table. Pausing without speaking felt like I was giving in to his verbal abuse. It was time I politely stood up for myself and got some respect.

"Chief, I have asked you many times to please not scream my name. Come to me if you need something. It is very disrespectful to sit there and yell someone's name when it is not an emergency."

Chief stood up so quickly his folding chair fell over backwards. He threw the newspaper down and pounded both fists on the table. He leaned forward on his knuckles and glared at me like a bull pawing the earth before a charge. I should have heeded the warning.

He swore at me.

I said the same swear back to him, demanding respect.

He flew around the kitchen table so fast I never saw it coming. There was no arc of his arm this time, there was only sudden impact. He hit me full on the jaw. I fell back into the door. I almost stumbled and crashed to the floor, but the vision of Chief kicking his ex-wife's teeth in as she was doubled up on the floor begging for mercy filled my head. I was not going to fall to the floor. And I was not going to beg.

I caught myself and stood up straight. I held my chin and the side of my face in the palm of my hand. "No. No, no, no. NO!" The last "no" freed my feet and brought a powerful will to live over me.

Just as he was swinging for me again, I miraculously ducked, released the latch, and ran out the door. Certain I would never make it, my feet moved faster than they ever had before as "flight" became my only option since "fight" had almost won me death.

I flew down the hill in my slippers and pajamas, running a mile across the acres to the nearest neighbor's house. I entered the kitchen, still holding my face, afraid to take my hand away and see my own blood.

The neighbor's kitchen was filled with women. Everyone was sewing and cooking and putting finishing touches on gifts. They all looked at me when I burst into the room.

I said, "He hit me."

I expected them to gather around me and hug me and let me cry. But they dropped their gaze and went back to work.

After a few moments, Deena came over and gently lifted my hand from the side of my face. Small, quick glances from the crowd evaluated the situation. They had seen worse. There was no blood, I still had my teeth, my jaw was connected and no bones were broken; they went back to work without comment.

I stood there, stunned, silent. Finally, a middle-aged woman spoke up very softly. "I thought it would be different this time. I thought you were the one to change him. He has hit us all." This woman, I realized, was Chief's most recent ex-wife.

She had spoken first, now the others felt free to offer whispered confessions. Deena said, "Dad's broken my nose a few times."

"Me too," said another woman, everyone looked at her; they nodded, remembering that injury.

Each woman came forward and told her story of how Chief had physically harmed her, too; his abuse spanned decades. I was horrified.

Yet, somewhere in the back of my mind, the stupid part of me still under his spell thought, "Wow, he must love me because after hearing these women's stories, I think at the last second he pulled that punch."

I suppose, looking back, I should also have been grateful as I was running across the prairie to the neighbor's house. Grateful Chief did not chase after me with his pickup truck and run me down like the last girl who tried to get away. I heard about that incident later from a non-reservation woman who knew him and the girl who came into his life a few women before me. He didn't kill her, but he chased her pretty hard with the truck at night across the prairie and left her for dead in a ditch.

The women let me use their phone to call my father; they listened as I told him what had happened. My dad said he knew it was coming; he'd get me out of there. I just needed a ride to the airport in Rapid. I offered a hundred dollars cash and a tank of gas for help to the women in the kitchen. Chief's ex-wife said her husband would be home soon with his good truck and she would ask him what he thought. I was choked up at the bond these women share; it has no boundaries. Here she was helping me with no hard feelings for being with her ex, when I had found it disconcerting to have her new husband perform my wedding ceremony.

It choked me up. I looked around at everyone who had been abused. I told them how sorry I was. "It's not right. All of you have been hurt because you are women. But you don't have a rich father who can bail you out and save you with a plane ticket to somewhere safe. You have to stay here and take it. I am so sorry. It's not fair. It is not right."

They nodded with silent agreement as they kept quilting, crafting, and cooking. I finally understood what it means to be a Lakota woman.

I realized my wallet was in the pocket of my sweatshirt back in the bedroom at Chief's house. I couldn't go anywhere without it. Someone suggested I call the tribal police and ask for an escort into the house. The tribal police asked if I wanted to press charges. The woman around me coached me to say no, shaking their heads, wide-eyed with fear. I said I only wanted an escort into the house to get my things. A woman officer picked me up and took me back to the house in her cruiser. The area was empty; Chief Two Bear Paws had vacated and swiftly padlocked all the doors. He was long gone in his pickup truck.

Earlier that same morning, I had been looking out over the prairie while I talked on the phone, listening to my father wish me a Merry Christmas. I saw the horses coming in to drink from the trough and I was overcome with a feeling I could not explain: it told me to unlatch the window. It did not make sense, but I had listened. It paid off in this moment; it saved my bird's lives. Chief would have killed them for certain.

When I was halfway through the bedroom window, the female tribal police officer stopped me and said, "How can I be sure you are not breaking into this house and stealing those birds?"

"Watch me through the window. They have strong beaks. They will step on my hand and easily go inside their pink travel carrier out of their own free will. If they were not my birds and I was stealing them, I would have to catch them, they would bite me, draw blood, and I would have to stuff them into a pillowcase."

She gave me a chance, but she seemed skeptical. The birds were easy and trusting as I had said. She watched me. I explained everything I was doing, the food I was taking for them, and the towel to cover the carrier from the cold. I put on my cowboy hat and hooded sweatshirt, knowing my wallet was in the pocket, and climbed with the travel cage back through the window. I said a prayer for Blue Fish and hoped he would survive without me. The policewoman still didn't seem to trust me, but she took me back to the house where my hundred dollar ride to the airport waited. I gave them the cash. They said they needed some gas now and a tank fill-up once we got there. I agreed. After all, this was Christmas day they'd be missing; it was two hours there and two hours back for them.

Thinks He Is Chief and Chief's ex-wife took me to the

airport in their extended cab truck. I leaned in between them from the back seat. Thinks He Is Chief said nothing the entire time, perhaps he felt he was doing wrong against Chief, or perhaps he realized I was not the woman he hoped I could be during the pre-marriage meeting. Or maybe I think too much and he was just driving and focusing on the road in simple silence.

While I was trying to figure it out and listening to his wife talk, Thinks He Is Chief lifted his index finger ever so slightly up in a half circle gesture. I looked at his wife, horrified she wasn't making a move to help him. I waited as long as I could. Time was ticking, he had spoken. A woman needs to react quickly when a man speaks.

I reached out and opened his soda can. He nodded and drank. His wife stopped talking, her mouth hung open with surprise. She looked at me and said, "How did you know he wanted you to do that?"

"He moved his finger."

"Well! I never notice those things. How am I supposed to see that? And how am I supposed to know what it means if I did happen to see it?"

Thinks He Is Chief looked at me with a sideways glance and nodded slightly; I took it to mean Chief Two Bear Paws had taught me very well.

My plane arrived in Connecticut around one a.m. My father was there to pick me and the birds up. He said I could stay one night in their home, tonight only, because it was so late. I had to spend the rest of my time in a hotel until I found an apartment and a job. I had hurt my family too badly; no one could bear to see me this time around. His words surprised me; I had discovered the boundaries of family love. I had tested the limits and broken them. My family was shattered and the apron strings were cut, just like Chief wanted. I cut deep when I cut the strings, slicing wounds that never healed.

For this, my one night, I set the birds and carrier in my

parent's finished basement and took a shower. My mother had put a clean nightgown out for me, since I had no clothes besides the ones I traveled in. I put it on and crawled into the futon in the loft area above the living room, it was more comfortable than the couch in the basement.

My legs were still scabbed up and itching. When I lay down on those crisp, clean, cool, white sheets, I felt all the pain, pressure, and itching release from my body. I could feel the bugs crawling out of my skin and setting me free. I thought I must be imagining it.

I slept five blessedly consecutive hours before my father woke me. It was time to go to the hotel before the rest of the family got up. I understood. That was fair. I grabbed the birds. He picked me up later that afternoon and handed me the classifieds, pre-circled. In between looking at apartments, I read over his suggested job offerings. The pay scale was no better than South Dakota, but Connecticut rents were outrageous. Dad and Amandah were willing to set me back on my feet. They offered to co-sign a lease for an apartment that allowed birds since my credit was shot from Chief's debts and desires; they even offered to pay the hefty deposit.

I contrasted the common, the rat race life I was about to get into against the fiery sunsets and horses of Chief's reservation ranch. I missed him. I still loved him and wanted that life to work out with all my heart. I was a fool. I knew he really hit me this time, and I knew I've always said if someone hurt me physically, I'd be gone for good. I learned the situation looks quite different when you're viewing it from the inside. I wasn't sure if I'd end up back with Chief, but I knew I sure wasn't cut out to live the 9 to 5 soul sucking city life.

I rationalized to my dad I needed to go back to my trailer in Hot Springs because it was cheaper than rent in Connecticut.

I checked Hot Springs want ads online, made a few calls, and got a job finishing sheetrock. There, now I had a good job and cheap rent at a trailer I was already paying for. How could anyone argue with that? Going back to South Dakota was only logical.

My family wrote me off.

I rented a car, bought new cages, and drove back to Hot Springs with my birds. My feathered kids were the happiest I'd seen them in a long time. I returned the rental and took the only taxi in town back to my trailer. The first sheetrock job was just down the street; my boss gave me a lift back and forth, since I had no vehicle. I bought him cigarettes. It was a start.

I was surprised to hear from my mother. She called to say she had bedbugs. She wanted to know if I knew anything about that. She had been sitting on the floor in the loft area above the living room, watching TV, leaning her back against the futon, when she started to itch. She noticed red bites, they swelled into welts and scabbed over, itching like crazy.

The doctor said he'd never seen anything like it, "It looks like bedbugs, but it's a type I've never seen before. Where did you contract something like this?" He was shocked she'd picked it up in the U.S. "Something like this would only be found in a remote, third world country."

He was fascinated. He gave her all the known bedbug remedies, and even some extra creams and salves he thought might do the trick. Nothing helped. She picked a scab and found a bug imbedded on the soft side. I said mine had been the same way. She also found relief in the blood-letting.

She later told me the only thing that cured her a hundred percent was summertime. She would sit on the deck by the pool during the hottest part of the day, burning and re-burning her skin hours at a time for weeks until it almost blistered. Only that killed the bugs completely and freed her of the torture. What a horrible, lasting Christmas present I had left for my parents.

Replaying the doctor's comments in my head, I felt certain the bugs must have come from Rosebud. I wondered who Chief was sleeping with now. I felt homesick for my Lakota family. I wanted them back. Chief was my husband; I missed him. I was sure it was time for his medication and he was not taking it.

JANUARY
through
mid-FEBRUARY

CHAPTER TWENTY-SEVEN:

Interference

The reservation still called to me; I could not shake it. The beauty is what got me. The beautiful people there among the sadness, the strength of those who seem to have nothing but have everything for a moment.

It's each day's goal to discover that beautiful moment among the tragedy. I never failed to find it. It was even more lovely when it found me, like the magpie on the fence, or the grandchildren hugging on me as I sketched, or the big paint horse that followed me up the hill. Beauty was there on the reservation more than anywhere else I'd ever felt. I would rather live in abject poverty with a much shorter life span but have moments of pure spirit and happiness than live forever as a billionaire with emptiness of heart.

It was never the poverty that deterred me, never the disease, unsanitary conditions, bugs or garbage, those things were never even a thought in my head as a reason for not staying. I kept looking for the good and always found it each day. I was happy on the reservation.

It would have all worked out if Chief could have been a little nicer to me. The only thing I was missing was love and respect from my partner. Maybe he had changed.

I called Two Bear Paws. He was surprised to hear from me. He said he felt very bad for what he had done. He told me he had smoked the sacred pipe and prayed to *Tunkashila* for forgiveness. "I have made a vow before *Tunkashila* never to hit a woman again. I am sorry I hit you. I have changed for good."

He had said the only words that would fix this, something I had been waiting a long time to hear. I knew this man offered apologies seldom, if at all, as he was deserving of so many that went unsaid from White Man. I chose to believe him and his vow. "Ok, tell you what, why don't we start over? I'm at my trailer, come see me."

He came. He was dressed up. I asked if he wanted me to cook dinner. He waved his hand, pushing the idea away. "Go to movie."

"Alright." I got dressed nice and was ready to accompany him.

"Bring the birds."

I froze.

"Get the birds!"

"Why?"

"They go with us."

"To the movies?"

Chief's face was stern, his jaw set firm. He stared straight ahead.

I knew that reply. I was not falling for this again. "Okay, look, why don't we just go to the movies. You and me, romantic, you know? After the movie, we'll come back here and spend the night in the trailer. We can be alone together without everyone else around. We can work on rebuilding our love. We'll go back to the reservation tomorrow in the daylight." I was trying to buy a little time so I could assess his behavioral change for longer than five minutes. If it all looked okay by daylight, I really would go back.

"No. I am taking you with me. Tonight. Last chance, get the birds or leave them here to starve."

I said okay, went to the bedroom and called the landlady. She never trusted that I had an Indian boyfriend and she thought it was a bad sign I was never at my trailer. But I paid the rent; she wanted to keep me alive. She said she knew from the beginning this day was coming. I hoped she would send her good-sized adult son, my neighbor, over to talk sense into Chief or escort him out. She said she was calling the police.

I went back into the kitchen.

"Where are the birds?"

"I'm not bringing them because I'm not going anywhere. You need to leave, Chief. I'm sorry but the police are coming."

He growled and pulled his arm back. I ducked and unlocked the back door. "Here. Go out this way." The cruiser's lights flashed through the window, bathing the kitchen walls in strobe light as White Man's police pounded on the front door. Chief took me up on my offer and sprinted out the back way.

The cops came inside and talked with me. They told me they knew Chief, he was wanted by the FBI. They said he's been in some serious trouble with the law, anytime he is off the reservation and on U.S. soil he can be arrested. One officer had been walking around the back of the trailer while the other banged on the front door. That officer said he saw Chief, but he jumped over a fence too fast to catch and he lost him. I was relieved. They told me I had to get out of my trailer right now.

"What? He's gone. I'm just going to lock the doors and go to bed."

"Ma'am, we can't allow that. Don't you have friends or family you can stay with?"

"No, I just moved here. I have nobody."

"Well then, we will have to take you to a women's shelter."

"What!"

"Anytime there is a domestic violence report we cannot leave the victim in the same setting. This Indian knows where you live. He or someone he sends will come by and kill you tonight if you stay here. That's how these Indians do it, we've seen it happen before. We know his kind. And we know *him*. You are in great danger. You need to leave with us right now."

I put the birds in a carrier together and grabbed my coat. "Ma'am, pets are not allowed."

Almost at the same time, the other officer said, "What's in there, a cat?"

"No, it's just a cat carrier with a perch inside. I have two parrots in here." The interested officer craned his neck to see inside. My babies chirped to say hello. He smiled.

I smiled back. "Come on, they are just little birds. Please let me bring them, it will be alright."

"Ma'm, you can't bring those birds with you."

The friendly officer straightened up and stood by his partner's decision.

"What am I supposed to do? They will die here alone without someone to care for them. Plus, I guess I have to let the trailer go, too, since you say I can't live here anymore."

"You are going to have to give the birds to a neighbor. Go, go on. Get rid of them now. We will wait for you. Knock on a few doors 'til somebody takes them in."

I was too devastated to show emotion. This couldn't be real. Getting killed by Chief's blow would have hurt less than parting with Snickers and R.D.

My neighbor, the landlady's son, said he'd take them. I handed him the pet carrier and the key to my trailer so he could get their cages and food. He told me he would keep the birds a few days, but their final home would be with his sister up in Rapid City. He said he would give me her name and phone number if I vowed to never ask for the birds back. Dizzy, I nodded, what else could I do. He wrote her information on a scrap of paper so I could arrange for a visit in the future.

The policemen took me to the station. It was all happening so fast; I was too stunned to realize I had lost my feathered babies for good. I would never see them again.

An officer asked me questions and filled out forms. The friendlier cop asked for my father's phone number. He called my dad and explained the situation. "Sir, your daughter is safe. We have her. We are taking her to a women's shelter."

My dad started to cry with relief. "Thank you."

The cop got choked up in response. "It's okay, sir. She's in good hands. We will take care of her."

Everything was happening too fast. It did not feel right to

me. At the women's shelter, they asked me to name my attacker. I had left that line blank intentionally. I was told it was a required part of the check-in process. Still, I refused to give a name.

"You can't stay here unless you write his name on this form."

I considered my lack of options. I chose what I felt would still honor Chief in some small way. "I will agree to *say* his name, but I refuse to write it."

I had argued so much by this point, she rolled her eyes and poised the pen above the clipboard. When I said his name, the four women in the room gasped and ushered me into the next room for counseling.

I sat on a sofa and waited. Two professional looking white women walked in and sat near me. They were reading documents from file folders, gasping and making fearful eyes at each other while they pointed at papers and whispered amongst themselves with hushed horror.

They handed me newspaper clippings from his past. "We are glad you are here. This man, he is a very dangerous man. He has a serious criminal record and a long history of hurting women. There are about twenty-three documented cases here from women he has abused over the past few years who have stayed at this clinic. Imagine how many unreported cases there are. You are courageous to come forward. It is imperative you stay away from him. We can help you."

I threw the newspaper articles aside; they were scraps of trash. "You are just trying to scare me with White Man's lies. I know his heart. He is a respected elder. He is Chief. Don't talk that way about him. I don't believe you. I want out of here. This has been a mistake."

"We cannot let you leave. The only way out is to go through the program."

I was instructed to follow an employee. As we walked down the hallways of the women's shelter, I looked into the bedrooms. The women were required to keep their doors open, most sat on beds or in chairs looking sad. I saw one victim with a little dog in her lap. That ticked me off—the cops had lied to me about no pets! I had lost my birds for nothing.

I was led to a clothing donation room, since all I owned was on my back. The shirt the woman chose for me to wear was a second hand Sturgis T-shirt. That was crazy.

After a few days, they transferred me to a maximum security place up in Rapid. This shelter was much larger than Hot Springs, every victim I saw here was an Indian, some even had babies and young children with them. These women were not all abused by Chief. There is a dense Indian population in Rapid City. Hitting Indian women seemed to be a common habit for men, even off the reservation.

Being relocated to Rapid worked out well for me, since that's where the next sheetrocking job was. I convinced the shelter to let me go to work. They laid the law down with my boss over the phone and put me through intense instructional training on "not contacting my attacker," after which, they reluctantly agreed to let me work a set shift. Armed with the security code to the front door, an emergency cell that only dialed 911, and a solemn swear to never give the secret location of the shelter away to anyone, I was allowed to go to work.

On lunch breaks, I would call Chief Two Bear Paws from the public library's payphone next door to the job. I told him I was sorry. I said I had paid the price for my mistake because they took my parrots away; the birds were somewhere here in Rapid City with their new owner.

Instead of compassion for my loss, Chief told me how he had suffered. He had been forced to wait in the cold darkness, hiding in the bushes for quite a while until the cops were gone and he could safely go back into my driveway for his car. I said I was sorry he had been cold, I expressed regret for his lost time. I never meant for it to be that way.

He was very upset I had called the White Man's police on him. For that, I deeply apologized and said I never meant for the police to come but the landlady had called them, there was nothing I could do but show him out the back way fast. I had given him warning, protected him, and let him escape; we were on the same side. I told him how the white counselors at the shelter tried to brainwash me with lies, but I did not listen to them. I stood up for him. I told him I still loved him and I wanted to come home. He was my life.

Chief said he'd take me back if I could get out of the shelter. He also advised me to quit my job because I was a woman and therefore talentless at a man's job like sheetrock. I told Chief my boss said I was the best finisher he has; my work was the only one he never had to go back in and sand. In fact, earlier today, I got a raise. Chief argued the only reason my boss would tell me my work is good is because he wants to sleep with me. Chief reminded me, "The only things women are good for is sex and cooking."

I tried to get out of the shelter, but they would only release me to family. Due to my exceptional circumstance, all the employees offered to chip in out of their own pockets and buy me a bus ticket back to my dad in Connecticut. They told me I needed to get away from South Dakota for good. I had to get away from them before that happened.

My sheetrock boss signed me out. He said he had talked to his wife about my situation and they felt a women's shelter was no place to live. The shelter interviewed them over the phone and faxed them some paperwork. As if I were a minor instead of a thirty year old woman, I was released into their protection, to the safety of their home and judgment. I was amazed people I barely knew could be so kind.

But I hadn't changed. I loved Chief. My boss's wife was beside herself with concern. She asked one of her best girl friends to come over to the house. They sat me down for a heart to heart talk. Her friend, a white lady, told me her personal horror story about dating a different Indian man who beat her severely. She said the situation never gets better.

They told me I was foolish for wanting to go back to Chief. Her friend had even lived on White Man's land with her Indian boyfriend and that did not stop him from beating her daily. They could say nothing to change my mind.

This family had been exceptionally good to me and for that I was grateful, but, in the end, they agreed it was my life and they had to let me go.

Chief was coming to pick me up a few blocks from their house. My boss's wife said her door is always open. She promised, if I changed my mind at any time, I could always come back and live with them. I thanked her for her kindness.

I would soon find out about another kindness a friend had shown me. Philipp was long gone from the reservation, he was already back in Germany by now. His thoughtful gift had been taking the U-Haul truck to the office in Rapid City. He knew how upset I had been over the stolen vehicle. He told U-Haul my story and apologized for the rental being extremely overdue, then took a cab to the airport. It touched me to realize, even though I was gone from the reservation when he returned from the Big Foot ride, Philipp still thought of me and wanted to help make things right in my life.

He got the keys from Chief by suggesting it would save everyone the hassle and gas of getting him to the airport in Rapid City, two hours away, if he just took himself there in the U-Haul truck.

It was a great idea and one much appreciated. Without it, I might have been writing this book from jail.

CHAPTER TWENTY-EIGHT:

Bingo Night

Chief Two Bear Paws picked me up at the gas station near my boss's house and took me to bingo night at the round building.

We stopped by Wal-Mart first and he picked out some bingo prizes for me to purchase. He chose things like a clock radio, CDs, slippers, tins of popcorn, spicy sausage, an eighty five dollar karaoke machine, and other sundries.

We went home, got dressed in our Western best, complete with hats, jewelry, fancy belts, and pointy tipped boots. Chief put a star quilt into his truck to raffle as the grand prize.

We set up the round building with long folding tables and chairs. Women began to come in with food they had cooked. Chief placed the prizes people could choose from on a table in the center of the room near the food. Many people arrived, we ate. Chief got the karaoke machine ready on the table at the head of the room, it sat next to a small, caged wheel with little numbered wooden balls inside. He picked up the microphone and began the festivities.

He called out numbers as I collected pennies from children and grown-ups placing bets. It was a family fun Bingo night and nobody lost much, as they didn't have much to lose. I don't think anybody lost more than three dollars in pennies the whole night.

I was hostess to Chief and proud. I walked around verifying bingo cards and slipping pennies to the delighted children so they could afford to place more bets.

On one of my rounds, I saw a woman Chief had abused badly in the past. I realized she was one of Chief's ex-wives. She had been in the house that day when I came crying after

Chief had hit me, but she hadn't spoken. She recognized me now and her face startled with shock and horror. She whispered, "I thought you got away."

"I came back. I love all of you so much. You are my family. The reservation is my home. And I love Chief with all my heart. I still want to marry him."

She looked at me with grave certainty. "He will kill you."

Either way it does not matter. Either way you die.

Or, in Chief's own words, "Annie Mae."

I shook the chills away and did not heed anyone's advice. The night wore on, but my happy luster seemed to have tarnished.

The party was over. Chief and I folded the tables up and put the chairs away. It seemed strange he would help. Hunter stayed with us, he picked up trash and coiled the extension cords. It took us more than an hour to straighten things up. We were the last to leave.

We opened the door to the round building and entered a world of white. The storm was dropping snow at a heavy rate quickly. Chief stood at his car and said, "Hunter goes with me in car. You take truck."

This made me nervous. "Uh, yeah, why don't the three of us go together in the car? We can come back tomorrow in daylight for the truck. It will be safer. I really don't want to drive in this. Besides, I've never driven your truck before. If I have to drive, can I take the car?"

"Keys in truck. Go now."

"Why don't I take Hunter with me? He can help me find my way home in case I get lost."

"No. You follow me." He closed the car door with Hunter inside and began to drive away. I had no choice but to follow in the truck.

The roads were blackness with no streetlights, the snow came down fast. Storms I've seen on the rez lead me to believe the roads never get plowed all winter.

Even South Dakota's White Man's roads seldom get plowed until after the storm has ended, which could be several days later. The eight foot drifts of snow get so bad the interstate shuts down. Highway on ramps have long metal bars welded in huge triangle shapes that serve as gates, cutting off access to the highway. It is not uncommon for the interstate to be shut down for months.

Chief told me every year the rez becomes inaccessible due to snow and drifts; people on the reservation are simply snowed in until spring.

It was shaping up to be one of those storms, the snow was deep and the road was slippery. Maine and New Hampshire snow storms did not prepare me for driving in this. To make matters worse, the truck was not four wheel drive, the empty bed was light, and I had minimal traction over the snow.

Someone had tried to rig the truck's steering column back together and they had done a sloppy job. At least I had a wheel to use instead of a screwdriver, but it did not feel right; it was too loose.

I could not see which way was forward without following the lights of Chief's car. He went faster. If I could not keep up, I would get lost on this endless prairie road. That is, if I could find the road. I could not tell the snow covered road from the snow covered grass. I was a white woman in a white truck in the middle of a snowstorm with nowhere to ask directions if I got lost and nowhere to walk if I got stuck. Chief drove faster still, his taillights faded. In a panic, I stepped on the gas to catch up. I slid off the road into a ditch. Chief kept going.

I had a new secret cell phone stashed in my pocket for emergencies. I called Chief's house right away, before he could get home. He hadn't been counting on that. Strong Bear answered. I told him roughly where I was. He came to rescue me. When he saw the depths of my situation, he had to round up a few more guys to help. They pushed with their weight and pulled with a chain and another pickup truck. Chief's truck was so far off the road and almost tipped on its side, but, blessedly, it hadn't flipped over.

When Chief saw me again, all he cared about was his truck. He yelled at me and said I could have damaged it. The truck was fine.

Things just weren't the same between us. The house had changed, too. All the elements of me were gone from our home. It felt like he had a new woman but dumped her that night because I was coming back.

At least the bedbugs were gone. Deena said Chief received a donation check and spent it on a new mattress; she said it was the only way to get rid of the bugs. Chief laughed as he told me he left the old mattress on the side of a reservation road. He thought it was funny a person who desperately needed a mattress would take it home and get more than they expected.

I went outside to get wood for the fire. I thought about how Philipp and I had stacked all this alongside the house when the weather was warmer, before the snow had rolled into town.

What was left of my heart got pierced by a barbed wire of pain when I saw two bird cages broken and rusted next to the scattered pile of wood in the side yard. Chief came out to see what was taking me so long. He found me standing there, staring at the cages, unable to move.

He laughed and said, "I took the cages outside to raise rabbits. But I gave up. Couldn't find any rabbits. Go," he pushed me sideways, "get the wood."

I tried to make things better between us. I listened, obeyed, cooked, never complained, never got angry or cried. We dressed up and went to a few dances and Indian gatherings, nothing brought the magic back.

Deena lost the baby. That explained why she had been spending most days sick in bed. I felt guilty about it; I secretly thought it was my fault. I caused her too much stress when I left, as she had to assume all the responsibilities of the household without me. It was a sad time.

Perhaps in an attempt to brighten things, Chief had me clean the entire kitchen top to bottom. I scrubbed the walls and did any task he dictated. After it was done, he wanted the computer moved to the kitchen. Chief and I still sometimes worked on the motorcycle ride. However, as things began taking shape with the event, Chief started to change. He either could not see my vision, or he was angry that White Man's woman had made a difference in such a short time.

He kept trying to downgrade the event into a one time party to show his friends how many new things he got for free in his back yard. He wanted to laugh and brag about how he swindled the White Man. He was more focused on giving AIM leaders free tipis than anything else. He told me to forget the bikers and make this an AIM gathering. He would not open his mind to see a larger concept, one that could serve his community for many years in the form of this ride.

I got the computer set up in the kitchen as Chief asked. I turned it on to be sure the connections were right and checked the email. My face lit up; I read Chief the news. Success was here, we had secured our big sponsor for the ride! Everything was going to work out. All we needed to do now was email the exact lumber specifications and construction tools needed to build the concert stage and list the rodeo supplies with the information for the rental company. If we agreed to put up banners with the sponsor's name on the rodeo fences and stage, we would have 100,000 dollars worth of supplies delivered for free.

Chief's face fell. Perhaps he hoped for a large cash donation, money he could keep for himself instead of specific materials for the event. I asked if he would sit with me and help figure out the sizes and quantity of lumber needed. He got angry. He ran over and shut the computer off. He pushed me. He pointed to the kitchen. "Cook!"

I stood up and looked at him with shock and sadness. "Cook? What do you mean, 'Cook'? It's all working out, can't you see?"

He waved his arm in a large swooping gesture, which meant his decision was final. "No more computer! You do not touch computer again. It is only for me to use. Women belong in the kitchen. Not computer! You cook. I have a *Tiospaye* meeting tonight. Seven elders will be here. Start cooking for them now!"

I made traditional Lakota venison stew, using dried meat from the deer we shot together. A pang of sorrow pinched my heart as I thought about how this deer was meant for our wedding day, which had fallen apart so tragically. Memories salvaged into stew, I cut the strips of meat into bite sized pieces, adding potatoes and onions. I shrugged and threw in a can of cream style corn, too; this surprise addition seemed to go over well.

I made biscuits and *wojape*. I knew how to make it the traditional Lakota way with wild chokecherries picked from the wilderness, sugar, water, and flour. I remembered how much the Lakota women smiled and laughed when I raved about their *wojape* and fry bread at the feed after the sweat.

I was confident the dinner I prepared for the *Tiospaye* meeting was *wash'te*; Chief would be proud. The men would soon arrive. I lit the candles and small sage bundle, I smudged the room and placed the sage in the seashell on the table by the door for the guests to use.

Chief said, "Put the fish there." I set my little friend as the centerpiece for the table, happy he had survived without me. Blue Fish swam in his tall glass container next to a plate of hot biscuits; the candlelight shimmered on the water and enhanced the steam rising from the bread.

I knew it was the woman's place to bring a cool drink to the man as soon as he arrives. I placed a glass of juice with ice in front of each man after he smudged himself and sat down. Only one man, Thinks He Is Chief, looked me in the eyes and smiled, greeting me. He also gave me a "good job" nod towards the ice. The others acted as if their drinks and food magically appeared in front of them because they wished it.

I watched Chief and waited for the smallest lift of his eyebrow muscle; this meant it was time to bring the stew. We never talked about his gestures beforehand; somehow, I just knew what they meant. Like I said, it's lucky I knew how to speak parrot.

The men spoke only in Lakota. I could understand a few words, mostly the words which made fun of me and white people in general. I filled each man's bowl. They gave a few nods to each other and to Chief as they tasted the stew, said *wash'te*, then exploded with more White jokes and laughter.

I kept myself removed, but close enough to watch for any command from Chief regarding more refills on soup or juice for himself or his *Tiospaye* members. If a member needed something, Chief would make the same small eyebrow gesture, but point with his lips ever so slightly towards the member who desired the refill.

I had been disbelieving of this gesture the whole time I knew Chief, but I finally realized he had never been pointing with his chin, it had always been his lips. This was such an odd gesture to me, but it was disturbingly etched in my mind from the night in the car when he pointed that way and told me to get in the house and go to bed with him. It had taken me a while to believe it was real, but I saw it now for what it had always been.

Meanwhile, small children were gathering around me in the kitchen. I realized the men had brought their grandchildren with them. But no women to help.

The children were hungry and standing around me, looking for me to provide. There was not enough of the *Tiospaye*'s food to feed them all, so I had to improvise. I put a large pot of water on to boil and I took the children to the living room. I gave them a big box of cardboard tubes I had been collecting, along with some string and ribbons. I figured their confusion at what to do with these non-traditional Lakota craft materials would buy me the time I needed to finish their non-traditional dinner.

I drained the pasta and melted a huge brick of government cheese over it, added milk, butter, and hot dog slices. I offered ketchup on the side. The kids went nuts for it. They all asked for seconds and thirds. They kept hanging on me, tugging at me, and kissing me, telling me the food was so good. That moment can still bring tears to my eyes, it was so spontaneously wonderful. They showed me their crafts, they had actually made some pretty creative things from the tubes and string; I was impressed and let them know. They kept eating and crafting while I checked on the men.

It was time to clear the table for *wojape*. As I was serving the men my favorite Lakota food, I realized I had not eaten but a cup of white mush this morning. There was still some *wojape* clinging to the sides of the empty pot; I disappeared into the deeper shadows of the kitchen and took a moment to myself while I licked the pot clean with my fingers.

As the night went on, the conversation over coffee got loud. The men began to yell hateful things against the White Man. They directed their anger towards me. I was white flesh standing before them, representing all that betrayed and oppressed them. I understood a few words but their faces and hand gestures spoke volumes about the rest.

The Lakota word *wasicun (wah-si-cun)* was spat against all my white relations, my ancestors who murdered them and my present day white relatives who continue to cheat, lie, steal, break treaties, and oppress the Lakota. The word *wasicu (wah-schee-choo)* was venom from their lips, it refers to an exceptionally bad white person, which we all seem to be, who is a selfish fat-taker, swooping in to grab the best parts of the meat for himself above all others. This word has a racial slur undertone such as the 'n' word—or 'Sioux' for that matter.

These Lakota words are used with valid emotions for

centuries of hate crimes still current in modern society. However, I was not exhibiting hate, quite the contrary. Only my skin color could be seen as I became the physical symbol standing before them for all that was wrong in their world; their conversation grew frenzied. Hate hung over them like a tapestry from the ceiling, the candlelight flickered with their energy as their words wove more darkness. Just as Mary Crow Dog is Lakota Woman, I am *Wasicu* Woman.

The air was thick with a blackness I could not remedy, perhaps smudging again with white sage would have helped cleanse the room of such electric negativity, but I did not want to linger long near the men. My mother's visions of gang rape and beatings danced in my head. The best choice was to remove myself from the situation and join the children in the living room where I was met with warm, small hugs.

Some time later, Chief yelled his grandchildren's names and they came running. He instructed them to say goodnight to their elders. The men motioned their own young ones forward and headed into the night without even a goodbye glance for me and my hospitable efforts. Chief went to bed without a word. I cleaned the kitchen until one in the morning.

I noticed Blue Fish was dead. Everyone had been dropping pennies into his water, making wishes and watching the coins drift to the bottom. The plastic plants and pebbles were covered in thirty cents worth of copper and germs, my poor little friend floated belly up; I was too tired and broken to even think of forming a single tear. I flushed him and half his water down the toilet, then flopped into bed exhausted. I was shaken awake at two with the "get the juice" ritual, four for the fire, then up at five to make breakfast for the masses.

Deena was up before me, she was already cooking the meat and mush. My eyes met with the empty glass bowl which had once been my little blue fish's entire world. It now held spatulas, large black plastic spoons, and the forty dollar professional chef pastry cutter my mother had given me as a splurge for my birthday in May, a few months before I skipped town and headed for South Dakota. I noticed when Deena had washed out the bowl, she had taken the coins and put them beside her children's breakfast plates.

The children sat at the table and their eyes grew wide with the discovery. They laughed and smiled and put the pennies in their pockets, taking them out to count them over and over, excited for their next trip to Wal-Mart so they could walk up and down the aisles and dream of what they might win at the next bingo night.

I looked from their happy faces to the pastry cutter. The irony at the cost of that fancy kitchen utensil and the joy on the children's faces when they saw the fishbowl pennies just about split my head in two.

Deena and I finished making breakfast while Chief sat at the computer and tried to use it. It only took him a few days to break it. It was a sad thing, cooking a few feet away, watching him sit there, trying to open emails, not knowing he had let a virus in. He never ran the anti-virus software.

Eventually, the hard drive crashed, the computer would not even turn on anymore.

The dream was over.

CHAPTER TWENTY-NINE:

Snickers

Another breakfast blended into another breakfast until all sense of time was lost and only cooking remained. Chief took his male friends outside because that's what men do, they leave the women in the kitchen.

While Deena and I did the dishes, I quietly confided in her the truth I had yet to speak, "This is exhausting."

She rolled her eyes in agreement. "Yeah, that's why we get jobs."

I thought, "Ah-ha! I can do that!" There was an ad in the paper for an internet help desk call center in Hot Springs, starting pay ten dollars an hour. I applied, did a phone interview, and got the job. This full-time, high hourly wage was unheard of on the rez. Chief had to let me work; the money was too good to turn down.

It was an hour's drive each way. Chief would take me to work and at the end of the day, a co-worker would drop me at the casino where Chief would be waiting to pick me up. Eventually, Chief trusted me enough to let me take the car by myself. He said I could borrow it with the promise I would come home to him every night. I agreed. I cashed every paycheck and handed Chief all I made; it was worth it to stop being a slave to the kitchen.

One afternoon, my shift ended early enough to inquire about an apartment down the road from my job. I wasn't sure what my intentions were, I was just curious and wanted to know the rental rate. In the back of my mind, perhaps I thought Chief and I could live here, if we wanted to get away, or maybe Deena could live here if she wanted to get away with her kids. I was examining options; I like the idea of knowing what's out there. The old, white landlord showed me the place and we got along well.

As I was driving out of the parking lot, he hollered to me. I came to a stop as he trotted over to Chief's car. "Hey, wait a minute! Are those reservation plates on your car?" I nodded. He frowned. "Well, I didn't notice that before. I coulda saved ya some trouble. We don't rent to people from the rez. You let one Indian move in and soon you'll have twenty. All drinkin' 'n' gettin' in fights when they're not layin' around bein' lazy. Sorry, but lose my number."

Chief seemed sad with me gone away to work. I think most days he just sat by the window and waited for me to come home. I'm sure, on the other side of the country, my mother was doing the same thing. What a melancholy mess I'd made.

Deena said, "Since you got a job, Dad's been more angry and extra mean to all of us. He makes us do everything for him like you used to do. We can't take it anymore. We're moving out."

Everyone moved out and left Chief Two Bear Paws alone in his big, empty house. Nobody came to visit anymore. Breakfast turned into a cup of coffee and toast with no company.

One morning as I got ready for work, a light snow began to fall. Chief stayed in bed long after I got up; I was dressed and ready to leave by the time he slowly walked into the kitchen. I had put his medicine, toast, and cup of coffee on the table. He walked right by them. He seemed very depressed. He was still in his pajamas, which he never wore around the house. He pulled a chair up in front of the window, sat down, and watched the snow. I gathered my things for work, but all of a sudden there was a change in the air and it felt like I was never coming back.

Chief turned to look at me openly for the first time since I had known him. It was just a normal, empty look without any games or anger behind it. As our eyes met, he sat there without a word. I walked over to him and wrapped my arms around his shoulders from behind. We were that way for a while, watching the snow fall together. I leaned down, kissed his forehead and said, "Goodbye. I love you."

I walked out into the snow, dusted off the car and got inside. When I looked back at the house, Chief was still there in the window. He lifted his hand and waved. I did the same.

It felt strange; I wasn't sure what had happened. I shrugged it off, figuring I was imagining things and I'd be home like usual that night. I always came home to Chief.

By the end of my work day, I had no explanation for how overcome I was with feelings for my parrot. I missed my little lost bird so much. I wondered if he was doing okay up in Rapid City. I used a payphone at a gas station and called his new owner. I asked if I could come up to visit, she said sure and told me how to get there. I called Chief to tell him I was going to be late. He asked why. I said, "I'm going up to Rapid to see Snickers."

Chief said, "Who's Snickers?"

My world imploded. In my mind I saw a wet, cardboard box collapsing inward upon itself. It flattened out and fell into its own shadow; I followed. Everything was blackness, spinning down, down, down into the hole. Chief was talking on the end of the phone line, but I was too deep within myself to hear his words.

I thought, "*All this—and you don't even know my baby's name.*"

Then, the fire of a mother buffalo protecting her calf lit within me. The flame caught low and yellow, a small flicker at my heels. It swept up to consume me, burning the darkness away, filling my body and mind with the warmth of awareness. I was alive again and free from the deep trance that once had a powerful hold on me. The spell was broken.

I heard Chief say, "Come home."

"No, you know what, Chief, I'm not coming home tonight and I'm never coming home again. You didn't even know my parrot's name, after all we've been through. The most important thing in my life that I loved more than anything and lost because of all this and you can't even remember his name. I'm done."

Chief said, "Oh, the bird. I thought you were talking about a person named Snickers. I forgot. Come home now. Bring the car. If you don't come home now, you will not be allowed to use the car again."

"Goodbye."

I drove to my old sheet rock boss's house. I told his wife, "I've left the Indian."

She jumped up and hugged me. "Oh my little girl, I am so happy!" She phoned her friend, she came over, the women hugged me and petted my hair and told me I was lucky to be alive.

I said I needed to return his car. It was registered in his name, I knew he would call the police and say I stole it. I wanted him out of my life. I had to get rid of the car tonight. They agreed to help me.

I called Chief and told him his car would be waiting for him at the casino. He could get a ride out there and the keys would be under the mat.

He said, "Ok," without a fight. He did not try to change my mind as he always had before. "One more thing. Do me a favor."

"What."

"Never call here again. Leave me alone." He hung up. I realized it was the day before Valentine's Day.

While I spent the lover's holiday alone, I heard Chief Two Bear Paws got a young Indian wife within a few days' time. He asked a girl he barely knew out to lunch, she was awed the chief would ask her and she accepted. Instead of going out to eat, he took her to the court house in Rapid City. She said she thought it was romantic and spontaneous.

They got married White Man's way on the first date. He made her introduce herself to people by saying, "I'm a fat sow." This was not her Indian given name, it was a put-down to humiliate her based on her size. He would laugh and make fun of her harshly, but she was quiet and could take it. Plus, she could cook.

For tonight, we were both alone and I was far from his spell. My white friends followed me down the road to the casino. At some point, a Hot Springs cruiser pulled up behind me, flashing his lights. It took me a while to notice him. I was crying hysterically.

The cop asked me to get out. He invited me to sit in the front seat of his car and tell me what was wrong. A cop friend later told me he did that so he could smell my breath and see if I'd been drinking. I had not.

In between heaves of sobs, I said, "I was w-with an I-Indian. We were s-supposed to get m-married." I could not think of any words to express my deep sorrow and conflicting emotions. It would have taken this entire book to tell him what was wrong.

I summed up everything by shortening it to something that wasn't quite true but expressed the depths of my pain: "He k-killed m-my p-p-parrots."

The cop was startled. "He *what*?!"

"He k-killed my parrots."

"Oh. I thought you said he killed your 'parents.' Where is this Indian now?"

"B-back on the r-reservation. This is the car I bought for him. It's r-registered in his n-name." I blew my nose on the tissue the cop handed me. "I'm d-dropping it off at the casino for him to pick up. I thought he'd call the police on me if I kept it."

"When did you break up with him?"

"T-twenty minutes ago."

"Well, you were weaving all over the road here, you looked drunk."

"I'm sorry, I was just crying so h-hard. I'm better now."

"Are those your friends in the other car?"

"Yes."

"I'll go talk with them. Do you think you can follow their car to the casino in a straight line and focus on your driving?"

"Yes. I'm sorry."

"Ok. Pull yourself together. And let your friends lead. Have a good night, Miss."

"You too, Sir. Thank you."

I followed my friends to the casino. I set the car up so when Chief started it, the CD would be playing in the middle of a Buffy Sainte-Marie love song. I hoped Chief would hear the words and know my love had been true. He probably didn't even notice. His prejudice and hate were stronger than my love.

I had been a fool and arrogant like my white ancestors to think I could make a difference in the lives of those who never wanted to be helped in the first place.

TATANKA SKA

A white buffalo calf is born in Goshen, Connecticut on June 16, 2012. My head and heart are still haunted by the joy and sadness of my time with the Lakota. I could never forget the significance of the white buffalo and the message White Buffalo Calf Woman brought to her people, a message of hope and survival, and the gift of the Sacred Pipe.

I moved from White Man's land in South Dakota to Connecticut just a short time ago. I live in the rat race city with a 9 to 5 job; my spirit is dying. I think back to what the dark horse said when I asked if I should stay on the reservation or go home to my sick mother: "*Either way it does not matter. Either way you die.*" I understand the cryptic message all too well now. In some ways, this spirit death is worse than the death my body would have faced on the reservation.

I left big sky sunsets and came back to the city to share what little time my mother had left in her earthly body. She is with me only in spirit now. For her, for Chief Two Bear Paws, for this fire that still burns in my heart, I knew I needed to go see the white buffalo calf.

It was there forgiveness released me. I found clarity in the long-forgotten smell of burning sage and sweet grass. I looked inside my heart, a place I hadn't dared go in years, and the memories from my past came flooding back to me on sacred smoke. The birth of this book began the same day I saw the White Buffalo Calf.

The newspaper article was the first I'd heard of the event. The article claimed elders from South Dakota's Pine Ridge Reservation would hold a naming ceremony for the white buffalo on July 28th, sometime between noon and two. With regards to a more specific time, it was said, "We are on Indian time here." I expected a long wait. That is, if the public was allowed to enter this private land at all. The article stated the general public was not officially invited, however, it is expected that hundreds of people will show up to attend the event.

Statistics say the chances of a white buffalo being born are one in 10 million. I was certain strangers would camp out in fields surrounding the bison ranch overnight. Extreme interest and curiosity would run rampant. Co-workers were talking about the white buffalo over the water cooler, never before saying the words "white buffalo" in their entire lives, now suddenly interested but not understanding the significance of the words they spoke, not knowing the Lakota people to whom this event was sacred.

The buffalo's temporary name in the month before the ceremony was *Tatanka Ska (Tuh-tahn-kah Skah)*, which means "White Buffalo" in Lakota.

The buffalo's public name, Yellow Medicine Dancing Boy, was announced at the ceremony in the late afternoon of July 28th, 2012. A Lakota voice spoke into the microphone for all to hear: "The white buffalo calf's true Lakota name is secret, spoken only by a few elders who participated in the naming ceremony last night. He will be known to the public as Yellow Medicine Dancing Boy. The untold Lakota name will be kept a secret. This will make the white buffalo calf safe. Only *Tunkashila* will know his true name and recognize the white buffalo's Spirit."

I hope the white buffalo calf who was slaughtered in Texas just two months before this ceremony was as equally known to the Red Man's god. I hope his spirit was recognized and well-met when the year old calf went to meet the Lakota's Grandfather Spirit.

The Texas ranch owner claimed it looked like a professional hit. He said someone trusted in the inner circle had to be the one who killed the buffalo. The killer knew what he was doing; he knew what to look for. The mainstream media didn't publicize that angle. The media called it a hate crime against Indians.

In my experience and opinion, I wouldn't be surprised if there was a Lakota out there with a very small white buffalo skin robe in his closet. He sleeps with a grin on his face at night, knowing his actions set the white buffalo's spirit free from the White Man's world. He gave it and its mother the honor of a traditional killing.

There is a lot to keep this Connecticut white buffalo safe from.

The newspapers quoted the Connecticut ranch owner as saying he is almost like the calf to the Lakota because he is the caregiver of the calf. That's like a pastor saying he is almost like Jesus to the congregation because he works in this church. The ranch owner means well, but I doubt very much the Lakota feel that way about him. He is a non-Indian man who didn't even know the white buffalo was sacred until an Indian neighbor told him. He really is nothing like the calf. In fact, I bet they would like to get the calf away from him.

I think, deep down, the Indians are trying to subconsciously influence the ranch owner to donate the white buffalo to the Lakota. They are giving him bracelets and gifts and letting him in a little closer to an almost real sweat lodge ceremony, trying to make him feel like he is special, an insider, so he will see the buffalo really belongs to the Indians.

They hope he will decide to do the right thing and give it to them. But, like all con-games the Indians play, the white buffalo would never really go to the true Lakota people like Chief Two Bear Paws and his family.

It would most likely be taken by a shiny, self proclaimed shaman or someone in the forefront who plays the Indian role well and shows outsiders the image they want to see. Someone like Turquoise Shaman, the almost white looking Indian with lots of turquoise jewelry and the smooth talking voice who was a prominent figure here today. I could see him keeping the buffalo for his own pet and trailering it around the country, charging people to see it, touch it, and take pictures with it. The sacred white buffalo calf would become a personal cash cow for one man.

I can see how white people are almost asking to be conned, though. They long for something to fill the emptiness, they search for something Red Sox games and hot dogs cannot fill. They are on a quest for a spirit, a sense of belonging. They are lost and looking for roots to a Sacred Tree that does not exist for them.

On the morning of July 28th, there were so many lost souls outside the bison ranch, hoping to be part of the naming ceremony. As I thought they would, some camped out in the field across the street the night before, waiting, not wanting to miss out on something bigger than themselves.

I figured the real ceremony had already happened, so I did not camp out. I believed white people would be kept out with a fence. There were no guarantees non-Indians would even get to set foot on the ranch owner's land. So, I took my time. I did not rush an hour down the highway early that morning. But I did fast. It is what we did the entire day of the sweat lodge ceremony on the reservation. Not eating or drinking felt like the right thing to do today.

I arrived around 11 a.m. to a thick crowd lining both sides of the narrow farm road. Free parking was available in a large field and from the way the sky looked, I hoped all the cars would not be getting stuck in the mud once those clouds decided to open up.

Thunder rolled across the sky. The crowd shouted and cheered, believing the thunder was a blessing. I believed we were all about to get very wet.

I walked to the end of the crowd and gazed at the field adjacent to the farmer's house. I saw a swimming pool and guests gathered around the pool. They ignored the thunder and ate lasagna. I knew it would be a while before today's ceremony began. The word in the crowd was we were all waiting for the elders to arrive.

A white woman educated her group of friends, "They said we are waiting for the elders to get here. Now, just because they call them 'elders' doesn't mean they are old." Her now enlightened followers murmured "mmmmm" and "oooohhhh."

While we waited, I heard many ignorant conversations.

I heard a White Man bragging to another White Man, he was passionately reciting all his Indian names. He claimed he had five, given from different tribes from various ceremonies he had attended in his life.

In my head, I said to this man, "Just because you think you went to an Indian ceremony, does not mean you really went to an Indian ceremony. You saw what they allowed you to see. You believed in smoke and lies and were fooled. You were celebrating. The Indians were laughing. All the way to the bank. You look like an idiot. Just because you've adopted a few words different from the name on your White Man's birth certificate does not make you some kind of honorary Indian. It just means the Indians are hoping for future donations even bigger than the one you already gave."

Based on how much money you give and your potential for giving more money in the future, you will get let into different levels of ceremony. The closest I saw to a White Man being allowed into the ceremonies was Philipp, our houseguest from Germany. He would give all the money he had and contribute his hard labor for a month, he committed to four years of Sundance, he carried a German/Lakota dictionary and tried his best to speak their native language. He listened to all the stories from the elders and remembered them with respect. He spoke little and listened much. He was let in closer than most white people ever would be. But still not as far as I was let in. I think my marriage ceremony to Chief Two Bear Paws would have been the closest to real. But the sweat ceremony we shared was also very real. I remembered how the Lakota bashed white people intensely in that ceremony, they spoke freely as if I were blood. They thanked *Tunkashila* for me, that I belonged to Chief.

I've seen the real thing, as close as any white person can get, and I am thankful for that, minus the almost dying. My time with the Lakota on their reservation brought clarity to my eyes which allows me to see the ignorance around me in White Man's world.

There are many emotions and I can see all sides. At this buffalo naming ceremony, I could understand Chief's viewpoints clearly for the first time. My own eyes opened. I could see why he is so racist against the White Man. I felt the same way hearing their ignorant comments.

Today, I decided to hold true to what Chief Two Bear Paws liked to say after we had relations. He would laugh and tell me, "You can say you have a little Lakota inside you now. I will always be part of your blood. My life is inside your veins, I am part of your body." I embraced that energy this day, even though he probably meant it as an after-sex joke. But, in truth, his cells and energy had met mine. Today, for the first time in so many years, I wanted to feel it. I stood away from the crowd, fixed my eyes on the horizon and felt Chief there with me.

The feelings mixed me up, like a rapist facing her attacker for the first time, but they also made me strong. I am blessed to be alive. Blessed with the ability to hear stupidity and call it out for what it is: ignorance.

As if to illustrate this realization, my meditations were peppered by overflowing snippets of ignorance I could not ignore. There were self-proclaimed enlightened white people telling stories to admittedly unenlightened white people who listened with adoring eyes. The pompous white people told their dances-with-wolves stories about their visits-with-Indians. They said stupid things like "our land" when referring to lands Indians called their own.

This irritated me deeply. The energy of Chief absorbed into my body burned with their words. I wanted my voice to boom out across the farmland saying:

"Listen! Even if you visited the Black Hills and still have a photo on your cell phone of you praying by a dark green pine, you are not an Indian. Listen! Even if you've tied colored ribbons in low branches on the paths around Devil's Tower, you are not an Indian. Listen! Even if you've kept a soft rock from the badlands that has since turned to dust in your pocket, you are not an Indian. Listen! Even if you've seen Niagara Falls, bought the T-shirt and felt the mist, you are not an Indian.

"Listen to me now and hear this above all else:

"The land is not yours; it was never yours to take in the first place. Even once you stole it, it remains to this day as it always was and always will be: *Not Yours*. You are white. Your hands are covered with the blood of murder. Your ancestors took that land from the Indians. You cannot speak of it as 'our land.'

"Just because you went to the craft store and bought a feather and tied it into your hair, this does not make you an Indian."

There were about five genuine Indians in the crowd from places other than South Dakota; however, I did not see any Puerto Ricans, there were no Muslims, no people from India, no African-Americans. It was amazing to me how this crowd was not diverse. This was not an accurate representation of the many different ethnicities and cultures living in Connecticut. There was a stark line on this land here today with only two bloodlines present: "Native Americans" and "Caucasian Americans." Blood and wannabes.

The white people ranged from original hippies straight out of a Woodstock poster still wearing their same vintage clothes, to grunge-type white people with dreads borrowing the other set of clothes the hippies saved from 1969. These modern day

Buffalo Soldiers wore Bob Marley style hats to this sacred Indian ceremony. An Indian looking upon this Rastafarian dress would be offended. An Indian would feel homage is being paid to the U.S. 10th Calvary. The 10th Calvary was an African-American regiment who were given freedom, promised Indian land and a mule in return for murdering Indians around the time of the Wounded Knee Massacre.

The mule was never given, but medals of honor were awarded to men who slaughtered Indians. As much as the truth may hurt and be offensive, there are always at least two sides to every story. The Black Man is guilty, so is the White Man. The colors of the medicine wheel do not unite us, as some sheep are lead to believe. Neither Black, White, or Yellow are equal to the Red Man in his own eyes. He stands alone for what is right. Only he knows the suffering his People have endured. The stolen land, rapes, and murders stain black and white hands red. We are not One.

Some in attendance that day modified the Buffalo Soldier look with the addition of gauged earrings, tattooed bodies, and multiple facial piercings. Piercing of the flesh is a sacred rite for the Lakota during the Sun Dance. I had left all my jewelry at home in case they let us attend some type of White Man's sweat, but that was far from happening. I was ready though. In my long cotton skirt and Sturgis T-shirt, I definitely fit in with all the lost souls. I had my cowboy hat with feather and hair flowing to my waist.

As I gazed into the distance and thought of Chief Two Bear Paws, a short white woman about fifty years old approached me and said, "Hi. I like your hat. Have we met before? Did you used to work at the health food store I go to?"

Literally, the muzzle of a gun to my head was a vision of comfort compared to a conversation with this lady. Without encouragement, she kept talking in her high pitched, chipper tone. She spoke non-stop rapidly, even though I had nothing more to say than "no" and "thank you." Using both words together within the same set of quotation marks was more than I wanted to offer, but occasionally I gave it, hoping she would go. It was no use.

She said, "Oh my gosh, okay, well, you look like someone I know. But that's okay if you're not her. Are you as excited to be here as I am? Oh boy, this is so great, I just love being here! The energy of all this, wow, you know, can't you just feel the 'Togetherness' of all people gathering here as 'One'? It's amazing! What time do you think the ceremony will start?"

I thought of the story Chief had told me about the white woman who reached climax in her pants with no physical contact, all she had to do was *look* at Chief to become that excited. I got ahead of this one.

I said, "I think the ceremony has already happened."

Her face fell with disappointment. "Oh, no! But they said it was happening today! What have you heard? Why do you think it's already happened?!"

I paused a moment. I turned to face her directly in the eye. Her small stature allowed me to look down on her as if I were disciplining a whining child who wants her way. I spoke slowly, calmly, "Do you really think they'd let White people into the *real* ceremony?"

Her illusion balloon popped with a dejected "Oh." She frowned.

I hoped she would go away at that point. I stared back into the distance, dancing with memories of my past, making my own peace with the pain. The pain in my heart was only lessened by a greater pain in my ass when she came closer.

"So, how do you know so much about this? Are you Native American?" She now had new hope, but I crushed it before she got too excited.

"No."

"Oh okay, but isn't this event beautiful? Everyone gathered together as One. . . that's how life should be, isn't it? I mean, right? How did you hear about this event? I heard about it on public radio this morning and I thought, 'White buffalo? Yeah, I'll check that out. It's close, you know? I'll just drive on over.' Oh, this is so exciting! What brought you here today?"

I finally understood Chief's stoic, reserved presence. His "man of few words" poise was the cap confining all the pressure about to blow. He stood in the face of ignorant white people like this and kept quiet, misleading them to think he was simply majestic. More often than not, this would lead to a donation of cash, sometimes thousands of dollars, even pickup trucks.

To the white observer, he appears thoughtful, mysterious. In reality, beneath that calm face, he wants to kill them with all his heart. Sometimes he took his stifled hate out on women he hit, but his resentment is bigger than that small release.

In this moment of understanding, I forgive Chief his violence against me. I realize he carries so much anger inside him from the scars of the past. Lakota culture is slipping away around him. He grasps the sands of the old ways in his hands; traditions and values slip through his fingers faster the harder he tries to hold on. He is left only with fists of rage. And sometimes women are on the receiving end of all he has left. It does not excuse his behavior or make it right. But, for the moment, I could understand how the pressure inside him could cause him to want to hurt others, never noticing their feelings or pain. His anger is not really for those at the ends of his blows, be they Indian or white. He fights to keep the old ways. His rage is a fire fueled by the White Man's lies, broken treaties, broken promises, stolen land, and stolen dreams. The white icing on this bitter cake is White Man believing "we are all one."

Mitakuye Oyasin, all my relations, yes, the Lakota are all one relation. It does not include other colors of skin. It can sometimes even exclude begrudged Indian tribes who do not get along with the Lakota due to past and present situations, and it especially does not include the White people. White people think Indians accept our apology shown without words by our unwelcome, respectful presence at their ceremonies. White people think Indians want us meddling in their lives, tagging along to their sacred ceremonies which we will never truly understand because the cells of our body do not hum with centuries of resentment. We still believe the Indian wants White Man's help, White Man's education, White Man's religion, White Man's words, or White Man's participation in sacred Indian events. The Indian did not want these things in the past and he does not want them in the present.

The bubbling ignorance stood before me in this perky little misguided white woman. All around me were reflections of my former self. I looked into the faces of the crowd and saw how I must have appeared years ago in a different life as I faced my family at the buffet table, leaving forever for South Dakota. A dumb little white girl thinking she could play Indian. With love and almost the price of my life, I earned this prejudice. It is a prejudice against both sides, removing me from both cultures and leaving me alone with nothing but my hurt.

I decided to level with this pesky woman. To give her, quite possibly, the only truth she will hear today. I said, "Today is all bullshit."

She gasped. A few white people who were wearing store bought Indian Halloween costumes moved away from me. I continued, "The White Man is not welcome here today. Anything we see is fake. They had their ceremonies yesterday, last night, another time. Even if they let us in we are going to be separated by a fence. And I guarantee you they will be asking for donations." I did not know any of this for sure; I could just feel it in my bones. It made sense. Today was a celebration of dreamcatchers made from yarn. The illusion of something real to hoodwink the masses for donations of cash. Those stupid enough to believe in yarn and craft store feathers did not deserve anything greater; they are not allowed to touch the truly sacred for their tainted blood could never understand.

Almost crying with confusion she said, "B-but, how do you know?"

"I used to live with them, the Lakota. They wanted to kill me. I left a few years ago. I escaped with my life. I am lucky to be alive. When I drove here today, my heart was racing. I felt like I was about to face my attacker. Indians do not like white people."

She immediately found a bright side to my potential death. "Well, rightfully so, I mean, gee, just look at all they've been through. They have a right to feel that way about white people."

"True. I agree with their prejudice against whites. They have every right. But I also feel that if there is one white person who gives everything, moves to the reservation with open arms holding nothing back, offers the rest of her life and commits her heart honestly to you and your people, then you should respect that one person by at least trying *not* to kill her."

She blinked. Thinking. "So . . . if you lived there, that means you must have attended some of their ceremonies?" She was getting herself wound up and wet in the knickers again.

"Yes. They let me in deeper than most."

"WOW! Amazing! Were you in a sweat lodge ceremony?" She almost panted the question.

"Yes."

"Oh my gosh!" She clapped her hands together and looked starry-eyed at me. "What were some things you learned from the sweat lodge? How was the ceremony? What can you tell me about it that was different from the inside?"

I silently stared into the distance.

"Well, at least, was there anything good and healing you took away from it?"

I almost had tears in my eyes. "If I were to think about it, it would take me back to a place I do not want to go. A time I do not want to remember."

She stared at me and said, "Now I know why you remind

me of the girl at my health food store. She was in the Army. She was raped by five men. When she told her superior officers about it, they did nothing. Because men in the Army think women are there to be used. Your eyes, they look like hers did."

I was thankful our conversation was diverted by an announcer driving his jeep through the crowd, telling everyone the ceremony was about to begin and out of respect no pictures were to be taken.

A few cars behind the jeep, an older couple was passing through. I looked inside their car as they slowly drove along and, to my amusement, I saw they had a standard poodle in the front seat. It was bright white. I laughed. I could hear Chief joking with me, saying, "Watch out! The white people are about to start worshipping that white poodle. They think it's the white buffalo!" It made me smile. I thought back to the sweat lodge story Chief told me about the rich white woman who prayed for her pet poodle to be blessed.

Around one thirty, women from the ranch came forward carrying lit smudge pots. The air filled with sweet smoke. It mingled with the humidity and impending rain, hanging low in the stormy summer sky, clinging around the crowd. The fragrance took me back to times and places I thought I had locked away deep enough so I could sleep at night.

Breathing in the sacred smoke opened me up and washed me with a flood of memories. When I got home that evening, I began to write this book. I had been pregnant with words for so long, it was time for this book to be born. Painful, but necessary. And, hopefully, like my mother said about giving birth, so beautiful after it is done that I forget the pain of bringing it into this world.

A man announced, "At this time, only those with Blood and those invited to Sundance can come forward." He opened the gates.

A White Man in the crowd laughed and yelled, "Sun

dance? Looks more like a *rain* dance to me!" The crowd exploded into laughter as the sky gave its reply in thunder; clueless people cheered and applauded the echoing reprimand.

Rightfully so, white people were segregated away from the event. When they were finally allowed to pass through the gate, non-blood were instructed to walk to the right away from the ceremony. They stood far away in a field of tall, wet grass surrounded by a chain link fence higher than their heads. White people were six rows deep, pressing against each other to see nothing and hear nothing.

Some white people had gotten inside the fence and near the drum circle. They were dancing their feet in a 2-2 rhythm and singing some non-English words. I knew they thought they were the special ones who got let into the "real" ceremony. Fools, this is all smoke.

A white woman squeezed in front of me, pushing her way to the front, clinging to the fence and peering into the field where the buffalo herd ran in time with the drum beat.

"Which one's the white one?" she asked. She was told it was the one with the lighter tan coat. "Well, it's not even really white!" She pouted, as if she had been lied to and cheated.

Another white woman said, "Are they going to catch it and bring it over to us so we can pet it?"

My stomach turned; I could not breathe. I made my way through the thick crowd into the clearing and all but ran away from the fence and the place where the white people had been corralled with their ignorance.

I walked back towards the entrance and stood there. It was amusing how there was a smudge pot burning when we entered the grounds, cleansing the whites just enough so they could be shooed past the Indian entrance and then directed to the outer field. What made me smile was, in order to get to the outer field, the whites had to first brush by the long row of Port-O-Potties.

I passed by the Port-O-Potties again, and then the smudge

pot. I stood there in the rain; it came down harder so I put up my yellow umbrella. A twenty-something, neo-hippie girl in a Wal-Mart cowboy hat came up to me and asked to share my umbrella. I denied in Chief's subtle fashion using lack of acknowledgement. She, not speaking Indian, smiled and helped herself to the front half of my umbrella, blocking my view of the field.

She turned to me with sunbeams from her smile and said, "Nice hat!" I nodded. It was a nice hat. It had buffalo nickels on it and feathers, Chief had shaped it properly for me on the reservation. I had no reply for her hat.

The Indian mother at the gate was turning someone away and sending her to the dumb herd of whites on the right. The white woman got snippy and yelled, "I was invited!"

Indian mother questioned, "Oh?"

The white woman put her nose in the air, tossed her chin-length hair, and huffed. "Yes, well, I *should* have been invited and I *should* be let in because I grew up in Montana!"

Indian mother replied with emotion breaking in her voice, "Montana? That's not the same thing. It's—it's not even the same culture. Just, just go. Go to the right."

The uppity woman stormed off in a huff. Snapping a "Well!" back over her shoulder, she went to the right.

It began to rain harder; Indian mother lifted up her purple shawl. She held it over her head using locked elbows so her shawl became a rain barrier tent. The young girl sharing my umbrella but not my conversation asked her, "Do you want to come under our umbrella?"

Indian mother answered, "This shawl has seen many more rains than you are old."

The young girl argued she was not really *that* old. Then, realizing how rude that might have sounded, she attempted to make amends by over-stating how pretty the shawl was. She was not given any conversation in return.

The rain came down much harder now; it was blowing a

chilling spray the umbrella could not combat, drenching my back and skirt. I took my blanket out of my bag, folded it in a large triangle and wrapped it around my shoulders. The young girl's eyes got wide; she smiled at my blanket as if it were a charmed, blesséd thing and said with awe, "Pretty!" I continued to gaze towards the field.

My silent thoughts replied, "This is not a prayer shawl, it is nothing special or sacred. It's not even pretty. It's a hunk of grey and tan fleece I grabbed from the backseat of my car. I got it on clearance for 2.99 end of season last year at Sears. You want to worship my 2.99 clearance blanket?"

Earlier, I had shared a smile and nod with another Indian mother inside the fence. My heart felt a fondness for her. Even though I did not know her, I felt love for her. We were well met in our gaze once again. I waved my fingertips for her to come to the edge of the fence so we could speak. She approached me and I left Wal-Mart hat girl standing alone in the rain.

I asked Mother if she knew the name of the man in the dark blue ribbon shirt. I said he looked familiar to me. She saw him, but did not know his name. I asked if there were any elders from Wounded Knee attending the ceremony. She said she did not know, as she was from a Connecticut reservation.

I said, "I used to live with the Lakota on the Pine Ridge Reservation in South Dakota." She looked deep into my eyes for truth, my gaze did not waver.

"Wow, that is amazing. You moved all that way, such a long way for you, and now they are here, all this way for them to Connecticut."

I nodded. "I do not know if those I lived with are here, as we have not spoken in several years. If I gave you some names of people I know, can you find out if they are attending?"

"I can do better than that. I can get you inside the fence in a little bit. Just watch that basket over there for me and I will come get you in a little while and bring you inside."

I agreed and went to the large wicker basket lined with red fabric. It was the donation basket I had been expecting. I knew there would be a few around.

It was darkly humorous for me to be collecting money from the white people. I felt like I had finally made it; I was now a true Indian. I poked at the dark humor inside myself as if it was a clot of congealed sap on a tree, but I could not quite pop it into a laugh. I thought about the irony, how I had been conned into giving more than I had because my heart was as big as my ignorance. And now, here I was, on the other side, collecting donations for the elders.

I stood in the rain with pride next to the basket. My long, brown hair soaked to black. My "pretty" blanket gently flowed into the folds of my buckskin colored, long, cotton skirt. White people gave me money.

White people thanked me for "allowing" them to attend "my" ceremony. They blessed "my people." I thanked them. I felt like a real Indian, stoic in the face of stupidity, being paid to hear their ignorance by taking their donations.

A small boy who was not white asked if he could put sage in the basket, I nodded. He gently placed it inside. I admired it, for it was the first real sage I had seen in years. The rain had extinguished the smudge pots and when I had looked inside them, I did not see sweet grass or sage, but needles from the same flat leaf pine tree that grows outside my apartment window in the city.

Later, I listened to an elder from Manitoba speak about the four medicine plants sacred to all North American Indians. They are tobacco, sage, sweet grass, and cedar. Everywhere on the continent of North America, one of these four sacred plants can always be found. They offer themselves to be used in smudges for purification before important meetings, to be used in sacred gatherings, meditation, and prayers. There is always a cleansing plant provided by our earth mother to help one focus, feel calm, and find peace.

A woman driving by in her BMW yelled to me and asked where she can buy sage for today's ceremony. I said at the Pequot museum here in Connecticut. She said she wanted it right now. I said I do not know a place that close. I thought, "It's not like it's growing among the wild horses. We're in Goshen, Connecticut. In a rainstorm. Nothing like the last minute to prepare, lady." But I said nothing of my thoughts and remained stoic. I was silently mysterious and this pleased her as she traveled onward, thinking she had spoken to a real drenched Indian.

An older white woman looked at the basket at my feet. "What's that for?"

"Offerings." I sounded totally authentic, like a cigar store Indian in a cartoon. White people like that.

She immediately knelt down before me in the muck, untied her long, gray hair, and dropped a single flower into the basket. "Lavender," she whispered, as if it were gold, or frankincense and myrrh for that matter.

"Thank you," I said nobly. But I thought, "Cash is better. What are the elders here or the ones 2,000 miles away going to do with a single, wet lavender stem?" I felt a touch of pity for this worn white woman, her body used up and her spirit still searching for something to believe in, craving to belong where she never will.

As hard as she tries, she is outcast and does not even know it. There she is, ruining her embroidered skirt by kneeling before me in her fantasy world, looking for a blessing from me—just another white chick in a skirt.

A rich white accountant walked up to me, dropped a 20 in the basket and asked, "What tribe is this?"

I said, "Lakota." I pronounced it with a very distinct sounding "L" because I could tell by looking at him he never heard of the Lakota people before. He lived up to my expectations.

"LA-kota?" he asked. "Huh. I don't know who they are.

Where are they from?"

"South Dakota. Pine Ridge Reservation." Geography wasn't ringing a bell for him, so I said, "Wounded Knee."

He looked like he might have heard about that event in history. Unsure, he still asked, "Where is that?"

"Lower south west of the state, almost near Nebraska." He nodded as if that made it as clear as his rain speckled glasses and walked away. I should have given him an Indian name. Well, for another 20.

About forty dollars later, an Indian woman approached me. She was wearing a ceremony dress, similar in style to the Connecticut mother who had assigned me the basket. She stopped to speak with me. "My child, put the basket there by the fence. Get out of the rain and go get some warm food." It was right to honor her request. She watched me place the basket by the fence and walk into the gathering. I found Connecticut Mother inside the feast tent welcoming and directing guests. I told her I watched the basket this whole time and, at the request of another, it is now beside the fence. She thanked me and said I am welcome here. She invited me to eat and suggested I go into the ceremony tent to find those I seek.

I look around me. There are many white people participating in the gathering now that today's ceremony is over. I was not going to be like the others who had stormed through the gates. I needed to be invited in, for I will never again tread where I am not welcome.

Honoring Connecticut Mother's invite to look for those I seek, I approach the drum circle. The drumming was on hold now as the men were being served plates of heaping food by their Indian women. The steam rises off their feast into the cold, damp air like the spirit of comfort a woman can give a man when she knows her place.

The men begin to eat.

While they dig in, I survey each one. There is Turquoise Shaman, the Indian who looks more like a rich White Man.

The ignorant white followers are gathered around him as if he is a thing of worship, as if he were a great leader of his people. I feel nothing for him. I have known true leaders, true elders like Chief Two Bear Paws; this man cannot even touch my Chief's shadow.

I dismiss him. He is not Chief. Turquoise Shaman claims to be Lakota but he has moved a thousand miles away; he is not staying behind with his people to help them remember the old ways, salvaging the traditions that are dying as young Indians try to be gangsters. Turquoise Shaman has moved on, gone away to make money off a name; to me he is a rich white actor playing Lakota Indian. I turn from him. I look at each member of the drum circle, searching for my eyes to meet a feeling in my heart.

There is a man who feels right to me. I bend to one knee beside him and softly ask if he is from Wounded Knee. He does not look at me but says he is from Pine Ridge and it's close to there. I nod once. "Do you know Chief Two Bear Paws?" I speak Chief's Lakota name.

At the sound of these words and the power of the elder's name, this younger Lakota man stops, fork full of food, frozen in mid-bite. He puts his food down on the plate and turns to me. He looks me in the eye and says yes. Yes, he knows Chief. He grunts in a way I know is Lakota. It means he is listening.

I say I used to live with Chief Two Bear Paws and his family. The man looks at me as if I am a ghost, as if he remembers the situation, or has heard stories of it. I ask if he will give something to Chief for me. A slightly different grunt expresses his Lakota consent.

For a moment, I think the man fears I will pull a gun out of my bag and shoot him; after all, that is the White Man's way. However, his grunt means he is ready for anything. He has agreed upon the honor of Chief's name to listen and accept what will be offered. He waits for what is to come.

I have a large zip lock bag full of fresh, loose tobacco; I set it on his knee.

This tobacco holds a story. Recently, I visited the Eastern Pequot tribe on their Lantern Hill Reservation in Connecticut. A man with Eastern Pequot Indian blood told me stories of his exterminated ancestors and how there are no full-bloods of his state recognized tribe left. He told me their reservation is so small that when he has a sweat and chants, the White Man stands a few feet away on the other side of the lake on non-reservation land and laughs.

People from the ignorant modern world yell heckling comments across the water at him and those gathered with him to pray; their judgment is voiced so loudly it drowns out his drumbeats. We shared understanding and names of elders we both knew from South Dakota who had visited his tiny reservation in Connecticut.

This tobacco was recognition for each other's life breath; it also blessed the life energy of those we knew across the miles.

I wanted those feelings to come full circle by including Chief, creating its own sacred hoop of respect, understanding, remembrance and friendship.

I was probably asking too much from a bag of tobacco for Chief to think of me in that way. He probably never even received it. But my intent was there.

"Please, tell him this is from the little white girl from Maine."

The man looks at the tobacco and waits. "Is that all?" he asks, still looking down at the tobacco.

I say, "Yes, that is the message, thank you."

He nods, picks up his fork and eats as I walk away.

EPILOGUE

A few weeks after the white buffalo ceremony in Connecticut, news comes my way that Chief Two Bear Paws has left the Pine Ridge Reservation. He has been gone a few years, but he still visits often. Those that see him as Chief and a highly respected elder still come to greet him when he spends time on the reservation from away. He has better health now, and money. Chief and "Fat Sow" parted ways when a better opportunity came along. Chief is now married to a rich white woman. They live in Texas.

Two Bear Paws spends his time touring powwows across the country, winning traditional Indian dance competitions, and riding horses on the ranch in Texas. He was given the honor of conducting the Pipe Ceremony and the Naming Ceremony for the white buffalo calf born in Texas. He now has a buffalo headdress, complete with horns and fur; he dances the Buffalo Dance.

When Chief left the reservation, he gave his house and property to his oldest son, Strong Bear, the one who always said he'd protect me. Strong Bear got out of jail and re-committed his life and Spirit to the old ways of the Lakota.

He was doing well at becoming a leader of his people, riding horses, speaking Lakota, living as an example of what is right and good while teaching and helping others remember and learn the ways of their Ancestors. Then, he was in an accident. He was not able to walk anymore.

It took a toll on his spirit; he began to drink. One night, everyone was drinking. A cousin made a remark about his crippled state, a rude remark about what a great leader he turned out to be as he could not even walk to lead them. Strong Bear suddenly spun around in his wheelchair and stabbed his relative in the stomach repeatedly, puncturing his lung.

The man died. Now Strong Bear is in prison for murder.

Things on the reservation with the people whom I loved have truly fallen apart. It saddens me to the depths of my heart. I wonder if there was more I could have done, if I had stayed longer, could I have made a difference in a positive way to help? Ah . . . and there it is. The voice of my real ancestors. After all I have seen, done, and understood, it remains within me. It is my scar, the white arrogance of wanting to help. For my ancestors it was motivated by hate, for me it is guised in the shroud of "love." As the dark horse said—either way, it does not matter.

The little voice inside me, my final shred of common sense, tells me I would have ended up dead, too, if I would have stayed on the reservation. Perhaps Chief Two Bear Paws heard a version of those same words within himself and knew it was time to go.

A friend who spends summers with the Indians in that area said to me recently, "There were two gravestones on the hill when my visit began. By the end of the summer, there were four. Something tells me it is not in my best interest to move there for the rest of my life."

My spirit will always remain at Wounded Knee. This part of me, no one can kill.

Date: Thurs, 29 Nov 2012 08:45:20
From: xxx@yahoo.com
Subject: Toniktuka hwo? (how are you)
To: xxx2@hotmail.com

Hello Dear (Deer),

Hehanni wash'te (good morning)

Just a few to let you know I am okay and hoping my money comes in this week. Our Tiospaye needs to do fund raising and develop web site to help the Museum in Wounded Knee and our people. I have idea that might work.

We meet with the family who still has the original flag captured at the battle of the little big horn. My people are the only Nation that ever captured the United States flag in the field of battle.

We still hold that flag today. The family that keeps the flag are from Chief Sitting Bull's band. I know that family and I can speak with them and borrow the flag.

We will take the flag to the White House in Washington and let the United States know we still posses their flag.

We can make arrangements to display the flag in museums and cities across the country and around the world.

We will raise funds for our people and the Museum in Wounded Knee with the donations we get.

We will travel with an entourage across the oceans of the world in support of our Indian Nation. What do you think?

I am looking for a full size van with bed in back so I can rest and not go to motel.

I am making plans so I can come pick you up now instead of waiting for spring or summer.

You ask why I still have a hold on you after all this time. It is because the grandfathers acknowledge you. When you walked into my tipi Tunkashila touched your spirit. You have a purpose in life. The grandfathers are watching.

You are a strong Lakota and Cherokee woman and I want you by my side.

Toksha! (later)

The Trail has no end. Only a new Beginning.

With the Spirit of Tasunke Witko (Crazy Horse)

Your Husband,

CHIEF TWO BEAR PAWS

index

casino . . . 176, 206, 321, 324, 325, 326

Cherokee (Indian tribe) . . . 31–32, 157, 352

Chief Big Foot Ride . . . 145, 169, 196, 209, 265, 267, 270, 277–279, 283–284, 287, 289, 290, 310

commodities . . . 31, 73, 178–180, 211, 237–238

Connecticut
    family . . . 7, 8, 9, 28, 31–33, 56–57, 94, 131, 134, 138, 177, 184, 189, 198, 212, 232–234, 242, 243–244, 252–253, 258, 261, 264, 278, 290, 297–298, 299, 306, 322, 327
        state of, statistics . . . 74

cradleboard . . . 212

Crazy Horse
    Oglala Lakota Warrior . . . 6, 24, 25, 53, 75, 121, 146, 352
    Memorial . . . 24–25, 145, 149, 266

Custer
    7th Calvary . . . 10–11, 21
    General . . . 10, 21, 38, 175, 237
    State Park . . . 21–22, 28, 38

Dakota War of 1862 (Sioux Uprising) . . . 236, 283

Dances With Wolves (movie) . . . 286, 332

Dennis Banks . . . 203

Devil's Tower . . . 21, 333

dreamcatchers . . . 37, 45, 46, 120–121, 128, 150, 225, 290, 337

About the Author

Little White Bird lived on the Pine Ridge Indian Reservation with the Oglala Lakota. She was arranged to marry an Oglala Lakota Chief who traveled two thousand miles to claim her as his wife. They lived together on the Lakota Indian reservation in the village of Wounded Knee, South Dakota, where her heart will always be buried.

Little White Bird currently resides in Connecticut; however, prone to wanderlust, no location is permanent.

Made in the USA
Middletown, DE
05 March 2020